S0-AEQ-254

DT
227.5
.C45
W75
1989

Wright, John L.

Libya, Chad, and the
central Sahara

| DATE DUE | | | |
|---|---|---|---|
| | | | |
| | | | |
| | | | |
| | | | |
| | | | |
| | | | |
| | | | |
| | | | |
| | | | |
| | | | |
| | | | |
| | | | |

# LIBYA, CHAD AND THE CENTRAL SAHARA

JOHN WRIGHT

# LIBYA, CHAD
## AND THE
# CENTRAL SAHARA

BARNES & NOBLE BOOKS
TOTOWA, NEW JERSEY

First published in the United States of America in 1989 by
Barnes & Noble Books, 81 Adams Drive, Totowa, NJ 07512
ISBN 0389-20860-4
© 1989, by John Wright
Printed in England on long-life paper

*For Mariateresa, Paul, Amina and Primavera*

# PREFACE

It was while living and working in pre-revolutionary Libya in the 1960s that I first became aware of Chad and its troubles. Travellers arriving in Tripoli from the remote southern province of Fezzan brought vague reports of injured Chadians seeking medical help in the provincial capital, Sebha, following bloody inter-tribal clashes in the even remoter northern provinces of their own country. Moreover, my own researches into the history of Libya from the earliest times to the Gadafi revolution of 1969, and from then till the early 1980s, inevitably touched on the history of the various territories and peoples which today comprise the Republic of Chad. For no country's history can be separated from that of its neighbours, even neighbours on either side of the Central Sahara.

Although I had written on Libyan and Chadian affairs for many years, it was not till 1983 that I attempted a brief historical explanation of continued Libyan interest in the Sahara and beyond. I presented a paper entitled 'Chad and Libya: Some Historical Connections' to the annual conference of the Maghreb Studies Association at the University of London in 1983 – one of those remarkable annual gatherings at which Dr Mohammad ben Madani brings together scholars and students of North African affairs from all over the world. That paper forms the basis of this book.

My purpose in writing has been neither to condone nor to condemn Libya's role in Chad, but rather to explain the historical background to Libyan intervention in the Central Sahara and the Central Sudanic lands, culminating in the bitter but unresolved confrontation over the disputed Aozou Strip, and to suggest motives for it. This background covers many countries. If a historical theme emerges, it is one of exploitation – the persistent exploitation of the natural and human resources of Black Africa by more 'advanced' North African societies and cultures. Others have experienced, and continue to experience, domination and exploitation by their neighbours, but perhaps few have endured the experience for so long and with so little reversal of roles as have some of the peoples living in what is now the Republic of Chad.

Yet, if only because they are neighbours, Libya and Chad seem destined to continue taking as justifiable an interest in each other's affairs as any other pair of neighbouring states; such as Russia and Poland, the United States and Mexico, Syria and Lebanon . . .

*Richmond, Surrey*                                JOHN WRIGHT
*March 1988*

v

# CONTENTS

# 1

# THE GREAT SAHARA

*'L'Historie c'est d'abord toute géographie'* – Jules Michelet

Africa is the most isolated of the three Old World continents: a peninsula cut off by water and desert from its neighbours. Only the bridge of Sinai and the narrows of the Red Sea exposed Egypt and the Sudanic and Ethiopian coasts to the exchange of influences with Asia, as the Mediterranean narrows exposed the northern coastlands to those of Europe. Nothing apparently ever reached Africa from the Atlantic Ocean until the age of European discovery. But the natural obstacles of the Indian Ocean and the Sahara have always acted as filters of outside influences, inhibiting rather than preventing human contacts with sub-Saharan Africa.

The Sahara in its present form is some 4,000 years old, and has been a formidable natural barrier ever since. Yet men have always travelled across it, exploited its meagre resources, and lived in its few more hospitable centres. The Saharan environment is difficult because it is barren, mostly waterless, and usually hostile, but above all because it is so vast. This largest of the earth's hot deserts is continental in its scale, stretching almost without a break from the Atlantic Ocean to the Red Sea, and from the Mediterranean coast of the Libyan Sirtica to Lake Chad and the River Niger – an area rather larger than the continental United States. Tripoli is as far from Lake Chad as it is from Paris, or London is from Malta. Tripoli is further from Nouadhibou on the Atlantic coast of Mauritania than from the north of Scotland, while the distance from Nouadhibou to Port Sudan on the Red Sea, across the full 5,400 km. width of the Sahara, is the same as New York-Madrid and rather more than New York-San Francisco.

Saharan Africa has not always been desert; the climate has fluctuated markedly in the past. A long, dry spell until about 15,000 years ago was followed by a wet phase lasting some 10,000 years. The lowlands became open savanna, ideal grazing country, while Mediterranean vegetation covered the uplands. The highlands of Tibesti and Hoggar may have been cool and humid, with higher annual rainfall than modern London. Lake Chad was an inland freshwater sea, a Mega-Chad as large as today's Caspian, contained in the basin between the foothills of Air, Hoggar, Tibesti, Ennedi and Darfur; according to Sikes, 'The development and persistence of Mega-Chad must have required sixteen times the present intake of water into the catchment basin'.[1] Possibly the only true desert of northern Africa at

1

that time was the Libyan, reaching as it does now from southern Cyrenaica to western Egypt and the Republic of Sudan.[2] The pastoral wealth of what is now Saharan Africa during the last wet phase is known from the many rock-paintings of species of wild and domestic animals now found only to the south of the desert.[3] Farming and perhaps stockraising reached Egypt from West Asia in the fifth millennium BC, and from there probably spread to other parts of Africa, although it may be unwise to attribute too many African innovations to Egyptian origins. Between the sixth and the third millennium BC, during Africa's first agricultural revolution, Egypt was not yet cut off by a desert barrier from the rest of Africa; the open country beyond Egypt was thus a natural outlet for Egyptian cultural and technical influences.

Northern Africa probably then offered many attractive centres of amenity to its inhabitants, both 'white' caucasoid and black pastoralists. The main divide between the 'white' northern Sahara and the black south may already have been apparent: 'Even at the beginning of historical times, there were important cultural differences between the Saharan peoples and the Berbers of the [Mediterranean] coast'.[4] But it is still likely that there was mutual cultural assimilation between northern and southern peoples from between about 5000 and 2000 BC, when a widespread, neolithic, pastoral culture flourished in what is now the largest of deserts.

The dessication of the Sahara over the last 4,000 years turned woodlands into savanna and savanna into desert. Lake Chad retreated towards its present shallow depression, and the great Erg of Tenere and the fossil dunes of Kanem emerged from the drying northern lake-bed. It was then that the natural east-west zones of Africa north of the Equator began to assume their present identities[5] of Mediterranean coastlands, north and south Sahara,[6] northern and southern Sahel,[7] northern and southern Sudan[8] and equatorial forest. Dessication was far-reaching, but may have been a sudden process; there is evidence that drought came quickly – 'apparently there was no gradual impoverishment, but everything was abandoned'.[9] The formation of the modern Sahara hardened existing geographical divisions and separated peoples. The triangular shaped stretch of land between Air, Borku and Lake Chad became nearly uninhabitable, and it is suggested that the resultant population shifts (roughly between modern Niger and Chad) marked the divide between two main language groups: Chadic to the west and Teda-Daza to the east.[10]

Drought appears to have forced the black Saharans southwards. They were replaced in the central desert by 'white' Libyan Berbers (quite possibly the ancestors of the modern Tuareg), although the black (but not negro) Tebu were able to hold their own in the Tibesti massif and the surrounding piedmont deserts.[11] People resettled in the oases[12] (including the Nile Valley) to the north of the desert and on its richer and wider southern fringes, a development that coincided with the first urban civilisation in Egypt. Although by then cut off from the rest of Africa by desert, the Nile Valley itself remained well within the cultural orbit of West Asia, and later of southern Europe. Both the Niger River valley and the Lake Chad basin appeared to offer some of the necessary conditions for the rise of an early urban civilisation on the Egyptian or Middle Eastern model. But at a decisive stage in their development, such sub-Saharan centres of amenity were denied the cultural fertilisation and influence that might have come from Egypt, as the newly-enlarged desert isolated inner Africa from the mainstreams of Old World evolution.[13] It is significant that the New Kingdom of Egypt (1580–1080 BC) knew little of Africa; superficial knowledge, especially when compared with that of earlier times, was doubtless a reflection of the difficulty and rarity of contacts up the Nile Valley, and particularly across the Sahara. Thus the great desert came to mark, as it still does, a deeper division of the African continent between the 'white' north, linked by geography, race, culture and history to the civilisations of the Mediterranean and the Near East, and sub-Saharan 'Black' Africa, of necessity remote, introverted and culturally largely self-sustaining. While North Africa had a Bronze Age and later an Iron Age, and was in close contact with, or even part of, some of the empires originating in the Middle East or southern Europe in the first millennium BC (Egypt, Persia, Greece, Carthage, Rome), the only parallel experience in sub-Saharan Africa was a late Iron Age. Such isolation might have been deeper had the Sahara formed a complete natural barrier, instead of providing the means for some continuing if selective access between northern 'white' and inner Black Africa, even if the initiative for such contact almost always seems to have come from the north.

Those who remained in the desert adapted to the increasing aridity by becoming nomads, as the best economic alternative to settled life.[14] Only constant mobility, at least during the summer, ensured grazing for their animals. Such true pastoral nomadism seems to have arisen in the Sahara about 3,000 years ago.[15] Nomads have always been forced by their harsh environment to widen their margins of survival. They have traditionally done so by raiding and exploiting the relatively prosperous sedentary communities in the oases or on the desert fringes, by trading with them, or by offering to 'protect' the desert trade of others. The patterns of seasonal transhumance have made many nomads close neighbours of such settled peoples for several months of every year. This proximity inevitably led to predatory exploitation of the sedentary cultivators, especially in the oases and at harvest-time, and eventually to domination on the one hand and servitude on the other.

It is important to distinguish between the Sahara proper and the pre-desert steppes to the north and south. Most of the Sahara is lifeless, but the steppes have supported pastoral, warlike peoples. Their mobility, and in particular their ability to mount swift, long-distance punitive raids, must always have been restricted until they acquired first the horse and later the camel, both of which gave them a remarkable new freedom of movement. The Sahara and its surroundings were always too poor to support a large and expanding population such as from time to time has burst from the deserts of Arabia or the steppes of central Asia to change the course of history. But the Sahara has nevertheless generated a continuous surplus of people who have had a notable impact on the lands to the north, and especially to the south, of the desert.

The Sahara of the pre-camel nomads of the first millennium BC was little different from today's desert, with human activity largely determined by the availability of water and pasture. What is generally called the Sahara in its broadest sense covers a great variety of terrain; much of it consists of steppes, vast plains of gravel, or broken, rocky plateaux. Pure sand deserts form only about one-fifth of the total, and the deep 'deserts within deserts', the terrible 'lands of fear', cover an even smaller part. Examples of the latter include the Ténéré of northeast Niger and the Libyan Desert of southern Cyrenaica and western Egypt, areas that travellers normally avoid. Then there are the relatively favoured regions. Three broad bands of country with slightly higher rainfall cross the desert from north to south: the westernmost, from Morocco to Senegal, runs inland from and parallel to the Atlantic coast; a second links Algeria to the River Niger; and the easternmost follows the high ground along the Red Sea.[16] The main centres of amenity, with sufficient water to support settled life, are either in the depressions or in the uplands. In the natural depressions, underground waters may be near enough to the surface to allow for irrigation from natural springs, wells or man-made subterranean aqueducts.[17] A few of the resultant oases are large, populous, prosperous and important; most are not. The mountain-blocks of the central Sahara, the Hoggar of south-east Algeria and the Tibesti of the Libya-Chad borderlands, the uplands of Air in Niger and Ennedi in Chad, all attract slightly more rain than the surrounding deserts and so combine natural defensive advantage with the possibility of subsistence cultivation and small-scale stock-raising.

Nomads may travel the Sahara for the sake of long- or short-range seasonal pasturing, for petty commerce, or to raid enemies. But travellers have habitually crossed the desert from North Africa to Sudan for one primary reason: trade. North Africa and the Sahara have, with few exceptions, never been prime sources of raw materials or manufactured trade goods. Rather, the ports of the Mediterranean coast and the trading oases of the northern Sahara have always been entrepôts, exchanging goods between two main markets: on the one side Europe and the Mediterranean basin (including Egypt and the Levant), and on the other Black Africa. Despite the Sahara's daunting extent, and the many difficulties of desert travel,[18] it has always been possible to cross it. The existence of trans-Saharan routes was perhaps first determined by nomads' transhumance and annual migration patterns,[19] by their need to attend harvests (especially of dates and grain) in those places where cultivation took place, and by the consequent growth of markets at suitable meeting-places of the desert and the sown. All such economic and social activity attracted a certain seasonal traffic, local and regional exchanges expanding as more distant markets (especially for Saharan salt in the Sudan) were opened up. Trade eventually became inter-continental in scope with the rise of the Mediterranean mercantile empires in the first millennium BC. In North Africa, the inflow of Levantine and European manufactured trade goods corresponded with a regular supply across the Sahara of Black Africa's gold, slaves and, for the Roman circus, wild animals.

The strong commercial pull exerted on North Africa by the Mediterranean lands in general and southern Europe in particular was felt as far off as Sudanic Africa, which exercised a reciprocal commercial fascination on North Africa, and a less direct one on the trading states on the far side of the Mediterranean. In marking the main divide between the cultures of Black Africa and those of the temperate Mediterranean lands, the Sahara has always been an important trading frontier.[20] And if trade has been the main incentive (indeed, often the sole incentive) for maintaining trans-Saharan contacts, the Sudanic lands have in the long run benefited from the many material and cultural influences carried across the desert by traders over the past two to three thousand years. Thus the destinations of trans-Saharan trade routes were determined by the location of the relatively few anchorages on the exposed and surprisingly inhospitable Mediterranean coast of North Africa, and by the corresponding location of markets and raw materials in Sudanic Africa. The route between such points was determined by terrain, the likelihood of meeting hostile or friendly desert peoples, and by the whereabouts of pasture. But the primary consideration was always the availability of water, a criterion perhaps even more critical before the widespread use of the Arabian camel from late Roman times onwards.[21] Mobility in the desert had before then been limited by the carrying capacities and endurance of bullocks, donkeys and horses, although a convincing case has been made for their adaptability to commercial desert travel, and of horses to desert warfare.[22] The proper horse is not a native of North Africa, but was brought from Asia to Egypt by the Hyksos invaders about 1700 BC, from where it spread into northern Africa. Horses were harnessed to chariots long before they were ridden,[23] and the use of such chariots is attested by many rock-art representations of them found in the Sahara. Much has been made of the fact that a series of known sites of such drawings reaches almost from the Mediterranean to the River Niger,[24] and a similar series crosses the desert further west. Yet these scattered sites do not necessarily mark the course of an ancient trans-Saharan trade route: the light vehicles depicted were used for hunting or in warfare, not for commercial transport, and much of the country where they are found is far too rugged to be crossed by any long-distance trade route, let alone one using wheeled vehicles.

At the southernmost sweep of the Gulf of Sirte at Agheila the Mediterranean penetrates deepest into the Sahara, and thus comes closest to central Africa. But there are no good natural harbours or means of settled livelihood on all that long, barren coast, and its hinterland is dominated by the Libyan Desert, the world's largest true desert, and a natural barrier to human traffic. The coast of Tripolitania, situated further north, offers shorter sea routes to Malta, Sicily and southern Italy; it has several good natural harbours, a moderately productive hinterland, and access to three routes into the interior. Two lead by different ways to the Fezzanese oases and from there via the Kawar oases to Lake Chad; the third goes south-westwards through the Ghadames oasis to Air and the River Niger. Tripolitania's close maritime proximity to Sudanic Africa was first recognised by the first international traders in North Africa, the Phoenicians. They found their way to that part of the Mediterranean simply by following the coast from their native Levant. From their original African settlements, first at Utica and then at Carthage in northern Tunisia, they built up trading contacts with the central and western Mediterranean, in addition to their existing commercial networks in the eastern basin and the Levant. Carthage dominated the central Mediterranean narrows between Africa, Malta and Sicily, but trading posts established some 500 km. further south on the coast of Tripolitania attracted the trade with inner Africa. That the Carthaginians found and developed at least three such Tripolitanian trading posts (Sabratha; Ui'at-Oea-Tripoli; Lpqy-Lepcis-Leptis Magna) suggests that openings for worthwhile trade with inner Africa already existed. There must have been greater commercial incentives than mere traffic in the low-grade products of local animal husbandry and subsistence farming; indeed, a case has been made for the import of precious stones into Tripolitania from across the Sahara.[25] The geographical advantage of northern Tripolitania in trans-Saharan trade ensured the survival into modern times of one of the three Carthaginian trading posts, Tripoli and its hinterland taking their names from the original trio of towns.

Tripolitania's role in the Mediterranean-Saharan entrepôt trade has always been closely associated with the natural corridor of the Fezzanese oases, which lie in a series of depressions with abundant underground water nearly in the middle of the northern desert, about one-third of the way along the shortest route from Tripoli to Lake Chad, and mid-way between the Nile and the Niger. They have always been an essential resting-place for men and their animals on the long desert journey, providing supplies of dates for desert travel, and serving as markets at this meeting-place of white and Black Africa. These oases have always had a certain 'Sudanic' character, in some respects having more in common with sub-Saharan Africa than with the nearer Mediterranean coastlands.[26] From these modest centres of amenity, routes lead to all parts of the desert: northwards to the ancient trading oasis of Ghadames (the entrepôt for Tunis and Tripoli) and to Tripolitania; north-east to Cyrenaica, Egypt and the Levant; eastwards to the Kufra oasis and eventually to the valley of the Upper Nile; southwards to the plains of Chad; and south-west of the Niger Bend country and western Sudan. From Fezzan, the ancient 'road' to Lake Chad skirts the natural barrier of the Murzuk Sand Sea to pass between the two great mountain blocks of the central Sahara, the Tibesti to the east and the Hoggar to the west. Both are huge: the Hoggar and the neighbouring Tassili are almost as large as France; the Tibesti is equal in area to Austria and Switzerland combined; both are volcanic in origin, and forbidding sources of danger to travellers. For these rugged uplands have long offered both refuge and subsistence to peoples forced by the harsh poverty of their environment to prey on travellers or to raid their marginally richer enemies and rivals. Although smaller than the Hoggar, the Tibesti is higher and even more rugged: Emi Koussi, an extinct volcano as large as Etna, dominates the southern range, reaching a peak of 3,400 m. (11,000 feet).

In this part of the central Sahara, settled life is only possible at over 1,000 m., where annual rainfall of between 50 and 100mm. is at least five times higher than in the surrounding plains. Rainwater that collects at the bottom of mountain valleys and in the craters of extinct volcanoes creates some pasture; run-off from the mountains sustains better quality, and more extensive pasture in the piedmont plains to the south. The Hoggar seems long to have been the home of white Berber peoples, ancestors probably of the modern Kel Ahaggar and

Kel Ajjer Tuareg tribal confederations, and of other Tuareg confederations now established further to the south and south-west. The Tibesti remains the home of a more ancient Saharan people, the black (but not negro) Tebu. Probably no more than 10,000 have ever lived there at any one time,[27] and the sum of their widespread communities in modern Libya, Chad, and the Niger Republic is less than 250,000 people. However, like the Tuareg, they have often decisively influenced the flow of trade between the Mediterranean and Lake Chad, and they have had much to do with the economic, political and military fortunes of the central Sudan.

Two-thirds of the way from Tripolitania to Lake Chad, and nearly in mid-Sahara, the oases of Kawar offer another essential restingplace for caravans, and an important source of salt for export to the largely saltless Sudan. Kawar consists of a chain of wells (some of them artificial), meagre and far apart, aligned roughly north-south, and marking a narrow path across the Ténéré and its natural extension, the great Erg of Bilma. While the Ténéré is not impassable to caravans, it has always been a barrier between peoples. Kawar's political importance, however, is due to its marking the natural divide between the eastern and western Sudan, between the white Berber Tuareg to the west and the black Tebu of Kawar itself and the higher country to the east.[28] South of Kawar, difficult but passable dune country finally gives way first to open bush-land and then to savanna near Lake Chad. Trans-Saharan trade routes led from other entrepôts in North Africa, and particularly from Morocco to the lands of the upper Senegal and Niger; but apart from the ancient track that linked Assiut in Egypt with the eastern Sudan at least from the time of the Old Kingdom (2800–2250 BC),[29] the central route from Tripolitania to Lake Chad seems to have been used in one form or another since very early times.

The relatively open and well-watered Sudanese grasslands south of the great desert are clearly ancient centres of amenity. They are fairly narrow, compressed between the pre-Saharan steppes to the north and the southern limits to cattle-herding imposed by the tsetse fly and the tropical forest-belt, but people, trade and ideas have flown relatively easily across the country that extends with few natural barriers from the Nile Valley to the Atlantic coast of Senegal and Guinea. Various breeds of domesticated Asiatic cattle were brought into this part of Africa from about 5000 BC onwards,[30] and an agricultural food-producing revolution took place during the third or second millennium BC after the diffusion of Neolithic techniques and the application of botanical knowledge to local cereals.[31] Nevertheless, the high population density and all the other necessary preconditions for an advanced urban civilisation on the Egyptian, Mesopotamian or Indus model were never achieved. It was only towards the end of the first millennium AD that outside influences eventually encouraged the emergence of a series of extensive, populous and powerful Sudanese kingdoms and empires. Such influences worked their way through from the settled lands of the upper Nile Valley, but most penetrated from the north through the Saharan nomads. As Sir Richmond Palmer put it, 'Ancient Sudanese routes of commerce and culture, long before the Christian era, spread the vestiges of upward progress among the more primitive prehistoric folk of Africa, and created a common heritage or nationality.'[32]

## NOTES

1. S. Sikes, *Lake Chad*, London, 1972, p. 3; *see* map 3, p. 4.

2. J.Ki-Zerbo, *Histoire de l'Afrique noire d'hier à demain*, Paris, 1972; see map, p. 55, 'Le Sahara au Néolithique'.

3. See H. Lhote, *The Search for the Tassili Frescoes*, London, 1959.

4. G. Camps, 'Beginnings of Pastoralism and Cultivation in North-West Africa and the Sahara: Origins of the Berbers' in J.D. Clark (ed.), *The Cambridge History of Africa, Vol. 1: From the Earliest Times to c.500 BC.*, Cambridge, 1982, p. 612.

5. R. Mauny, *Tableau géographique de l'Ouest Africain au Moyen Age*, Dakar, 1961, fig. 54., p. 214.

6. *Sahara*, the Arabic for desert; 'Sahara Desert' is tautological.

7. *Sahel*, the Arabic for 'coast'; some read it as 'plain'.

8. *Sudan*, from the Arabic *Bilad al-Sudan*, 'Land of the Blacks', the broad belt of savanna south of the Sahara and north of the tropical forest of West and Central Africa extending from the Senegal River to the Nile.

9. O. Davies, 'The Neolithic Revolution in Tropical Africa', *Transactions of the Historical Society of Ghana*, IV, II (1960).

10. H.F.C. Smith, 'The Early States of Central Sudan' in J.F.A. Ajayi and M. Crowder (eds), *History of West Africa*, vol. I, London, 1971, p. 162.

11. R. Mauny, 'Trans-Saharan Contacts and the Iron Age in West Africa' in J.D. Fage (ed.), *The Cambridge History of Africa, Vol. 2: 500 BC to AD 1050*, p. 337.

12. For the survival of fish and other aquatic life in the Saharan oases, see G. Scortecci, *Sahara*, Milan, 1945, pp. 169–94.

13. J.D. Fage, *A History of Africa*, London, 1978, p. 17. See also R. Mauny, *Tableau géographique*, pp. 195–6.

14. A.M. Khazanov, *Nomads and the Outside World*, Cambridge, 1984, p. 200. Nomadism is not necessarily a precursor of settled agriculture; the reverse may be the case.

15. *Ibid.*, p. 107.

16. S. Baier, *A History of the Sahara in the Nineteenth Century*, Boston, Mass., 1978, p. 4.

17. For the workings of the foggara, see C.L. Briggs, *Tribes of the Sahara*, Cambridge, 1960, pp. 10–12.

18. For modern accounts of the hardships and dangers of traditional Saharan camel travel, see G. Moorhouse, *The Fearful Void*, London, 1974; R. Trench, *Forbidden Sands*, London, 1978; M. Asher, *In Search of the Forty Days Road*, London, 1984; T. Edwards, *Beyond the Last Oasis*, London, 1985; M. Asher, *Impossible Journey: Two Against the Sahara*, London, 1989.

19. See Khazanov, *Nomads and the Outside World*, pp. 37-9; J. Chapelle, *Nomades Noirs du Sahara: Les Toubous*, Paris, 1982, pp. 210-16.
20. Fage, *History of Africa*, p. 70.
21. Mauny, *Tableau géographique*, p. 202, notes that Saharan wells, especially in rocky places, could only be dug with *metal* tools.
22. Briggs, *Tribes of the Sahara*, pp. 20-1; E.W. Bovill, *The Golden Trade of the Moors*, London, 1970, pp. 15-17.
23. R. Law, *The Horse in West African History*, London, 1980, pp. 1-2.
24. See, for example, R. Oliver and J.D. Fage, *A Short History of Africa*, Harmondsworth, 1962, map 4, p. 55; Lhote, *The Search for the Tassili Frescoes*, map facing p: 22; Lhote, *Les Chars rupestres Sahariens*, Toulouse, 1982.
25. B.H. Warmington, *Carthage*, London, 1964, p. 66; Bovill, *The Golden Trade*, pp. 20-1, 26-7.
26. See E.F. Gautier, *Le Sahara*, Paris, 1950, p. 134; *Il Sahara Italiano*, I: *Fezzan e Oasi di Gat*, Rome, 1937, pp. 451, 495.
27. *Tou* in Teda means 'mountain' and *Tubu* 'man of the mountain'. B. Lanne, *Tchad-Libye: La querelle des frontières*, Paris, 1982, p. 137.
28. See K.S. Vikor, 'The Oasis of Salt: The History of Kawar, a Saharan Centre of Salt Production', unpubl. thesis, University of Bergen, 1979.
29. The so-called *Darb al-Arba'in* of the later Arab traders, so named because it usually took forty days to travel.
30. See B. Davidson, 'Africa in Historical Perspective' in *Africa South of the Sahara*, London, 1982, map, p. 5: 'Early Movements of Different Kinds of Cattle'.
31. Oliver and Fage, *A Short History*, p. 28; Lhote, *Les Chars*, pp. 47-62.
32. R. Palmer, *The Bornu, Sahara and Sudan*, London, 1936, p. 3.

# 2

# WHERE AFRICA BEGINS

*'Ex Africa semper aliquid novi'* – proverbial, from Pliny

The people known to the classical world as 'Libyans'[1] lived in North Africa west of Egypt and were the ancestors of the modern Berbers. Few in number, widely scattered between the Mediterranean and the central Sahara, they had little culture or political organisation.[2] There were no large settlements, no towns or cities until the Phoenicians and the Greeks founded them.[3] One possible exception was the tribe or tribal confederation of the Garamantes, first mentioned by Herodotus in the fifth century BC. He described them as a powerful people (*ethnos*) living ten days' journey west of Augila, that is, in the central Fezzan. According to him, these people used four-horse chariots to hunt the swift-footed Ethiopian troglodytes (this is the first written confirmation of the evidence of Saharan rock-art).[4] The brief passages of Herodotus on the people of North Africa tell of a presumably 'white' Garamantean people, socially organised and with a relatively advanced technology, exploiting the natural resources of the central Fezzanese oases, and hunting down the primitive Saharan blacks, presumably to enslave them (the 'Ethiopians' he refers to were not necessarily negroes, but probably ancestors of the modern Tebu).[5] The Carthaginians' trans-Saharan trading contacts, either from Carthage itself or through the Tripolitanian emporia,[6] were carried on through the Garamantes. They occupied the oases connecting the most direct route from the Mediterranean to Central Africa, the so-called 'Garamantean road'; outsiders would have been excluded from desert trade, its profits and its secrets, just as they were in later times. Although the Greek cities established in northern Cyrenaica from the seventh century BC had a stronger agricultural base than the Carthaginian emporia of Tripolitania, they also traded indirectly with Central Africa, through the Augila oases.[7] From Augila, trade passed south-westwards through the Garamantes, rather than by the long and difficult route leading directly south from Cyrenaica through the Libyan Desert to Kufra. If the Garamantes did indeed control the trade of the central Sahara, they are more likely to have had pack-animal caravans rather than the horse-drawn carts that rock-paintings suggest they might have used,[8] for there is no firm evidence of a system of Saharan commercial cart-roads.[9] The fact that the horse was first introduced into West and West-Central Africa from the north as an animal to be ridden rather than driven,[10] and that the wheel was for

11

long unknown south of the Sahara, would seem to weaken the case for trans-Saharan trade by wheeled transport in the distant past.

The use of iron and iron-smelting are thought to have reached the Sudan from two possible sources. One was the 'white' Kushitic kingdom with its capital at the great iron-working centre of Meroe on the upper Nile, which flourished in the last pre-Christian centuries and in the first century AD. The other, and perhaps more likely source, was Phoenician-Carthaginian North Africa.[11] Iron weapons were being imported into Sudan from North Africa by the third century BC,[12] but the techniques of iron-working did not reach Fezzan and the lands south of the desert until much later.[13] Once the techniques were known, iron metallurgy flourished in the Sudanese savanna, where iron ore and wood for fuel were plentiful,[14] and places that had had no Bronze Age enjoyed a belated Iron Age, with all its attendant technological and socio-economic transformations.

The Garamantes next appear in written history in the first century AD when coastal North Africa was under Roman rule. The account by Pliny the Elder of the expedition by the Proconsul of Africa, L. Cornelius Balbus[15] tells of a show of force directed against the Garamantean capital at Garama (Germa) in the Wadi Agial of central Fezzan in AD 19. This and other expeditions[16] during the first century AD seem to have convinced the Romans of the futility of trying to hold lines of communication into the interior and of gaining mastery over elusive desert peoples. In Tripolitania imperial frontiers never reached far into the desert, and by the third century the flow of traffic on the three main trans-Saharan trade routes came to be controlled by large frontier forts. These were sited at Ghadames on the trans-Saharan route from the port of Sabratha to the River Niger; at Gheria al-Garbia on the direct north-south route from Oea (Tripoli) to Fezzan across the Hammada al-Hamra; and at Bu Ngem on the old, circuitous road from the port of Leptis to the oases of Fezzan.[17]

Roman North Africa, spread along the Mediterranean from Egypt to Morocco, occupied only the cultivable strip north of the pre-desert steppes. The Romans themselves knew little of the Sahara and even less of what lay beyond; the second-century Alexandrian geographer Ptolemy knew the desert only as far as Tuat and Fezzan. The classical world had far better knowledge of the East African coast, with its direct access to the rich cultural and trading milieu of the Indian Ocean.[18] Nevertheless, through the agency of the Garamantes, the Romans traded across the desert. According to Ptolemy,[19] the latter made two trans-Saharan expeditions in Garamantean company about AD 100, one of which may have gone as far as Sudan, for he reports that it reached the unidentified country of Agysmiba, frequented by the rhinoceros. Such expeditions were intended to assess the trade prospects of inner Africa and the produce that might profitably be imported into the Roman world: ivory (by that time rare in North Africa itself), possibly carbuncles and other gems, civet and slaves.[20]

Slaves driven across the desert by the Garamantes were presumably taken in raids along the southern Saharan fringes; wild animals for the Roman circuses, and Sudanese ivory, were similarly raided and traded. Carbuncle stones, although an important item of trans-Saharan trade at that time, have not been identified, nor has their source. There is little evidence for a central Saharan gold traffic in Roman times, although the Carthaginians did trade in West African gold. Overall, the Garamantes' relations with the Sudan were as much predatory as commercial; they took slaves and ivory directly, without payment, although other commodities may have been exchanged for foodstuffs or Saharan salt.[21] However certain goods always penetrated the Sahara as long as it was in the interests of middlemen that they do so. Thus arms and metals were imported into the Sudan from the north from early times.

The size and wealth of the three seaports of Roman Tripolitania – Sabratha, Oea and especially Leptis Magna – reflected their role as the Mediterranean outlets of a flourishing trans-Saharan trade. This was second in importance only to the export of local agricultural produce, and in particular low-grade olive oil. Although trans-Saharan trade in Roman times seems to have had limited cultural impact on the peoples of the desert, 'it was a source of a constant trickle of fresh negro blood which has continued ever since to seep slowly and irregularly into most of them, both sedentary folk and nomads'.[22]

Even if they never permanently penetrated the desert or established their own communities beyond the pre-desert fringes, the Romans built up a flourishing trade with the Garamantes. The remains of the Garamantean capital at Germa (Garama) in the Wadi Agial of central Fezzan, and the thousands of graves found nearby, have yielded many Roman products from the late first century AD onwards.[23] Such remains suggest that the Garamantes came under considerable Roman material and technical influence. There is no evidence however that Rome and its works were ever known beyond the Sahara, as they were known beyond all the other, but less inhibiting frontiers of the empire; written records are both brief and vague, the archaeological evidence is non-existent.

During the Carthaginian period, and especially during the more than four centuries of Roman occupation, northern Tripolitania was largely detached from its Saharan hinterland. The pre-desert became a frontier between the civilised world and the 'barbarians' beyond.

The pre-desert steppes themselves were not worth conquering, and their nomadic tribes were an elusive foe, beyond even the Romans' ability to control. Tripolitania was thus brought into the international Mediterranean civilisation as a minor province of the Roman, and eventually Christian, empire. Christianity, among the other 'Roman' influences, spread from its vital centres of Alexandria and Carthage into all the remoter regions of North Africa, and reached up the Nile Valley to Nubia and Ethiopia. But there is no evidence that it ever crossed the Sahara, at least not from the North African provinces; and it never spread into the Western Sudan.[24] During the Byzantine sixth century, Christianity is said to have reached the northern Saharan oases (Siwa, Augila, Ghadames and others) and the Garamantes.[25] The few discernible Christian influences among the modern Tuareg possibly reflect some penetration of the Sahara at that time, but Jewish rather than Christian influences seem to have played a greater role in the evolution of desert society.[26]

After prolonged religious and civil strife and economic decline, Roman North Africa was overrun by Germanic Vandal invaders in the late fifth century. This collapse coincided with, and partly prompted, the social and strategic changes that were to set North Africa on a different historical course, partly reopening it to the Saharan hinterland and the lands beyond the great desert. The Byzantine reconquest of the sixth century only postponed what had by then become an inevitable process.

In the first Christian centuries the Romans were able to control the influx of nomads seeking seasonal pasture and trade within the imperial frontiers. But the nomads themselves were acquiring greater mastery of the steppe lands immediately north of the desert, and eventually those to the south of it as well. The key to this revolution was the Arabian camel. Though not a native of Africa, it was probably brought into Egypt by the invading Persians in 525 BC. It took a further thousand years to spread through the Sahara, despite its obvious advantages over any other pack or riding animal. The Romans may have brought the camel into Tripolitania and the Maghrib, and the traders of Leptis Magna were probably the first in Africa to organise camel-caravans, perhaps in the third century. About AD 500 the value of the camel in desert warfare was demonstrated when the horses of mounted Vandals refused to charge a defensive ring of tribesmen's camels. The coming of the camel opened a new era for the northern half of Africa.[27] It could travel over longer distances faster than other animals, needing food and particularly water at much longer intervals, and was in all ways better suited to the harsh exactions of the desert. Thus nomadic tribes taking to the camel (or perhaps becoming nomadic in the process of adopting it) became more mobile: distances were shortened and even the remotest pastures could be exploited. The Sahara, though still a formidable natural barrier, became relatively easier to cross by raiding-parties, trade-caravans and herders seeking pasture. 'It was an economic revolution, without exaggeration comparable to that of the railway, the automobile and the aeroplane.'[28] The result of this new-found freedom of movement was the rise in the fifth and sixth centuries on the pre-desert steppes of a new social order represented by the camel-mounted Berber pastoralist, organised into large predatory tribes or confederations of tribes. As E.-F. Gautier puts it:

The camel is livestock, inseparable from the man that raises it and makes use of it. This man is the nomad, the great camel-nomad, grouped into formidable tribes, each one of which, with no previous training, is a sort of natural regiment, speedy, elusive, liable to appear at any moment, as unexpected as a catastrophe, from the unguarded wastes: a powerful military machine. And this great nomad, inured to the privations of the desert, is as a result consumed with overwhelming lusts, greedy for possessions and power; in his wretched poverty, this human savage confusedly pursues a constant dream of pillage and domination.[29]

While excluded from the settled lands of the Romans, the nomads' political power and coherence seem to have been increased by an influx of migrants, refugees and exiles from Roman North Africa, and possibly from further east. On the pre-desert steppes of southern Tunisia and Tripolitania there arose in the fifth and sixth centuries the great tribal confederations of the Zenata and the Lawata, camel-mounted pastoral nomads who augmented their meagre resources by frequent pillaging raids into the settled coastlands. The Zenata roamed southwards into the desert grazing-grounds after the first winter rains and spent the summer in the northern mountains: the Gebel Nefusah of northern Tripolitania is named after an important Jewish tribal element in the Zenata confederation. Indeed, Jewish influence and possibly leadership is thought to account for the unusual political coherence of the Zenata – unusual, that is, by the standards of fractious Saharan tribalism.[30] The Zenata and the camel appeared in the Maghrib at about the same time, and together revolutionised Saharan society.[31] The collapse of Roman power, the Vandal occupation and the Byzantine reconquest in the fifth and sixth centuries resulted in a period of upheaval encouraging the dangerously mobile Berber nomads to greater boldness, both in their raids on the poorly defended coastlands and in the penetration of the Sahara and the lands beyond.

The formidable barrier represented by the Sahara even after the widespread adoption of the camel was nevertheless the means by which outside influences permeated to the Sudan. Egypt has always

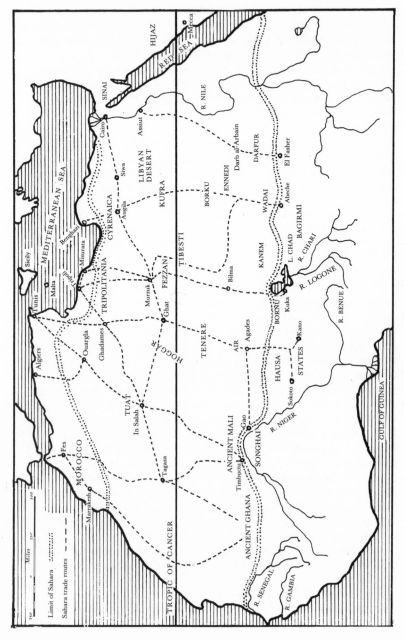

Trade Routes of Northern Africa

been a wellspring of ideas and influences, spreading deeper into Africa via the uniquely favourable route of the Nile Valley. But evidence of their further diffusion from the Upper Nile into the Sudanic savanna remains meagre. It has been suggested that the destruction of the Meroitic civilisation in the Nilotic Sudan in the fourth century by the rising power of Ethiopian Axum may have dispersed remnants of that civilisation throughout the lands between the Upper Nile and Lake Chad.[32] But traces of any such influence are slight. It seems, for instance, more likely that knowledge of iron metallurgy reached West Africa from across the Sahara (where iron spears are clearly shown on rock-paintings), rather than from Meroe.[33] There is plentiful evidence of successive human migrations into the Sudanic lands by way of the Nile Valley, but these migrants seem to have imparted no new elements of civilisation to that region of Africa.[34] And it has been argued that, 'Before the coming of the Arabs, West Africa was practically cut off from the worlds of Egypt and the Mediterranean, and evolved on its own with the least outside influences, along age-old ancestral patterns.'[35]

Any nomadic tribe is a political rather than a territorial organisation, particularly in its relations with the sedentary world, but also with the nomadic one.[36] Nevertheless, three main nomadic groups – the Tebu, the Tuareg and the Moors – came in due course to be associated with the respective parts of the Sahara where they were clearly paramount, and where intruders went in risk of their lives and property unless suitable tribute was paid or protection sought. What is not clear from the evidence is how and where the great Tuareg confederations of the central and south-western Sahara, down to the Niger Bend, came into being; also unclear is their relationship to the Berber confederations of the Zenata and the Sanhaja. It is tempting to assume a direct ethnic, cultural and political ancestry, but in fact the processes of evolution seem not to have been so straightforward. What is known, however, is that the 'white' nomadic forerunners of the Tuareg moved into and dominated all the desert from western Fezzan through the uplands of the Hoggar, Air and the Adrar of the Iforas, where the topography guaranteed their safety and water was sufficient for their needs. There was a tendency over the centuries to retreat before irresistible hostile pressures from the north by moving southwards and westwards towards the Niger Bend, and even beyond it. These white, Berber-speaking Saharans, with their own distinctive, partly matrilineal, societies of veiled men and unveiled women generally dominated the black (but not necessarily negro) and largely aboriginal inhabitants of the oases, reducing them to the state of serf-cultivators, the *haratin*.[37] Tuareg society also had the most unusual institution of slave-herdsmen.[38] But there were distinct geographical limits to the ascendancy of the Tuareg and their nomadic ancestors. In the west, a different people emerged, eventually attaining their modern identity, the so-called Moors, through a far greater Arab admixture with Berber stock than the Tuareg ever experienced.[39] And to the east, the Tuareg never penetrated the formidable natural barriers of the Libyan Desert or the Tibesti Mountains. From the remote oases of Taiserbo and Kufra in the north-east to Kawar in the south-west, through the jagged lunar landscapes of the Tibesti Mountains, the Ennedi plateau and the Borku depression, to the savannas of Lake Chad, the black Tebu and related peoples in all their ramifications have never been fully overcome or absorbed by outsiders.

According to Chapelle, 'this is a free people, which in the course of centuries has known how to preserve the independence of its tents, live in its own manner and make itself feared and respected by its neighbours.'[40] The Tebu and similar peoples probably owe their survival from the Saharan Neolithic to the present day to a rare combination of factors. Among these are their singular hardiness and endurance; their ability to survive (if need be in small, isolated family groups) in a desert environment and climate harsher than even the Tuareg can endure; the extreme poverty and remoteness of their surroundings, which long discouraged intruders; the extraordinary mobility of at least the men, whether in trading, raiding or escape; the almost complete lack of a social hierarchy and the consequent resilience and fluidity of their social and political allegiances; their lack of a strongly identified cultural or religious inspiration or even of a cultural, religious or political centre; and their dedicated and predatory ferocity towards their many enemies, far and near. Their origins and history however are quite obscure. It is generally supposed that they are the same people as the 'Ethiopians' described by Herodotus.[41] But 'having never founded a state, having never fought great battles, having never kept chronicles and archives, the Tebu place their historiography . . . before a disquieting void.'[42]

The Tebu are a family of people with certain common characteristics. Occupying a central role and place in the Sahara, they (rather like the Germans in Europe) are known to themselves and to their neighbours by many different names. Such names also in part depend on geographical location – Tebu, Teda, Teda-Tou, Daza, Daza-Gada, Kreda, Gorane, Bidayet, Zaghawa, Braouia, Ikaraden.[43] Physically, the Tebu in the Tibesti region may look like the negroid *haratin* serfs of the Saharan oases. Their skin-colour is 'normally very dark in all respects' yet their colour is combined with 'clear European traits'[44] and their blood-group is quite different from those of both the *haratin* and the Sudanic negroes. But it is so similar to that of the

Berbers that it has been suggested that the Tebu might originally have been Berbers, 'however outwardly negroid they may have become in relatively recent times'.[45] On the other hand, their dialects, now classified as 'central Saharan', seem most closely related to certain negroid Sudanese language groups and show no greater Berber influence than can be explained through long contact with Berber-speaking neighbours.[46] Such contradictions make the Tebu and their near relations the most enigmatic of all Saharan peoples. But their characteristics are believed to be aboriginal, and not of recent origin. E.-F. Gautier has called them 'a prehistoric humanity', the last representatives of an 'Ethiopian' Sahara and of a people who used to extend as far north as the Atlas Mountains.[47] Their characteristics are high nervous tension, impulsiveness, temperamental instability, unsociability and an inveterate mistrust of their fellow-men.[48] Personal status is judged by the number of a man's enemies, and the threshold of mortal offence is accordingly very low: sarcasm, innuendo, moral or material harm, the wounding of an animal, are enough to bring the daggers into play.[49]

A people as diffuse as the Tebu, without effective political, religious or military leaders, and with no identifiable political centre – 'the principle of freedom raised almost to the level of anarchy' – [50] are not readily overcome, absorbed, or eliminated by others. The northeastern Tebu outposts of Taiserbo and Kufra, protected for centuries by their extreme remoteness, only fell to Arab invaders in the eighteenth century; and it was not till the early twentieth century that the Turks attempted the military control of the Tibesti massif itself. This forbidding natural fortress seems always to have been, as it remains today, the heartland of the Tebu people. It is not necessarily a political, religious or cultural homeland, but rather a centre of attraction and dispersion for many different Tebu groups over the centuries.[51] It is a place of relative amenity and final refuge which, in a largely hostile world, a handful of men may successfully defend. Water is always present, as are thin mountain pastures just sufficient for flocks, if not herds, and upland valleys where a few palms and crops may be tended. 'Here, in a remote corner in the depths of the Libyan Desert refuge, a little piece of the ancient negro Sahara has preserved itself more or less intact.'[52]

The Tebu and related people may feel little 'familial' solidarity among themselves, little allegiance to the greater racial whole (although this is not necessarily how they are perceived by outsiders). But they are clearly distinguishable from other Saharan and Sudanic peoples by language of several dialects; by a 'strangely homogenous physical type'; by similar manners and customs; by the same social ideas; and by common attitudes, gestures and reflexes, all of which contribute to the identity of a Tebu – man woman or child – living between the 13th and 23rd parallels.[53]

Although divided into many different clans, the Tebu of Borku, Ennedi and Tibesti acknowledge no supreme clan that imposes tribute or laws on others.[54] The Tebu clan is not like a traditional nomadic tribe, living and moving under the authority of a chief. All members of a clan are equal; this 'acephalous social system' consists of free and independent men and women, dispersed in space, but united by blood.[55] Clans tend to disintegrate over a period of time through the powerful centrifugal pressures of Tebu life and society. Nevertheless, the Tebu are socially stratified, with the 'noble' warrior clans carrying the greatest prestige. The Azza clans form a broad subservient class or caste, comprising several occupational groups (and generally despised as such) – hunters, smiths, tanners and woodworkers, with the women working as weavers, potters and basket-makers.[56] They occupy much the same position as the 'vassal' tribes in Tuareg society; they are not warriors, but look to 'noble' clans for protection as 'clients'.[57] At the bottom of society are the black slaves brought from Sudan who traditionally did all the hardest work; the Tebu had a reputation for treating these people harshly.[58]

The Tebu have never had a state of their own, yet they have spread themselves across an immense area of the central Sahara and the southern savannas, some 1,300 kilometres square, covering some 1.7 million square km., or the equal of modern Libya. Few in number (perhaps an estimated 200,000 today) and widely dispersed, they have in some respects lived outside the main currents of Saharan history. Despite, and yet also partly because of, their own anarchic and turbulent traditions, they have been a constant and usually malign presence in mid-Sahara, endangering (yet never wholly severing) the always precarious communications between the two sides of the central desert. They have long been an unquantifiable, unpredictable factor in relations between, to the north, the settled Mediterranean coastlands of Tripolitania, as well as the inhabited oases of Fezzan, and to the south the populous Sudanic countries beyond the central Sahara. The Tebus' relationship with the northern Saharans and the peoples of the Maghrib has either been briefly opportunist, offensive and predatory, or defensive and passive, depending on circumstances. But the relationship with their southern neighbours has more usually been openly aggressive; and if the Tebu peoples have never had, or been able to make, an identifiable state of their own, they have sometimes played a central role in the processes of Sudanic state-formation on behalf of others, a role that has continued right up to the present time.

Like the Tuareg, the Tebu have over the centuries slowly been giving way to the irresistible pressure of stronger and more numerous enemies from the north. They have in their turn increased their own pressure on weaker and more numerous pastoral peoples in richer lands to the south: towards the Niger Bend country in the case of the Tuareg, and towards Lake Chad in the case of the Tebu. Thus if the Tebu are no longer found in such northern Saharan oases as Augila (except perhaps on brief trading visits) and apparently only remain in oases such as Kufra on suffrance, they are most numerous in central and north-central Chad. Their presence across an immense area now covered by southern Libya, north and central Chad, the north-east of the Niger Republic, the westernmost areas of the Sudan Republic, and even north-east Nigeria, remains a common historical factor in all these places. It is a presence underlying, influencing and at least in part explaining the course of events in a part of Central Africa with complex ethnic, linguistic and cultural divisions. The Tebu, in particular, provide the constant human link, the common point of reference, between lands extending from one side of the central Sahara to the other.

The Tebu of southern Libya, the Tibesti and north-west Chad are the Teda. They call themselves Tedagaza, or speakers of the Tedagaza dialect of a language group closely related to Dazaga and Kanuri. Broadly defined as camel-herders who have economic links with the date-palm groves of northern Chad, they are divided into at least twenty clans, of which the most 'noble' and prestigious, and considered the most 'pure', is the Tomaghra. But such attributes confer no special authority. The second great northern group is the Daza or Dazagada (those who speak Dazaga); they tend to dominate the great camel-raising country of the Borku depression and the Ennedi plateau. Southern groups of Tebu people are spread across the Sahelian provinces of modern central Chad. The most important groups are found along the usually dry waterway of the Bahr al-Ghazal (the Kreda), in the dune country of Kanem north and north-east of Lake Chad (frequented by at least six mixed groups), and in the higher lands of Wadai and Biltine to the east and across the border into the Sudanese Republic through the uplands of southern Darfur as far east as El Fasher (Zaghawa and Cherfada).[59] Outside Borku, Ennedi and Tibesti, the Tebu are a minority: a nomad minority adjacent to and constantly moving among a partly-settled majority. They have never been easy people to control and administer, most of them displaying, as noted above, a character 'turbulent et batailleur'. Their very presence across wide stretches of pre-desert country suggests a long history, reaching back over at least the past thousand years, of turbulent relations with an extraordinarily complex mosaic of neighbours hardly more amenable, governable or settled than themselves, all of whom have usually competed for the same resources in marginal country where drought or other natural phenomena can make the difference between a state of peaceful prosperity and warring want.

Because the Tebu can survive under the most harsh conditions and have long been used to raiding and trading over great distances (even to Siwa in the Western Desert[60] and the Nile), they are found in some of the remotest and most desolate corners of the Sahara. The Gebel Arkenau is a granite massif rising over 600 m. from the desert plain at the junction of the modern Egyptian, Libyan and Sudanese borders. It was only mapped when the Egyptian explorer Hassanein Bey reached it and the nearby mountain oasis of Uwaynat in April 1923, finding a small group of Tebu refugees ('Goranes') in residence.[61] Tebu had from time immemorial been in Kufra, which seems to have been a centre of Tebu attraction and dispersion until its Arab conquest and Islamisation in the eighteenth century. Its name, 'pagan' in Arabic, reflects the long preservation of its pre-Islamic Saharan character. Other oases within a range of 200 km. – Taiserbo, Bou-Zeima, Ribiana and Kebabo – were also Tebu outposts.

Tebu have long been present in the southern oases of Fezzan, a reminder of the more truly 'Sudanic' African character of this area up until at least the Middle Ages. There are a few Tebu in Murzuk, and some more at Al-Gatrun, Al-Bakki, Madrusah and Tajarhi along the Wadi Ecnema and the main north-south trade route between the Mediterranean and Lake Chad. After leaving Murzuk, this route skirts the Murzuk Sand Sea to reach Tummo and the important salt-producing oasis of Kawar. Off this main route, but on the trail linking Kawar to the oasis of Ghat, Jado is a rocky and impenetrable place, but with enough water to support half-a-dozen or so small Tebu settlements. It has long been an important half-way house between Mediterranean and Sudanic Africa and its people have always been seasonal travellers and raiders, especially into the important south-Saharan entrepôt of Air. The Kawar oasis-chain, further south, is doubly important both as a producer of the salt traditionally exported to the saltless lands to the south and as a source of water and supplies at the approximate mid-point on the Mediterranean–Chad route. Like the nearby salt-producing centre of Fachi, it has long been disputed by rival peoples and powers, and if the Tebu are predominant there, the economy is largely in the hands of the Air Tuareg.[62] Kawar is separated from Air by the forbidding, fearful Ténéré desert; the latter, though an effective barrier to the mingling of peoples, is not necessarily an obstacle to trade. Small groups of Tebu live in other, less important oases in the nearly empty north-east of the Niger Republic.

All these Tebu centres, most of them insignificant dots on the modern map, represent the reference-points of a historical, widespread Tebu entity, joined by a network of caravan trails of varying importance. A chain of oases as remote as Kufra may have long remained unknown to the outside world, but to the Tebu it was a centre from which contacts were maintained with Cyrenaica, Tripolitania and Fezzan, with the Western Desert of Egypt, Borku, Ennedi and Tibesti, and with Kawar and the main trans-Saharan routes leading to the Niger Valley and Lake Chad.[63] These far-flung relationships involved at most a few tens of thousands of people scattered across a bitterly hostile terrain of sub-continental dimensions. Only by exploiting the resources of a large area, by travelling far to find water and pasture or to raid and trade, and by an almost superhuman mobility and endurance, could the average Tebu survive. His survival depended above all else on his willingness and ability to move great distances for possibly very little reward, while the women stayed put, tending crops and animals.[64] Thus his presence, whether as a benign herdsman and petty long-distance trader, or as a malign predator and imposer of 'protection' on the trade of others, was an influence felt throughout the central Sahara from at least the Middle Ages to the present century.

## NOTES

1. The name 'Libyan' comes from the ancient Egyptian 'Lebu' or 'Rebu', applied in the second millennium BC to a tribe or groups of tribes in Cyrenaica. The Greeks gave the name to all the Hamitic (non-negro) peoples of North-West Africa. D.E.L. Haynes, *The Antiquities of Tripolitania*, Tripoli, 1965, p. 18.
2. For a harsh opinion of these people, see Sallust, *Bellum Jugurthinum*, XXI - *African initio habuere Gaetuli et Libyes . . .*
3. For a fuller account, see J. Wright, *Libya*, London, 1969, pp. 36–8.
4. Herodotus, *The Histories* (trans. de Selincourt), Harmondsworth, 1954, bk. IV, 183, pp. 303–4.
5. Chapelle, *Nomades noirs*, pp. 33–7; Briggs, *Tribes of the Sahara*, p. 181; Camps, 'Beginning of Pastoralism', p. 621. Palmer, *The Bornu*, p. 4, thinks the Garamantes are the Garawan of medieval Bornu writers: 'They are now called Teda or Tebu.'
6. *Emporia*, the name the Greeks gave to the Carthaginian ports of Tripolitania, recognises their primary commercial function.
7. F. Valori, *Storia della Cirenaica*, Florence, 1961, pp. 20–1.
8. C. Daniels, *The Garamantes of Southern Libya*, London, 1970, pp. 12–13; Camps, 'The Beginnings of Pastoralism', p. 619.
9. But see Lhote, *The Search for the Tassili Frescoes*, pp. 127–8.
10. Law, *The Horse*, p. 2. For the general amazement that a *wheeled* cannon caused in Agadez (north-east Niger) in the First World War, see C. Boccazzi, *Il condottiero dei Tuareg*, Milan, 1982, p. 100.
11. P.L. Shinnie, *The African Iron Age*, Oxford, 1971, p. 17.
12. P. Huard, 'Introduction et Diffusion du Fer au Tchad', *Journal of African History* (hereafter *JAH*), VII, 3 (1966).
13. *Ibid.*
14. Shinnie, *The African Iron Age*, p. 70.

15. Pliny the Elder, *Natural History*, V.5.
16. For a sober reconstruction of possible Roman incursions and conquests in Fezzan, see map 'Itinerari di Guerra' in B. Pace, 'Storia Antica' in B. Pace *et al.*, *Il Sahara Italiano, Fezzan e Oasi di Gat*; see also Sir M. Wheeler, *Rome Beyond the Imperial Frontiers*, Harmondsworth, 1954, pp. 132-3, and A. Merighi, *La Tripolitania Antica*, Verbania, 1940, vol. 1, pp. 149-226.
17. Haynes, *The Antiquities*, p. 39.
18. Mauny, *Tableau géographique*, p. 191.
19. Ptolemy, *Geography*, I, 8.
20. See Daniels, *The Garamantes*, pp. 22-23; Wheeler, *Rome Beyond*, pp. 129-30; Bovill, *The Golden Trade*, pp. 40, 42.
21. R.C.C. Law, 'The Garamantes and Trans-Saharan Enterprise in Classical Times', *JAH*, VIII, 2 (1967).
22. Briggs, *Tribes of the Sahara*, p. 263.
23. Wheeler, *Rome Beyond*, pp. 123-8; Daniels, *The Garamantes*, p. 25; see also S. Sergi, G. Caputo and E. Pesci, *Scavi Sahariani*, Rome, 1951.
24. J.S. Trimingham, *A History of Islam in West Africa*, Oxford, 1970, p. 15.
25. Merighi, *La Tripolitania Antica*, II, pp. 301-2; A. Fakhry, *The Oases of Egypt*, Cairo, vol. I (1973), pp. 90-1; vol. II (1974) pp. 67, 120-1, 165.
26. Briggs, *Tribes of the Sahara*, p. 90.
27. Bovill, *The Golden Trade*, p. 43.
28. E.-F. Gautier, *Le passé de l'Afrique du Nord*, Paris, 1937, p. 209.
29. *Ibid.*, p. 209.
30. Wright, *Libya*, p. 70. See also Gautier, *Le passé*, pp. 225-6.
31. Gautier, *Le passé*, p. 227.
32. Oliver and Fage, *A Short History*, pp. 42-3.
33. J. Ki-Zerbo (ed.), *General History of Africa*, Vol. I: *Methodology and African Prehistory* London (UNESCO), 1981, p. 629.
34. Mauny, *Tableau géographique*, pp. 195-6.
35. *Ibid.*, p. 196.
36. Khazanov, *Nomads and the Outside World*, p. 151.
37. See Briggs, *Tribes of the Sahara*, pp. 66-7.
38. Khazanov, *Nomads and the Outside World*, p. 181; 'had' because what was true of such societies in the 1930s and even in the 1950s is no longer necessarily so.
39. See H.T. Norris, *The Arab Conquest of the Western Sahara*, Harlow, 1986.
40. Chapelle, *Nomades Noirs*, p. 37.
41. Herodotus, *The Histories*, bk. IV, 183, pp. 303-4.
42. Chapelle, *Nomades Noirs*, p. 37.
43. *Ibid.*, p. 5; A. Le Rouvreur, *Sahéliens et Sahariens du Tchad*, Paris, 1962, p. 264.
44. Chapelle, *Nomades Noirs*, p. 11; he suggests that in their physical make-up there are '*de caractères négroides et de caractères europoïdes juxtaposés*' (European and negroid characteristics juxtaposed).
45. Briggs, *Tribes of the Sahara*, p. 168.
46. *Ibid.*
47. Gautier, *Le Sahara*, p. 172.
48. Chapelle, *Nomades Noirs*, p. 17.
49. J. Chapelle, *Le peuple tchadien*, Paris, 1980, p. 167.
50. Briggs, *Tribes of the Sahara*, p. 170.
51. See Chapelle, *Nomades noirs*, pp. 41-8.
52. Gautier, *Le Sahara*, p. 136.
53. Le Rouvreur, *Sahéliens et sahariens*, p. 267.
54. Chapelle, *Nomades noirs*, p. 341.
55. *Ibid.*, p. 345.
56. Briggs, *Tribes of the Sahara*, p. 186.

57. But see *ibid.*, p. 187.
58. *Ibid.*, p. 185; Chapelle, *Nomades noirs*, p. 343.
59. See *ibid.*, annexe 1, pp. 405-6.
60. See Fakhry, *The Oases of Egypt*, vol. I., p. 66.
61. A.M. Hassanein Bey, *The Lost Oases*, London, 1923, pp. 203-4, 206.
62. P.E. Lovejoy, *Salt of the Desert Sun*, Cambridge, 1986, pp. 153ff.; K.S. Vikor, 'The Early History of the Kawar Oasis', *Maghreb Review*, 12, nos 3-4 (1987).
63. See map 'Caravan Routes Passing through Kufra', appendix A to K.D. Bell, 'Kufra' in *Handbook on Cyrenaica*, Cairo, 1945.
64. Khazanov, *Nomads and the Outside World*, p. 20.

# 3

# AL-DAR AL-ISLAM

*'Il est . . . accepté par tous les Sahariens, comme axiome proverbial, que, pour s'enrichir, il suffit de faire un voyage au Soudan'* – H. Duveyrier

The coming of the camel-nomads marked the decline of North Africa's long association with the classical, Mediterranean world and the beginnings of the medieval revolution. These processes were hastened by the seventh-century invasion of North Africa by Bedouin Arabs who brought with them the compelling new message of Islam. Following the Islamic conquest of all its southern and eastern shores, the Mediterranean was no longer the centre of the Roman world-empire, but became instead a frontier disputed between the powers of European Christendom on the one side and Afro-Asian Islam on the other. While it was being replaced by Islam in North Africa and subjugated in western Asia, Christianity was converting the heathen in remoter Europe: Scandinavia, Germany and, eventually, Russia. The reciprocal and contemporary progress of Islam was towards Central Asia, the Indian subcontinent and Saharan and sub-Saharan Africa. Following the swift Islamic conquest of the Arabian Peninsula, the Fertile Crescent and the Persian empire in the 630s, the Arabs conquered Egypt in the early 640s, making it their base for an advance across North Africa. Arab mastery of the desert was their main advantage in their conquest of the *Jazirat al-Maghrib*, the Island of the West, as the invaders called all the lands between Barqa (Cyrenaica) and the Atlantic.[1] Nevertheless, even if the Byzantine defence was weak, Berber resistance was such that the conquest was not completed and consolidated until the early eighth century. Indeed, active Berber resistance to Arab conquest, and passive resistance to the processes of 'Arabisation' have continued to this day.

By the time the Arab invaders reached North Africa, religious zeal had largely given way to more temporal motives.[2] That they may from the outset have been interested in Saharan trade with Black Africa is suggested by the various southward forays made during the main conquest of the North African coastlands. Thus during the conquest of Cyrenaica in 641–2, Arab contact may have been made through the oasis of Augila with Zawila in Fezzan, which may therefore already have had some of the greater commercial fame it was later to acquire. Again, during the conquest of coastal Tripolitania by Omar Ibn al-As in 642–3, a detachment was sent down the main trans-Saharan route (the so-called Garamantean road) as far as the trading oasis of

26

Waddan. Then, in 666-7, shortly before the establishment of Arab power in *Ifriqiya* (Tunisia) by Okba bin Nafi, Waddan and the former Roman frontier post at Ghadames were occupied. Okba next led an expedition into Fezzan, captured all its strong-points, and forced the king of the Garamantes into formal submission; he finally pushed on as far as the trading and salt-producing oasis of Kawar, conquered it and imposed tribute of 360 black slaves.[3] This suggests that the slave trade was at that time an established operation, at least within the Sahara itself. But this was a mere raiding expedition; these conquests, almost up to the very frontiers of the Sudan, were abandoned, and no more was heard of Arab military activity in this area. Although the sources for the early Arab penetration of the Sahara are not reliable,[4] they do suggest the existence of interior oases of sufficient political and commercial importance to divert an Arab general from his main objective of conquering the central Maghrib.[5]

Like other would-be conquerors of North Africa, the relatively few Arabs of the first invasions had great difficulty in overcoming the Berber tribes and extending their rule beyond the main coastal towns and forts. Yet the Berbers, both Christian and pagan, were in the long run surprisingly receptive to the message of Islam, and not only because of the economic advantages and social prestige enjoyed by converts. The divisions and weaknesses of North African Christianity, and its failure to penetrate the Berber soul, were all too obvious by the time of the first Arab conquest. In the confrontation with pristine, vigorous and militant Islam, the North African church was not uprooted, but simply withered away.[6] Pagan Berbers, prepared for Semitic monotheism through the thousand-year influence of Semitic Carthage, and centuries of Christian and Jewish infiltration, simply grafted the new beliefs onto their traditional ones.[7] Arabs formed only a very small part of the largely Muslim Berber armies that in the early eighth century completed the conquest of the Maghrib, invaded and overran the Iberian Peninsula, and began probing forays into the Western Sudan, where they were attracted by the golden entrepôt trade of Ancient Ghana, centred on what is now southern Mauritania.[8]

Islam triumphed in North Africa after taking on the form of a national movement opposed to the Arabs. Traditional Berber hostility to foreign domination and foreign institutions found expression in support for schismatic movements. The most notable was Kharijism (Ibadism)[9] with, among other features, its rejection of orthodox ideas of the caliphate; its original followers were 'stern, uncompromising and fanatical',[10] although its Berber adherents were not necessarily so. The Arab conquest and the initial Islamisation of North Africa gave an impetus to Berber nationalism, and the state-formation that had largely eluded the Berbers in the past. An Ibadite state existed briefly in Tripolitania and Tunisia in the mid-eighth century, and Ibadism was by then also established in two separate states in Fezzan. One was centred on the former Garamantean capital of Germa in the Wadi Agial; the other was at Zawila on the north-east rim of the Murzuk Sand Sea. Zawila may thus have existed since at least Byzantine times.[11] Followers of the Ibadite chief Abu al-Khattab (the Bani Khattab) made Zawila their capital in about 760, and it very quickly became the main market of the central Sahara and a point of contact between expanding Islam and the central Sudan. It remained a centre of Ibadi political influence for more than two centuries.[12]

While the trade in gold through Ghana and its successor-states brought prosperity to the caravan-routes and oasis towns between the western Sudan and the Maghrib, and helped finance the medieval Hispano-Mauresque civilisation, the trade in black slaves brought considerable, if not wholly comparable, prosperity to the central Saharan trade dominated by Zawila. The demand for slaves of all races in the new Islamic lands of North Africa, Egypt and the Middle East presented opportunities that the Ibadite Berbers of Zawila, and the lesser Fezzanese trading centres, were well-placed to seize. The Holy Koran legitimised the enslaving of non-Muslims (a distinction often ignored in practice); slavery was a well-established institution in Islam, and both Europe and Black Africa supplied suitable infidels or pagans. By the tenth century, Zawila slavers were renowned throughout Islam for the number of captives they brought across the desert from central Sudan.[13] Slaves taken from various Chadian peoples were acquired by local rulers who sold them to traders from Zawila operating through Kawar, which itself became closely associated with the trading enterprise of Fezzanese Ibadite Berbers and was populated or dominated by them.[14] Zawila was particularly noted for the re-export of eunuchs taken mainly from the country west of Lake Chad, and destined for the harems of Islam. They were unusually expensive – mortality from castration was estimated at 90 per cent. By the tenth century, most of the black slaves sold in Muslim countries were imported through Zawila, which gave its name to the whole of medieval Fezzan.[15] Blacks, both slave and free, were settled in *Ifriqiya* and also formed an important element in the Ibadite communities of the Gebel Nefusah of north-west Tripolitania, which in turn had strong links with the centres of widening Ibadite commerce in central Sudan. The village of Jado in the Gebel Nefusah thus had close links with Jado, north-west of Kawar.[16]

Zawila lay astride the main Mediterranean-Chad route, which divided at Kawar, with one branch crossing the Téneré to Air and the Niger. Its traders were thus able to control commerce with the emerging political and economic centres east of Lake Chad, while also commanding the open roads northwards to Tripolitania and north-eastwards through the oases of Augila. The Augila road was in turn connected via the Siwa oasis to the Nile valley and delta, and the great new Fatimid capital of Cairo (founded 969).[17] This route, which also carried many of the Maghrib's new Muslims on pilgrimage to the holy cities of the Hijaz, was shorter, easier and safer than Egypt's alternative connections with central and western Sudan. These either passed through Kufra (a route later abandoned and forgotten) or along the Darb al-Arbain (the 'forty days' road') from Assiut in Upper Egypt to El Fasher in Darfur, and from there across the Sudanic lands to Ghana.[18] The road from Zawila entered Cairo by the Bab Zawila (still standing), which used to be on the southern edge of the medieval city.[19] But the twelfth-century Spanish-Jewish traveller, Benjamin of Tudela, mentions that Helwan (then well outside Cairo) was where caravans bound for Libya and Fezzan assembled.[20]

According to the early Arab geographers, Zawila was in effect a frontier-post of the Maghrib, the point at which Black Africa began. This was not necessarily an exaggeration, for medieval Fezzan still had much of its original 'Sudanic' character. In the mid-twelfth century the Spanish-Arab geographer Al-Idrisi (who was at the court of the Norman King Roger II of Sicily) saw Zawila at possibly its most prosperous. He described it as 'the gateway to the country of the Blacks',[21] and found it small, but full of bazaars. Zawila drew merchants from the cities of Khorasan in Central Asia and Kufa and Basrah in Iraq; indeed it seems that Ibadites from the original centre of Kharijite dissent in southern Iraq played some part in the development of trans-Saharan trade at that time.

Slaves were only the most valuable of the merchandise taken northwards across the central Sahara from the Middle Ages onwards. Zawila was also noted for a special leather known as zawiliyya, and it is possible that this (like the famous so-called 'Moroccan' leather) was imported from Sudan.[22] The main southbound medieval trade seems to have been in cloth, strips of red cloth being exchanged for slaves. The size of trading caravans (by this time, camels did all the load-carrying) was limited only by the availability of water en route. Larger caravans were more secure, and the fourteenth-century historian Ibn Khaldun mentions trains of up to 12,000 loaded camels plying between (probably) Fezzan and Sudan.[23] Most travelling was done in the winter, when water and pasture were more plentiful and the weather rather more clement. The Ibadite Berbers of medieval Fezzan combined economic enterprise with missionary zeal,[24] carrying the message of Islam deep into the Sahara and into the lands of Black Africa beyond it through the commercial contacts they made. No

Muslim armies crossed the Sahara to impose the new religion through war and conquest.

From the early Middle Ages, a series of large and powerful states or empires arose in the narrow but relatively well-watered country lying between the Sahara and the tropical forest-belt, and extending without a break from the Atlantic in the west to the Red Sea in the east. The salient feature of these 'Sudanic' civilisations was the incorporation of so many different African peoples into states with institutions so similar that they seem to have derived from a common source.[25] At the head of these states were kings accorded divine powers. The states themselves tended to cluster in groups, with a number of small, outlying kingdoms dominated by one large kingdom, all held together by a strongly-centralised political structure. The typical 'Sudanic' state has been compared to a bureaucracy in which power was wielded by officials appointed by the king, from four chief ministers to provincial and district chiefs. 'The main concern of such administrations was the raising of tribute for the support of the king and the semi-urbanised inhabitants of his capital . . . External trade was always in some sense a royal monopoly.'[26] The earliest and most westerly of such empires was ancient Ghana. It was first mentioned in an Arabic source in the eighth century, but seems to have existed well before the Arabs first arrived in North Africa.

There is still much controversy over the nature and degree of 'white' North African (Berber and Jewish) influences on the rise of such states, and the role played in the processes of state-formation by 'white' technology, including the use of iron and (possibly very much later) of war-horses.[27] The superiority of iron weapons, for instance, enabled those who acquired them by trade from North Africa (or learned how to make them) to conquer and dominate peoples without them, and thereby create larger political units. Bushland and forest were more easily cultivated with the iron tools also essential for digging deep wells in all but the softest ground. It has been argued that the Saharan Berber nomads, particularly before the coming of the Arabs, had themselves so little experience of political organisation and state-building that they were incapable of so influencing others.[28] Nevertheless, it seems to be the case that the typical 'Sudanic' state only acquired a certain pre-eminence *after* it had come into close contact with a variety of nomadic and trading infiltrators from the north.

Nomadic pastoralists have always tended to encroach on sedentary agriculturalists. Accustomed to defending their own rights and property against others, they have not usually respected the land and property of peoples living in scattered settlements on the desert fringes. South of the Sahara proper, where pre-desert steppe merges into bush and savanna, the Sudan must always have appeared as a land of abundant wealth to those who approached it from the north. For centuries, these relatively rich frontier-lands just beyond the great ethnic and cultural divide represented by the southern Sahara have been raided, infiltrated, conquered and settled by 'white' desert peoples, themselves in contact with and influenced by the urban civilisations of north and north-east Africa.

Clearly, the earliest Sudanic kingdoms emerged from entirely local, ancient, Black African cultural origins. It is nevertheless significant that such states apparently owed their early pre-eminence to their favourable geographical position near, or on the edge of, the Sahara, the sole avenue of stimulating influences from the north. Ancient Ghana, in particular, was centred on the southern pre-desert, rather than on more favoured areas further south, suggesting that trans-Saharan contacts and trade may have played a vital role in stimulating the rise of the earliest of the great Sudanic monarchies.[29]

Social turmoil within the Sahara in the early Christian centuries reflected contemporary upheavals in northern Africa, which may in turn have prompted the migration southwards and south-westwards of large numbers of camel-mounted Berber and Berber-Jewish peoples; the need to escape the Arab domination of the Maghrib from the seventh and eighth centuries onwards again stimulated this Berber migration. The repercussions of this prolonged and widespread movement were in due course felt south of the Sahara, where these 'whites' brought with them the germ of a higher political organisation. As Urvoy puts it:

Small in numbers (to have been able to cross the Sahara), combative and highly mobile, they took with them, despite the anarchic atavism of the nomads, the sense of empire, the reflection of the political notions of the Orient and the Mediterranean, and a certain pride of race.[30]

Thus while the nomads first 'insinuated themselves into the immense uncultivated spaces left between the fields' in Sudan to create a new mosaic of peoples and cultures, the Sahara remained a means of access for successive waves of desert peoples – 'the brave, the ambitious, the greedy'-[31] and the ideas and trade-goods they carried with them. In due course, these migrants not only brought Sudanic Africa into fuller contact with the outside world, via the long and precarious Saharan trails, but by processes that are not entirely clear, they themselves founded Sudanic dynasties and empires.

The existence of an ancient and important trade route right across the central Sahara implies that organised, trading societies existed from early times at its southern as well as its northern end. Trade brought Sudanic rulers the means of extending and consolidating their powers: it brought them weapons and war-horses; luxury goods to buy or reward the fidelity of subordinates; a means of raising revenues from import and export dues; and an opportunity profitably to dispose of surplus slaves and captives. But the open, transitional country east of Lake Chad was not necessarily a point of origin of southern trade goods (and particularly not slaves), nor the final destination of imported products. Rather, it was a place of transit trade, concerned with the collection and preparation of tropical materials for export across the desert, and with the transfer of imports from camel caravans to the transport of the Sudan – oxen, donkeys, porters and waterways – for onward shipment towards the forest-zone of eastern Sudan. Like ancient Ghana, the empire of Kanem that eventually emerged east of Lake Chad in the ninth century, and caught the attention of early Arab chroniclers, owed much of its wealth and prestige to its favourable intermediate position and the contributions of trans-Saharan and Sudanic entrepôt trade to its political, military and economic pre-eminence. Kanem's open, ambiguous geographical situation was reflected in its amalgam of African peoples of the desert, the pre-desert, and the sown: the nomadic, the semi-nomadic and the settled.

Lake Chad, at best an amorphous and rather inaccessible stretch of fresh water, has always been a geographical objective, a terminus in its own right. It has long attracted cultural influences from the Maghrib and Fezzan, Egypt and the Nilotic Sudan, and has in turn been an important centre of cultural diffusion.[32] The transitional country north and east of Lake Chad thus offered several encouraging conditions for the rise of Kanem.

Kanem's historical origins are associated with the So or Saw people – possibly migrants from the upper Nile valley – who established towns east and west of Lake Chad typical of the smaller political units of the pagan 'Sudanic' civilisation. The semi-desert plains and fixed dunes of Kanem (the former lake-bed of Mega-Chad) may provide fair cattle-country, but seem a poor environment for building an empire, even a Sahelian one. However, the climate may have been rather better in the Middle Ages;[33] the historical record of Lake Chad's levels suggests a wetter phase (*ca.* 1150–1350) contributed to Kanem's pre-eminence at that time, but that there was no climatic incentive to the processes of state-formation during the long, dry spell of earlier centuries.[34]

Imperial Kanem was established east and north-east of Lake Chad by Zaghawa immigrants, who achieved political dominance over the locals. ('Zaghawa' is the earliest Saharan or Sudanese ethnic name to appear in an Arabic source – Wahab Ibn Munabbih, early eighth century.)[35] Originally nomads from the eastern Sahara-Sudan, the black Zaghawa are part of the Tebu family of people,[36] with Berber and Arab additions, and their language belongs to the Teda-Daza group. The Zaghawa – or perhaps those they conquered – eventually covered, and partly settled, a vast area of the central Sahara from Fezzan to Nubia; today they are confined to Wadai in eastern Chad and Darfur in western Sudan. Zaghawa migration into the country known as Kanem (derived from the word for south – *anem* – in Teda and Kanuri speech) was one symptom of the general restlessness of Saharan peoples in the centuries following the decline of the Roman empire in North Africa and the rise of the camel-nomad, combined with apparently unfavourable climatic changes in the Sahara and Sudan: the level of Lake Chad was low between perhaps 750 and 1150.[37] The Zaghawa settled peacefully among the peoples east of Lake Chad about 700 and eventually dominated a cluster of vassal kingdoms. By the ninth century, Arab sources confirm,[38] the Zaghawa formed a state, known by the Arabs until the eleventh century as 'The Kingdom of the Zaghawa'.

According to tradition, the first ruler of Kanem was Sef (Saif), founder of the Saifawa dynasty that was to wield power in the Chad region until the nineteenth century. The first centre was at N'jimi, which was later to become the capital of Kanem, and which controlled the trans-Saharan trade routes to the north and their continuation eastwards to the upper Nile.[39] The main export – indeed possibly the only one – to the north seems to have been a steady supply of slaves for the Zawila market. Domination of the open country of Kanem and its settled agricultural and partly urbanised negroes by Zaghawa nomads has generally been attributed to their use of cavalry;[40] however, this view has been strongly challenged.[41] Horses had probably been known in West Africa from the first millennium BC,[42] but were breeds not necessarily suited to warfare, and may not have contributed to state-formation. Horses in themselves have no military significance: their military potential is realised by fitting them with the equipment needed to wage successful warfare. Thus the decisive use of cavalry in Kanem and other parts of the Sudan may well have had to await the arrival, perhaps in the thirteenth and fourteenth centuries, of larger breeds from across the Sahara,[43] together with the use of saddles and stirrups which greatly increased the rider's stability and security, especially when wielding weapons.[44] In the typical Sudanic state, the domination of people has always been more important than the possession of territory, and the geographical extent of states and empires was never clear in a region of few natural boundaries; booty, and especially human booty, was a main source of state revenue.[45] The Zaghawa kingdom was not unusual in its exploitation of subject peoples for state purposes, a practice that the coming of Islam encouraged rather than mitigated.

Kanem remained wholly pagan until about 1100. Merchants, responding to North Africa's traditional fascination with the Sudan and its commerce, were the first to bring Islam to inner Africa. But 'the efforts of Arab traders were individual and voluntary and the spreading of Islam and Arab culture was not their primary objective.'[46] Scholars, geographers, diplomats, men of religion and plain travellers no doubt followed them, but Islam was a creed that developed in an urban, mercantile setting; the Prophet had himself been a merchant and is credited with the saying, 'Pitch is the cure for scab in camels; the Sudan is a cure for human poverty'. Traders were held in high esteem in medieval Islam, as Morsy points out: 'the ethics and practice of trade play an important role in the Islamic worldview'.[47] In Sudanic Africa Islam's image was enhanced by the public prestige of the visiting Arabised-Berber Muslim merchant and craftsman as a literate and numerate representative of a distant but powerful and wealthy culture of high spiritual inspiration, as well as intellectual and technical attainment.

In medieval Sudan, where Islam was a minority faith, all Muslims were aware of their part in an international social order: simply to be a Muslim there and at that time was to have a cosmopolitan outlook. Islam was established across the central lands of the known world, and Muslims thus came to dominate communications and trade between the three Old World continents, exercising a control by both land and sea that was not challenged until the rise of European maritime power. Their mission was helped by the ease with which they set themselves up in alien lands, with the *sharia* governing the rules of communal and commercial life wherever they settled, and Islam providing followers of any race with an *entrée* to a universal world of trade, civilised affairs and scholarship. With the contact, favour and fraternity of fellow-Muslims wherever he went, the North African Muslim trader could travel all over the Sudan in relative safety.[48] By contrast, the African *kafir* (unbeliever) rash enough to penetrate the *Dar al-Islam* was in danger of being enslaved. Merchants tended in time to settle in the Sudan, establishing a North African Muslim *medina* alongside the main native market towns, for Islam first rooted itself in an urban and commercial milieu.[49] Such towns were linked to the Saharan trade routes, and their Muslim settlers took local women as wives, concubines and domestic slaves. Such markets continued to dominate the trade of all northern Africa until, and even after, the arrival of the Europeans from the fifteenth century onwards.

Traders were allowed full freedom by tolerant local rulers both to practise and propagate their religion,[50] not least because they did so with moderation, and fair tolerance for local pagan practices. Sudanic rulers and merchants were especially receptive to Islam, which, 'perhaps more than any other religious system, provides for its practitioners a blueprint of a near total social order'.[51] It offered a means of consolidating increasingly important ties with rulers and traders in Islamic North Africa and the Middle East, and provided a relationship with the outside world of Islam, with its Sudanic adherents becoming part of the greater Islamic *umma* or religious community. Islamic *sharia* law based on the precepts of the Koran, and literacy in Arabic – the language of the Koran – both proved valuable and in due course necessary tools for the administration of expanding Sudanese empires, for the upkeep of diplomatic and administrative correspondence, as well as historical and other records, and for the regulation of commerce. The spread of Islam was thus accompanied by the diffusion of a prestigious literacy in Arabic[52] and the processes of Islamic *sharia* law.

But Islam's appeal was usually limited to those whom it could obviously and immediately benefit. Rulers became Muslim to enjoy the reflected power and prestige of an international religion transcending the limited authority of localised pagan cults. The royal court and leading officials and agents of the central authority usually followed their ruler's example, and further converts may have been readily found in the trading towns where there lived mostly de-tribalised inhabitants cut off from traditional tribal religious influences. Trimingham identified another source of converts: 'Islam is a necessary passport for animist traders working in Muslim areas. They become Muslim less from conviction than as a matter of course, just as they accept their de-nationalizing dress.'[53] But the diffusion of Islam throughout the population took many centuries: indeed, in Chad and other states of Sudanic Africa, the slow process of conversion continues to this day. Even the acceptance of Islam by a Sudanic ruler and his entourage was often something of a façade:

If it were more than this, then it would destroy an essential basis of their power, as successors to the founding ancestors of their societies, the original pagan kings who had first made the compacts with the world of the spirits and gods on which the prosperity of their peoples and their agriculture were popularly thought to depend.[54]

Writing in the mid-eleventh century, Al-Bakri described Zawila ('a town without a wall, standing in the middle of the desert') as the beginning of the country of the blacks. Kanem, forty days' off, was inhabited by a race of black pagans, among whom lived Umayyad Muslim refugees from Abbasid persecution.[55] Apart from these refugees, Islam was by then known in Kanem through the influence of traders and other Muslim travellers penetrating via Kawar[56] from Fezzan and further north. It is doubtful that Islamic influences permeated at this time from the west, from beyond the natural barriers of Lake Chad and the Erg of Ténéré, or from the east where the Christian kingdoms of the upper Nile formed a most effective barrier to the spread of Islam from Egypt into north-east Africa.[57] Despite the prolonged influence of traders, refugees and possibly missionaries, Islam seems to have made its first notable convert in Kanem only with *mai* (king) Houme (1085–97). Mohammed Ibn Mani, the learned *mallam* who instructed the *mai* in the principles of Islam, was rewarded with the hereditary imamate of Kanem and his family with hereditary immunity from taxation. Although Islam was confined largely to the royal court and the main business centres, Kanem's Muslim rulers began to fulfil duties such as the *hajj* (pilgrimage) to Mecca; indeed, *mai* Houme died in Egypt on his way there. The *hajj* was perhaps the best way newly-converted black rulers could familiarise themselves with the practical principles of the faith, with the Islamic world of North Africa and the Middle East, and the striking international character of Islam as witnessed at the annual *hajj* ceremonies at the Holy Cities of western Arabia. *Mai* Houme and his successors drew to their courts educated Muslims who brought the cultural, legal and political standards of contemporary Islam to a country that had up to then been largely isolated from the outside world. But if Kanem's main trade link remained, as always, with Kawar, Fezzan and the traditional Tripolitanian and Cyrenaican outlets, the main intellectual influences came primarily from Cairo and other centres of learning in the Arab *mashriq*. Indeed, by the mid-thirteenth century, so many Kanemi pilgrims were passing through Cairo that the Ibn Rushiq *madraseh* was founded in the capital for their accommodation.[58]

The formation and expansion of Kanem is a subject still shrouded in much uncertainty, but by the eleventh century the four essential elements of Sudanic state-formation were present: the nomadic intruder; the divine king; long-distance trade; and Islam.[59] Even as the nomadic ruler imposed his authority, the constant dangers posed by further intrusions from the desert prompted the formation of larger, more powerful, confederated states to counter the threat. Trans-Saharan trade enabled the ruler to levy the taxes on imports that probably provided most state revenues; and trade also brought in the men and ideas of the wider Islamic world – in particular the skills needed to administer an expanding empire. The conversion of a dynasty of nomadic rulers and a military aristocracy to Islam, the introduction of 'Arab' and Islamic culture, and of political norms and a legal system based on the *sharia* coalesced to produce a typical Sudanic sultanate, 'combining a black peasantry, a nomadic aristocracy and a Muslim veneer'.[60]

Kanem perhaps differed from other Sudanic kingdoms in that once Islam had begun to spread, even the common people in due course abandoned their ancestral pagan religion. This, it has been suggested, may have been the result of Kanem's close contact with the desert nomads,[61] and so with Fezzan, Tripolitania and the rest of North Africa. Kanemi society emerged from a fusing of nomadic and settled peoples whose rulers continued to marry nomads, especially those from the noble Tomaghra Tebu clan.[62] While contacts were further stimulated by the practice of the *hajj*, the rise of a new Islamic court and the emergence of an aristocracy and a citizenry open to North African cultural influences in turn generated demand for luxury manufactured goods that only North Africa could supply. The processes of state-building, the spread of Islam, and the consolidation of trade-links started in the eleventh to twelfth centuries and were to continue with varying fortunes for hundreds of years. In the thirteenth century Kanem rose to imperial greatness through the victories of militant Islam, the conversion of conquered nobility and the institution of the Maliki school of law as the official standard of justice,[63] all processes and institutions reflecting North African originals. North Africa, meanwhile, had undergone its own revolution. The first Arab invaders had always been few and, apart from the influence of Islam, had hardly changed the essentially Berber character of the lands west of Egypt. But the invasion of the mid-eleventh century was altogether larger and more far-reaching, setting in motion processes of Arabisation in the Maghrib and the Sahara that continue to this day.

The Bani Hilal and Bani Sulaim arrived in upper Egypt from western Arabia in the early eleventh century, and by about 1050 these nomads were loosed on the Maghrib. The fourteenth-century historian Ibn Khaldun compared them to an army of locusts destroying everything in their path; and it has been estimated that up to 1 million men, women and children spent nearly a century moving from the Nile Valley to Algeria. Cyrenaica was overrun by the Bani Sulaim, becoming the most typically Arab land outside the Arabian peninsula itself. Other sections of the Bani Sulaim moved into Tripolitania and southern Tunisia, bringing settled life outside the towns to an end and appropriating all the land as one open range for their flocks and herds. Islam became yet more firmly established, and from the beduin Arabic spoken by the invaders originated most of the modern Arabic dialects of the Maghrib and the northern Sahara. Except in the mountains of Tripolitania, Algeria and, especially, Morocco, and in the south and south-west Sahara, Berber tribes were assimilated by the newcomers and the old tribal groupings were replaced by a new pattern of Arab, Arab-Berber and Berber tribes. The Arabs in due course moved into Fezzan, undefined in its extent and always defenceless against invaders. From the Bani Sulaim descended many of the main Arab tribes (and principally the Awlad Slaiman) that later dominated southern Tripolitania, the Sirtica and Fezzan,[64] and thus the northern stages of the Tripoli-Chad trade route. By the end of the fourteenth century, when the first Muslim Arab nomads were penetrating the Chadian lands from the north,[65] Arabs were also coming in from the north-east, following the Muslim conquest of Christian Nubia.[66] Although these movements lasted many centuries, and some even persist to this day, one early consequence was increased pressure on the Saharan Berbers. They in turn put pressure on their black sedentary neighbours to the south, claiming a living space that would only be satisfied through a dominant role in the processes of early Sudanic state-formation. While the whole of the northern Sahara (with the exception of some of the larger oases) was Arabised by the 1400s, the Tuareg in the south-west Sahara and the Tebu in the centre resisted Arabisation, and continued to do so until the twentieth century.

The importance of trans-Saharan trade to both Tripoli and Kanem was reflected in their constant concern to control and protect it. But no state has ever achieved the ideal objective of simultaneous domination over both ends of the central Saharan caravan routes. While Kanem and its successor-states in central Sudan have always tried to exert authority over the route at least as far north as the oasis of Kawar, Tripoli's commercial interest in Fezzan has led to varying degrees of political control. Only once in the past has the balance of power between the two sides of the central Sahara tilted decisively to one side, with Kanem's imperial expansion into Fezzan in the thirteenth century. As early as the mid-eleventh century, there were 'Bornu or Kanem colonies' in Kawar,[67] the one place on the northbound road to Fezzan to offer proper facilities for travellers, in addition to its own commercial attractions as a salt-producing centre. Urvoy believes that the road from Lake Chad to Fezzan was largely man-made, since nature only provided reliable water-supplies at the lake itself, in the relatively humid valley of Kawar some 600 km. northwards, and at Jado, at a further distance of 400 km.[68]

It is certainly in large part a political creation of the *Mais* of Kanem, who possessed in it a trail of their own, which led them, without their own dominions, to the borders of Fezzan . . . The careful spacing of the wells on these stretches was no doubt due to efforts to control a route of such importance.[69]

But Vikor[70] questions whether Kawar was ever fully integrated into the Kanemi state: 'for this, the distances were too long and the contact too infrequent. We have therefore no tradition of any Kanemi political institutions in Kawar. The traditions are those of military expeditions.' Similarly, effective control over Fezzan from Kanem was not in the long term a practical proposition.[71]

The free flow of trans-Saharan trade has always depended on the security of the central desert, and particularly of Fezzan. The domination of Fezzan gave simultaneous control of the north-south trade (Tripoli/Tunis - Kanem/Bornu), and the east-west trade between Egypt and Ghana, Mali, Songhai and other west Sudanic states. Kanem had no real alternatives to the Chad-Tripoli route for its long-distance trade with the Mediterranean; alternatives such as the Wadai-Benghazi route were only opened and exploited much later. The protection of wells and staging-posts as far north as possible was thus a prime objective of Kanem's foreign policy.[72] So long as the Bani Khattab Berber dynasty controlled Fezzan, and Kanem's authority reached out from the south most of the way to Fezzan, nomadic predators were kept in check; but in 1172-3 the Bani Khattab were overthrown by a Mamluk adventurer, Sharif al-Din Karakush, and trade was badly affected. In the mid-thirteenth century, the expanding power of Kanem enabled *mai* Dunama Dibalami (*ca.*1221-59) to intervene. In order to protect his vital trade with Tripolitania and the Middle East and to prevent its diversion to secondary routes, he annexed Fezzan (most likely with Tebu help), installing a governor (probably a Tebu) at a new capital at Traghen between Murzuk and Zawila.[73] It is possible, however, that *mai* Dunama's political and military initiative was able to build upon a north-bound penetration of people and influence going back much further.'[74]

*Mai* Dunama is reputed to have had between 30,000 and 40,000 cavalry horses.[75] His main purpose in Fezzan may therefore have been to protect the Saharan trade in horses that supplied the Kanemi cavalry with relatively bigger and heavier mounts derived largely from the Barb breed of North Africa.[76] Kanemi power eventually reached as far north as Zella in the Sirtica (on one of the main roads to Egypt and the Levant) and Waddan in the Giofra oasis commanding the southeast access to Tripoli. There is, as mentioned above, much doubt about the political and commercial power Kanem wielded in Fezzan; yet during this period Kanem opened diplomatic relations with the new Hafsid dynasty in Tunis and had close diplomatic, religious and commercial ties with Egypt.[77]

Although the Kanemi governor at Traghen declared himself independent (perhaps at the end of the thirteenth century) and founded a black dynasty, the Bani Nasur, certain Sudanic influences on parts of Fezzan proved remarkably persistent.[78] The territorial extent of thirteenth-century Kanem may have been exaggerated, but 'that Kanemi intervention in the Fezzan did have a lasting effect seems indicated by the survival, even into the 19th century, of Bornu titles even in the administration of the Fezzan . . . a similar Bornu influence may be traced in some Fezzan place-names.'[79] (There are other survivals in Fezzanese buildings and street plans).

While there was a strong Tebu element in the ruling Saifawa dynasty of Kanem, this was also manifest in Kanemi imperial expansion into the Sahara and Fezzan. All the Sudanic empires relied to a greater or lesser degree on the Saharan nomads for the organisation, guidance and 'protection' of the trading caravans, while the nomads themselves contributed to this trade livestock and salt from the Saharan centres of production.[80] In the central Sahara, Tebu families have long maintained quite complex trading relationships to provide some of the necessities (and small luxuries) that their own harsh environment denies them and have always travelled great distances, often for only slight gain. The economies of the nomads, the oasis-dwellers and settled communities north and south of the desert are largely complementary, with each group able to supply necessities the others lack. The nomad had surplus livestock to sell or to hire out for transport, and in turn needed dates, grains, condiments (tea and sugar in later centuries), textiles and arms. The oasis-dweller produced salt, dates and a little grain, but required extra grains, meat, textiles, tools and utensils, skins and draught-animals. The Sudanese people produced millet in abundance, but had to buy in wheat, dates, salt, meat and skins; the markets to the north of the desert provided textiles and manufactured goods from Europe, Egypt and the Levant.[81] In the central Sahara, the nomadic Tebu provided the essential contact between these different markets and demands. Patterns of international trade that had evolved across the central Sahara by the Middle Ages were thus based on well-established nomadic knowledge, practices and contacts extending from Wadai to Fezzan, and from Bornu to Kufra.[82]

Tebu domination of the central Sahara and its trade, and the tradition of Tebu intermarriage with the Saifawa rulers of Kanem, encouraged a special relationship between the state and these unruly peoples: 'The sovereigns had to show indulgence toward the turbulence and indiscipline of their relations.'[83] While their close personal ties with the Tebu often gave rulers the influence necessary to play a formal role in the affairs of the central desert, the Tebu remained dangerously on the fringes of the state, always ready to take advantage of any perceived weakness in the central authority.[84] Indeed, in alliance with the Bulala, the Tebu were partly responsible for the overthrow in the late fourteenth century of Kanem and the transfer of Saifawa dynastic power to the west of Lake Chad, leading to the rise of the Empire of Bornu at the end of the fifteenth century.

Goods traded across the Sahara had to be transportable, imperishable over months of very rough travel, and of an intrinsic value justifying the costs of the desert crossing; transport charges alone were said at least to have doubled the cost of most products carried.[85] As Sudan's main exports by value over the centuries, gold and slaves met all these conditions. If medieval gold exports across the Sahara ever did reach nine tons a year,[86] only 100 camels would have been necessary for its transportation. Slaves, of course, provided their own transport, even the children being herded across the desert on foot; but they always proved much more troublesome to move and trade than gold: if travel for members of a caravan was normally extremely harsh and dangerous, slaves had the worst of such conditions. But if many slaves died (and even the survivors usually reached North Africa in poor condition), the profits of the trade usually more than compensated for such losses. Both gold and slaves were traded across the desert in response to strong North African demands generated even further afield. Gold found its way to Europe, where it was used to buy European slaves, raw materials and, later, textiles and manufactured goods; and it stimulated commerce between Europe and the Levant and Asia in general.[87]

Slaves were in demand throughout pagan and Islamic Africa and the wider Islamic world. It was an institution almost endemic in, and a common feature of, West African pagan societies, to the extent that when an external demand for slaves arose, West Africans were readily able to meet it. Thus commercial slavery and slave-trading developed with the growth of states, as a form of labour-mobilisation to meet the needs of an expanding system of foreign trade.[88] If the coming of Islam changed some of the terms and precepts of slavery, it also endorsed slavery as an institution, and in particular the unlimited number of slave-wives that could be taken in addition to the legally-recognised four.[89] In the Arab world, the main demand for black slaves was as army recruits (in Cairo, the barracks of the black troops was at Bab al-Zawila), as eunuchs for harems and government service, and as concubines and domestics; and slaves were circulated as tribute, alms and gifts, as well as commercially.[90] While gold was the main source of exportable wealth in western Sudan, as ivory was in the east, in the centre, 'slavery was an essential economic enterprise, for without it the central Sudan had little with which to balance its payments in foreign trade . . .'[91] Moreover,

slaves contributed the main 'merchandise' exchanged for imports from the north and they were obtained by organising raids against the non-Muslim peoples of the south. It was therefore not in the interests of the kings of Kanem to facilitate the expansion of Islam beyond certain limits.[92]

As slaves usually failed to maintain their numbers naturally,[93] the slave population had to be replenished constantly. Estimates of the number of slaves taken across the Sahara vary greatly, from as many as 20,000 per annum in the later Middle Ages to more than 10,000 a year in the sixteenth century;[94] but these figures seem excessive. According to other estimates, between 3,000 and 8,000 slaves crossed the Sahara every year by six main trade routes – an average annual flow for each route of about 1,000 slaves.[95] Exports perhaps reached a peak annual average of 8,700 in the tenth and eleventh centuries (giving an estimated total of 1,740,000 slaves for the two centuries) falling thereafter to between 4,000 and 5,500 a year up to 1600.[96] The tradition of slave exports that had begun centuries earlier when Kanem was the centre of the state[97] was maintained by the kings of Bornu, the expansion of their state in the fifteenth century probably increasing the supply of slaves to the trans-Saharan trade by the Lake Chad–Murzuk route.[98]

Driven out of Kanem in the fourteenth century, the Saifawa kings of Bornu recaptured their former country a century later and made it a tributary state; but they never settled in Kanem again. This may well have been because Bornu, west of Lake Chad, was agriculturally more productive and better placed as a trading centre than Kanem, with richer sources of slaves immediately to the south, and more direct access to the northern trade route through Fezzan.[99]

Horses brought across the desert were another medium of exchange. Leo Africanus, writing originally in the mid sixteenth century, had the following to say about Bornu:

. . . in this country, they use to exchange horses for slaves, and to give fifteen and sometimes twenty slaves for one horse. And by this means were abundance of horses brought: howbeit the merchants were constrained to stay for their slaves until the king returned home conqueror with a great number of captives, and satisfied his creditors for their horses.[100]

Although the king had great wealth in terms of gold, being 'extremely covetous', he preferred to pay his creditors in slaves – for which he raided once a year – rather than in gold.[101] In the early sixteenth century, the ruler of Bornu countered attacks by neighbouring peoples and extended his slave-raiding capacity – by building up a cavalry force of 3,000 'Barbary' horses, although it is suggested that they came from Egypt through Fezzan and Kawar, rather than from Barbary (north-west Africa) itself.[102]

Compared with the staples of slaves and gold, the other Sudanic trans-Saharan exports were quite modest in volume and value. They were all unprocessed raw materials, but had obtained the status of luxuries by the time they reached the markets of North Africa, and were even more so on arrival in Europe. The trans-Saharan trade in ivory dates from late Roman times, when the native North African elephant was hunted into extinction, while the trade in ostrich feathers began in at least the twelfth century. The raw materials for making perfume (especially civet) were always in demand, and the kola nut, a mild stimulant acceptable in Islam, reached Tripoli from West Africa. In the other direction went the manufactures of North Africa, Egypt, the Levant and Europe: metal goods, arms and glassware, there being an insatiable demand for glass beads for the Sudan trade.[103] By the fourteenth century, Venetian merchants established in Tripoli could organise, though not accompany, their own trading caravans into the interior.

While Bornu became a leading power in the fifteenth and sixteenth centuries, the rise of both Portuguese sea power and Ottoman power by sea and land had a noticeable, if indirect, influence on inner Africa. Portuguese navigators trying to reach the sources of West African gold made their first contact with Black Africa in the mid-fifteenth century, and by the early sixteenth century all the coasts from the Senegal River southwards to the Cape of Good Hope and northwards up to the Red Sea were open to their trade, a trade which effectively by-passed the Muslim trans-Saharan caravans and competed directly with the Islamic sea-borne trade of the Indian Ocean. By the mid-fifteenth century, the trade of the western Sahara was being disrupted by the barter of slaves and goods with Portuguese and other European ships at Arguin island (Mauritania), on the Senegal River, and further south.[104] The success of European trade on the west coast, the gradual exhaustion of the traditional sources of west Sudanic gold, and Morocco's attempt to seize the sources of Sudanese wealth by conquering the Songhai empire at the end of the sixteenth century, all contributed to the decline of the west Saharan trade routes, and to the rising prosperity of the alternative central and eastern roads. This eastward shift in the bulk of trans-Saharan trade was not a steady process; yet it continued for over 400 years, up to the early twentieth century, reflecting the varying fortunes of trading states on both sides of the desert, as well as the security of trans-Saharan communications.

After building up their military strength in Anatolia in the fourteenth and fifteenth centuries, the Ottoman Turks occupied Egypt in 1517. From there Ottoman seapower extended westwards into North Africa, although they never conquered Morocco. Tripoli, Tunis and Algiers all became *pashaliks* of the Ottoman empire, and bases for the corsair fleets that were to harry the Christian Mediterranean coasts and shipping for the next three centuries, thereby supplying the North African states with their main revenue.

After the troubled fourteenth and fifteenth centuries, in the 1500s the rising power of Bornu needed to ensure the security and continuity of the trans-Saharan trade on which the prosperity of the state and the prestige of its rulers depended. Indeed, between the sixteenth and eighteenth centuries, Bornu's consistent policy was one of maintaining cordial relations with Tripoli, which controlled the trade route's northern stretches.[105] Tripoli itself had also had difficulties, and was still experiencing them when the first embassy from Bornu arrived in 1512, two years after the town had fallen in a grim struggle to the expanding power of Catholic Spain. The visit resulted in an agreement by which black slaves were re-exported through Tripoli to Spanish Sicily.[106] A second Bornu embassy arrived in Tripoli in 1534, when the town had been taken over by the Knights of Malta; but the third embassy in the mid-1550s had the more satisfactory outcome of an agreement between *mai* Dunama bin Mohammad and the Turkish corsair admiral, Darghut Pasha, who had captured Tripoli from the Knights in 1551.[107]

The Turks realised that the prosperity of their Tripoli *pashalik* (regency) – apart from the profits of corsairing – would depend largely on keeping the Saharan routes open to the safe passage of trade to and from Bornu. But Turkish authority in Tripolitania reached only as far as Misurata to the east and Garian to the south. The main tribes of the interior – the Awlad Slaiman of south-east Tripolitania and the Al-Mahamid and the leaders of the hill country to the south of Tripoli – were unconquerable;[108] indeed, when the Turks returned to Tripoli some three centuries later, they had very similar difficulties with the descendants of the same peoples. Although unable to exercise proper control over the interior, the Turks promoted Tripoli's traditional interests in Fezzan, as a means of controlling at least the northern stages of the trade routes.

Fezzan in the early sixteenth century came under the rule of a Moroccan *sharif*, Mohammad al-Fasi. The Ulad Mohammad dynasty, with its capital at Murzuk, took a leading role in Fezzanese affairs for the next three centuries, despite Tripoli's persistent attempts to impose its direct rule over the country, which often seemed likely to fall again into Bornu's sphere of influence. The Turks briefly conquered Fezzan in 1577, but were unable to hold it against popular resistance (possibly aided and encouraged by Bornu). *Mai* Idris Alooma of Bornu for his part sent an embassy to the Ottoman Sultan Murad III at Constantinople in 1577 to complain of meddling by Turks from Fezzan in Bornu's trade and other interests in its sphere of influence in the central Sahara, described by one historian as 'one of the deepest penetrations into the Sahara ever made by the Turks'.[109] They had apparently seized a fortress on the road between Fezzan and

Kawar, and the Bornu embassy demanded its return. The mission had the further objectives of maintaining uninterrupted trade with Tripoli; of acquiring Turkish firearms and the help of Turkish troops in using them; of seeking Turkish military help in Bornu's war against the Hausa state of Kebbi; and of gaining for the *mai* recognition as a great Muslim leader by the greatest of contemporary Muslim rulers.[110] In the event, there was no effective alliance between the Turks and Bornu, for *mai* Idris sought help from Morocco instead. But the embassy might well have given the Ottomans an inflated impression of the allegiance and sovereignty they nominally exercised in central Africa, and were indeed to claim in the face of European expansion into Africa at the end of the nineteenth century.

The reply *mai* Idris received from Constantinople[111] was both patronising and discouraging – the missive of 'a superior giving instructions to a subordinate'.[112] It was not Turkish practice, he was told, to cede fortresses under Turkish control to anyone, no more indeed than territories or other places under Turkish jurisdiction. But there seem to have been no further Turkish encroachments on Bornu till the nineteenth century, for in the intervening period Tripoli was incapable of projecting its power so far across the Sahara.[113] However, the embassy did apparently have the positive result of opening Bornu to the supply of Turkish arms. In 1577-8 'a gift of fine horses and firearms' went from Tripoli to Bornu, possibly the first import of such weapons into the central Sudan, despite the fact that they had been in use in Egypt and North Africa for well over a century. *Mai* Idris may well have been the first Sudanic ruler to recognise the value of firearms. The desire to acquire these new arms, together with powder, shot and Turkish gunners as armourers and instructors, was clearly a prime objective of his embassy to Constantinople, and of his policy of establishing close relations with Turkish Tripoli.[114]

The extraordinary military success of Bornu in the late sixteenth century owed much to the use of firearms (hand-guns rather than cannon). The accumulation of firearms under centralised state control began to have noticeable effects on the internal balance of power and on military organisation in particular;[115] but these were slow processes, and cavalry remained the most decisive force on the open plains of Sudan till the nineteenth century.[116] This was largely because guns and ammunition had to be imported over great distances – locks and barrels, at least, from Europe – and were accordingly very expensive. North African armourers were also needed to service stocks of firearms. And it has been suggested that only in the nineteenth century did the cheapness and availability of guns so increase as to upset permanently the balance of political power in the central Sudan.[117]

Besides receiving gifts of fine horses from both Tripoli and

Morocco, *mai* Idris bought horses from Fezzanese merchants who imported them from Egypt. But the number of horses taken across the Sahara probably declined during the later sixteenth century as the local breeding of larger horses became established.[118] Much of the equestrian equipment of the central Sudan was either brought or copied from North Africa and Egypt;[119] chain-mail armour was imported from Tripoli and Egypt after being made obsolete there by the widespread adoption of firearms in the sixteenth century.[120]

The Turks held Fezzan with difficulty, and leaders of the frequent local revolts in the late sixteenth and early seventeenth centuries used Bornu as a base and place of exile.[121] Successive Ottoman *deys* at Tripoli clearly had problems in imposing any authority or taxation on the peoples of the interior; the tribes' acknowledgement of the Sultan at Constantinople as *caliph* did not imply any willingness to obey his laws, serve in his armed forces, and least of all to pay his taxes.[122] But in the case of Fezzan itself, a settlement was reached in 1626: Turkish forces were withdrawn, the hereditary authority of the local Ulad Mohammad ruler was recognised, and Fezzan undertook to pay a yearly tribute of 4,000 golden *mithqal*, half in gold and half in slaves.[123] The Fezzanese were responsible for delivering the slaves to Sokna in the Giofra (and for making good any losses), and were also expected to give annual presents to senior state officials. Fezzan's tributary role at least ensured some security for caravans between Tripoli and Bornu, although from time to time the *deys* of Tripoli had to assert their right to tribute by force.[124]

Embassies between Bornu and Tripoli were quite frequent throughout the seventeenth century. The French consul in Tripoli in 1686 reported that twice a year the *dey* sent a caravan of about 100 camels into Fezzan, carrying mainly Venetian trade-goods – beads, coarse paper, brassware and textiles – and returning with gold-dust, senna and a total of 600–700 slaves in one year.[125] In 1698 another French consul reported the export through Tripoli into Sudanic Africa of a wider range of goods from Venice, Leghorn (Livorno) and Marseilles. Leghorn, in particular, imported from Tripoli senna and ivory sent up from Bornu.[126] Compared with the value and volume of worldwide trade then being opened up by the European maritime powers, this trans-Saharan exchange was tiny in extent: the *dey's* twice-yearly caravans carried at most 20 or so tons of goods, equal to the capacity of one small (and very slow) merchant ship. There were, of course, other caravans and other towns engaged in the trade, but what may in the Middle Ages have been a substantial traffic was no longer considered so by the greatly enlarged commercial standards of the late seventeenth century. Even Tripoli's most lucrative import, black slaves, represented a quite modest flow of wealth for a region obliged to seek its main sources of income from state-sponsored piracy in the Mediterranean. But to all those taking part in it, the small scale of trans-Saharan trade was only relative: it was an operation of such profit and importance that it had to be maintained at considerable hardship and constant risk to human life.

Tripoli always found it difficult to exert effective influence over Fezzan, and more so to interfere in the Saharan interests of Bornu, so long as its administration was preoccupied with Mediterranean and domestic matters. In 1672 a succession of mostly strong Turkish *deys* came to an end, to be followed over the next four decades by twenty *deys*, most of whom were ineffectual, some holding office for only a few months.[127] Revolution, and with it an end to any further pretence that Turkey still had any real political or military power in the regency, came in 1711. Following the example of both Tunis and Algiers, a local *Cologhli*[128] cavalry officer, Ahmad Karamanli, overthrew the ruling *dey*, massacred leading Turkish officers and sympathisers, and sent lavish gifts to Constantinople to buy the Sultan's recognition of himself as an effectively independent *Pasha*. In 1716 and again in 1718 he invaded Fezzan, which had not met its tribute obligations. Karamanli in effect reasserted Tripoli's traditional rights to uninterrupted commercial access to the Sudan, imposing on Fezzan the quite modest annual tribute of fifty slaves and ten pounds of gold-dust. The Pasha also brought Cyrenaica more firmly into Tripoli's orbit and originated the practice of sending younger members of the ruling family to govern that notoriously unruly province. Quite possibly his main purpose in doing so was to maintain Tripoli's control over trans-Saharan trade even when it diverged from the main Chad-Tripoli road (as it tended to do in times of upheaval and found alternative outlets through Augila and the Cyrenaican ports such as Derna, which had their own trading contacts in the eastern Mediterranean).[129]

The road from western and central Sudan through Fezzan and Augila to Cairo owed its importance to its use since the Middle Ages as a main route for Sudanese pilgrims able to meet their travelling expenses to Mecca by trade (at the height of the *hajj* season Mecca took on the character of a great international fair);[130] those unable to do so tended to keep to the traditional pilgrim routes south of the Sahara. Augila was also a centre for pilgrim caravans from the Maghrib. The pilgrimage was a vital factor in sustaining trade between the western Sudan and the large and generally stable Egyptian market; in the seventeenth century the Sultans of Bornu sent annual caravans to Egypt by this route, but did so less often in the following century.[131] Egypt had a close relationship with the rulers of Fezzan, whose territory was 'an essential "port of call" ' on the route from the western

Sudan', although 'the central stake in the trade along this route was held by the inhabitants of Augila.'[132]

Throughout the eighteenth century the slave trade continued to provide the main bond of Karamanli Tripoli with the sultanate of Bornu, as also with the Hausa states, the main centres of slave collection and distribution on the Niger. Most slaves arrived in Tripoli from Bornu through Murzuk in Fezzan, with the rest coming from the Niger country through Ghadames. The traffic varied considerably from year to year, presumably reflecting fluctuations in the sources of supply and the security, or lack of it, of the Saharan trails. In the early 1700s slaves were imported into Tripoli at an average rate of only 500–600 per annum, increasing to 2,000 by the 1750s and falling to an average of around 1,500 a year by the end of the century. The total number of slaves imported over the whole century may have been 150,000.[133]

Estimating slave mortality on the desert crossing is not easily done, but a loss of one in five is generally accepted. More accurate estimates had to await the closer observations of slave routes by Europeans in the nineteenth century. The profits of the trade were considerable: in the late 1800s the value of slaves bought in Bornu tripled by the time they reached Fezzan, and more than doubled again when sold in Tripoli.[134] A century later, slaves bought in Hausaland for between £2 6s. 8d. and £5 were re-sold in Tripoli for between £16 and £20, anything between a four- and seven-fold increase in value. From such profits had to be deducted the costs of the desert crossing: food, guards, and import dues and taxes, as well as any losses incurred. Slaves taken to Tripoli were either bought for local use, or were re-exported (mostly in French ships) to other parts of the Ottoman Empire: Constantinople, Greece, Crete and the Aegean. Miss Tully, sister of the British consul Richard Tully who served in Tripoli in the 1770s and '80s, tells how 'unfortunate blacks' were frequently brought to the city. 'They are carried to the bazaar, or market house, where they are bought by the rich people of the place, who occasionally sell them immediately to merchants waiting to re-ship them to other parts.'[135] The very idea, she wrote, of a human being 'brought and examined as cattle for sale, is repugnant to a feeling heart; yet this is one of their principal traffics.'[136] In Tripoli itself, slaves from Sudan were conscripted into the Pasha's black guard; others did the heaviest work (particularly in the quarries) alongside white Christian slaves mostly taken during corsair raids in the Mediterranean. Women and girls were bought as domestics and concubines. Profits from the slave trade enabled the Pasha's administration to finance the Mediterranean corsairs. Thus a recession in the slave trade resulting from a lack of security on the desert roads resulted in less corsair activity, a fall in revenues, and little or no pay for the janissaries, the troops entrusted with the protection of the trade routes. So the vicious circle was completed with the further neglect of desert security,[137] an increasingly common situation during the forty-year rule of Ali Pasha Karamanli (1754–95), who in his later years seriously neglected affairs of state.

It is often said of slaves taken across the Sahara that once bought and settled with their new owners in North Africa or within the Ottoman Empire, they were far better treated than those taken to the American plantations. As the German traveller Gustav Nachtigal remarked in the later nineteenth century, 'Islam generally brings with it a mild administration of the institution of slavery'.[138] In practice much depended on the age and sex of the slave, the place of sale, and the race and character of the new master. While it was true that many domestic slaves lived like members of the family, many others were harshly treated.[139] What is not at all clear is what influence, both racial and cultural, black Sudanese slaves may have had on the societies of North Africa and the Middle East into which they were introduced in quite large numbers. A general darkening of the native population through the influx of so many blacks over the centuries may in some ways have been offset by the corresponding influx of Circassians and other whites from Georgia, the Caucasus and south-eastern Europe. It is also not clear what influence, if any, slaves from sub-Saharan Africa had on the pervading Islamic host-culture, as their greater numbers so obviously had on the more receptive cultural milieux of the Americas. While the Karamanlis married off their daughters to European slaves to avoid dynastic rivalries, 'it would have been unthinkable for an Arab or a Berber . . . to consent to his daughter marrying a Black African, slave or freed'.[140]

After the first expansion of the Arabs in the seventh century, Islam became common to most of North Africa and the Sahara and, over the next thousand years, widely diffused in the Sudan. The penetration of Islam beyond the Sahara gave North Africans a religious, cultural and commercial entrée into Sudanese societies previously largely isolated by geography from such outside influences. If the trade between the two sides of the Sahara from the early Middle Ages onwards was mutually beneficial, as well as profitable, associated cultural, technical, social and other influences flowed essentially from north to south. But the political relationship, the limits of power between the one side of the Sahara and the other, remained in rough equilibrium for many centuries, with the exception of Bornu's short-lived expansion into Fezzan in the thirteenth century and Morocco's foray into Songhai in the late sixteenth century.

Desert nomads sometimes threatened to upset the balance of power in Tripoli, and actually did so in the Sudan; but no state was able to project its power across the Sahara till the north-south relationship was again upset in the nineteenth century with Egypt's invasion of the Nilotic Sudan. Although Tripoli was unable to emulate Egypt militarily, Tripoli and more especially Cyrenaica did in the nineteenth century alter the terms of the traditional trans-Saharan relationship, exploiting their central Sudanic hinterlands economically (particularly for slaves) and exerting there a far greater degree of political-religious influence than had ever been known before. Many more enduring connections were thereby established between the lands which now form part, respectively, of modern Libya and modern Chad.

## NOTES

1. More specifically, the *Maghrib al-Wasith*, the 'Middle West', was Tunisia and Tripolitania; Morocco (*Maghrib*) was specifically the *Maghrib al-Aqsa*, the 'Far West'.
2. Bovill, *Golden Trade*, p. 57.
3. See, in particular, Ibn Abd-al-Hakam, *Futuh Misr*, edited by C.C. Torrey, New Haven, 1922, pp. 194–6.
4. J.-C. Zeltner, *Pages d'histoire du Kanem, pays Tehadien*, Paris, 1980, pp. 33–4. Zeltner, for instance, doubts the extent of Okba's Saharan expedition.
5. K.S. Vikor, 'The Early History of Kawar Oasis'.
6. J.S. Trimingham, *A History of Islam*, p. 17.
7. Oliver and Fage, *A Short History*, p. 71.
8. Bovill, *Golden Trade*, pp. 69ff.; P.B. Clarke, *West Africa and Islam*, London, 1982, pp. 8–10.
9. E. Rossi, *Storia di Tripoli e della Tripolitania dalla conquista araba al 1911*, Rome, 1968, pp. 37–8.
10. N.A. Guillaume, *Islam*, Harmondsworth, 1956, p. 113.
11. 'Byzantine influence is also evident at Zawila . . . where there survive a city-wall and a domed tomb built in Byzantine style.' Law, 'The Garamantes and Trans-Saharan Enterprise in Classical Times'. Zawila was an early objective of Arab conquerors of Cyrenaica; see A. Gateau (ed.), *Ibn Abd-al-Hakam: Conquête de l'Afrique du Nord et de l'Espagne*, Algiers, 1947, p. 37.
12. Vikor, 'The Oasis of Salt', p. 102.
13. B.G. Martin, 'Kanem, Bornu and the Fezzan: Notes on the Political History of a Trade Route', *JAH*, X, 1 (1969).
14. Vikor, 'The Oasis of Salt', p. 105.
15. Indeed, the name persisted till the nineteenth century. G. Nachtigal, *Sahara and Sudan*, I: *Fezzan and Tibesti*, trans. and ed. by A.G.B. Fisher and H.J. Fisher, London, 1974, p. 149.
16. Martin, 'Kanem, Bornu and the Fezzan'.
17. Mauny, *Tableau géographique*, fig. 74, p. 429: 'Principles routes commerciales du VIIIe au Xe siècle'.
18. J.Ki-Zerbo, *Histoire, de l'Afrique Noire*, pp. 15–16, map 'Routes commerciales à travers le Sahara au Moyen Age'.
19. See E.W. Lane, *The Modern Egyptians*, London, 1908, p. 237.

20. R.L. Hess, 'The Itinerary of Benjamin of Tudela: A Twelfth Century Jewish Description of North-East Africa', *JAH*, VI, 1 (1965).
21. R. Dozy and M.J. de Goeje (eds), *Description de l'Afrique et de l'Espagne par Edrisi*, Leiden, 1866, p. 158.
22. H.F.C. Smith, 'The Early States of the Central Sudan' in J.F.A. Ajayi and M. Crowder (eds), *History of West Africa*, Vol. I, London, 1971, p. 171.
23. Mauny, *Tableau géographique*, p. 401.
24. N. Levtzion, 'The Sahara and the Sudan from the Arab Conquest of the Maghrib to the Rise of the Almoravids' in J.D. Fage (ed.), *The Cambridge History of Africa*, Vol. 2, Cambridge, p. 197.
25. Oliver and Fage, *A Short History*, p. 44.
26. *Ibid.*, p. 45.
27. H.J. Fisher, 'The Horse in the Central Sudan', part I: *JAH*, XIII, 3 (1972); part II: *JAH*, XIV, 3 (1973).
28. P. Munson, 'Archaeology and the Prehistoric Origins of the Ghana Empire', *JAH*, XXI, 3 (1980).
29. Fage, *A History of Africa*, p. 70.
30. Y. Urvoy, *Histoire de l'empire du Bornou*, Paris, 1949, p. 22.
31. H.J. Fisher, 'The Eastern Maghrib and the Central Sudan' in R. Oliver (ed.), *Cambridge History of Africa*, Vol. 3, *c. 1050–c. 1600*, Cambridge, 1977.
32. Trimingham, *A History of Islam*, p. 104.
33. A.T. Grove, 'Desertification of the African Environment' in D. Dalby *et al.* (eds), *Drought in Africa/Séheresse en Afrique 2*, London, 1977, p. 56.
34. See D.J. Schove, 'African Droughts and the Spectrum of Time', fig. 4.2, 'Lake Chad Levels since about AD 700' in *ibid.*, p. 39.
35. Levtzion, 'The Sahara and the Sudan', p. 680.
36. *Ibid.*, p. 680; Trimingham, *History of Islam*, 2, p. 104; Chapelle, *Nomades noirs*, p. 54.
37. Schove, 'African Droughts', fig. 4.2.
38. See Zeltner, *Pages d'histoire*, pp. 27–37.
39. G.T. Stride and C. Ifeka, *Peoples and Empires of West Africa*, London, 1971, pp. 114–5.
40. Levtzion, The Sahara and the Sudan', p. 681; Oliver and Fage, *A Short History*, p. 64.
41. Fisher, 'The Horse in the Central Sudan'. See also Law, *The Horse in West African History*, pp. 181–92.
42. Law, *The Horse*, pp. 3 and 7.
43. Fisher, 'The Horse'.
44. Law, *The Horse*, pp. 121ff.; p. 177.
45. Fisher, 'The Horse'.
46. Y.F. Hasan, 'The Historical Roots of Afro-Arab Relations' in K.E.-D. Haseeb (ed.), *The Arabs and Africa*, London, 1985, p. 34. Early traders from North Africa were of course Berber rather than Arab.
47. M. Morsy, 'Arbitration as a Political Initiative: An Interpretation of the Status of Monarchy in Morocco' in A.S. Ahmed and D.M. Hart (eds), *Islam in Tribal Societies from the Atlas to the Indus*, London, 1984, p. 51.
48. Mauny, *Tableau géographique*, p. 521.
49. J.S. Trimingham, *Islam in West Africa*, London, 1959, p. 25. See also I.M. Lewis, 'Agents of Imperialism' in I.M. Lewis (ed.), *Islam in Tropical Africa*, London, 1980, pp. 20–31.
50. Trimingham, *A History of Islam*, p. 31.
51. Ahmed and Hart, *Islam in Tribal Societies*, p. 3.
52. See J.O. Hunwick, 'The Influence of Arabic in West Africa: A Preliminary Historical Survey', *Transactions of the Historical Society of Ghana*, VII, (1964).

53. Trimingham, *Islam in West Africa*, p. 28.
54. Fage, *A History of Africa*, p. 74.
55. Al-Bakri (trans. M. de Slane), *Déscription de l'Afrique septentrionale*, Paris, 1965, pp. 28–9.
56. Zeltner, *Pages d'histoire*, p. 44.
57. Smith, 'The Early States of the Central Sudan', pp. 171–2; Oliver and Fage, *A Short History*, p. 66.
58. See Zeltner, *Pages d'histoire*, p. 50.
59. Fisher, 'The Eastern Maghrib', pp. 287–8.
60. Urvoy, *Histoire de l'empire*, p. 24.
61. Levtzion, 'The Sahara and the Sudan', p. 682.
62. Trimingham, *A History of Islam*, p. 116.
63. Stride and Ifeka, *Peoples and Empires*, p. 117.
64. Rossi, *Storia di Tripoli*, p. 62.
65. Smith, 'The Early States of the Central Sudan', p. 204.
66. I. Hrbek, 'Egypt, Nubia and the Eastern Deserts' in R. Oliver (ed.), *Cambridge History of Africa*, Vol. 3, p. 79.
67. Nachtigal, *Sahara and Sudan*, 1, p. 149
68. Urvoy, *Histoire de l'empire*, p. 148.
69. *Ibid.*
70. Vikor, 'The Oasis of Salt', p. 119.
71. Fisher, 'The Eastern Maghrib', p. 263.
72. See D. Lange, 'The Kingdoms and Peoples of Chad' in D.T. Niane (ed.), *General History of Africa*, IV, UNESCO, Paris, 1984.
73. Chapelle, *Nomades noirs*, p. 50.
74. Fisher, 'The Eastern Maghrib', p. 263.
75. Law, *The Horse*, p. 8.
76. See *ibid.*, pp. 28, 48.
77. Lange, 'The Kingdoms and Peoples of Chad'.
78. Zeltner, *Pages d'histoire*, p. 50. See also Nachtigal, *Sahara and Sudan*, I, p. 150, esp. n.4; and E. Scarin, *Le Oasi del Fezzan*, Bologna, 1934, I, p. 21, n.5.
79. Fisher, 'The Eastern Maghrib', p. 263; see also H.Duveyrier, *Les Touareg du Nord*, Paris, 1864, pp. 279, 282.
80. Mauny, *Tableau géographique*, p. 219.
81. Chapelle, *Nomades noirs*, pp. 210–11.
82. *Ibid.*, fig. 8, p. 213, *Circuits caravaniers familiaux.*
83. *Ibid.*, p. 55.
84. *Ibid.*, p. 57. See also D. Lange, 'L'Eviction des Sefuwa du Kanem et l'origine des Bulala', *JAH*, XXIII, 3 (1982).
85. P. Wickins, *An Economic History of Africa from the Earliest Times to Partition*, Cape Town, 1981, p. 148.
86. Stride and Ifeka, *Peoples and Empires*, p. 169.
87. Wickins, *An Economic History*, pp. 141–2.
88. See J.D. Fage, 'Slavery and the Slave Trade in the Context of West African History', *JAH*, X, 3 (1969).
89. Trimingham, *Islam in West Africa*, p. 164.
90. Fisher, 'The Eastern Maghrib', p. 270.
91. *Ibid.*, p. 272.
92. Lange, 'The Kingdoms and Peoples of Chad', p. 253.
93. For reasons, see P.E. Lovejoy, *Transformations in Slavery*, Cambridge, 1983, pp. 7–8; see also P. Manning, 'The Enslavement of Africans: a Demographic Model', *Canadian Journal of African Studies*, 15, 3 (1981).
94. Wickins, *An Economic History*, p. 149.
95. Lovejoy, *Transformations in Slavery*, p. 24.

96. *Ibid.*, table 2.1, 'Trans-Saharan Slave Trade, 650-1600'.
97. *Ibid.*, p. 25.
98. *Ibid.*
99. A.G.B. Fisher and H.J. Fisher, *Slavery and Muslim Society in Africa*, London, 1970, p. 60.
100. J. Pory, *A Geographical Historie of Africa, Written in Arabicke and Italian by John Leo a More, etc.*, London, 1600, p. 293.
101. *Ibid.*, p. 294.
102. Law, *The Horse*, p. 49.
103. Bovill, *The Golden Trade*, p. 105.
104. J. Mercer, *Spanish Sahara*, London, 1976, p. 93.
105. K. Folayan, 'Tripoli-Bornu Political Relations, 1817-25', *Journal of the Historical Society of Nigeria*, V, 4 (June 1971).
106. C. Feraud, *Annales tripolitaines*, Tunis, 1927, p. 34.
107. Folayan, 'Tripoli-Bornu Political Relations'.
108. Rossi, *Storia di Tripoli*, p. 152.
109. Martin, 'Kanem, Bornu and the Fezzan'.
110. *Ibid.*
111. For relevant text, see Zeltner, *Pages d'Histoire*, pp. 183-4.
112. *Ibid.*, p. 183.
113. Folayan, 'Tripoli-Bornu Political Relations'.
114. See Martin, 'Kanem, Bornu and the Fezzan'.
115. J.P. Smaldone, 'Firearms in the Central Sudan: A Reevaluation', *JAH*, XIII, 4 (1972). In addition to 'Turkish' musketeers, the Sultan had numerous household slaves who became skilled in firing muskets. See Palmer, *The Bornu, Sahara and Sudan*, p. 227.
116. Law, *The Horse*, p. 133.
117. H.J. Fisher and V. Rowland, 'Firearms in the Central Sudan', *JAH*, XII, 2 (1971).
118. Law, *The Horse*, p. 49.
119. *Ibid.*, pp. 96ff..
120. *Ibid.*, p. 132.
121. See E. Rossi, *La Cronaca Araba Tripolina di Ibn Galbun*, Bologna, 1936, pp. 88-9; 'Storia del Medio Evo' in *Il Sahara Italiano*.
122. Rossi, *Storia di Tripoli*, p. 172.
123. For the relative values of the slaves, see Rossi, *La Cronaca Araba*, pp. 89-90 and 'Storia del Medio Evo', pp. 339-40.
124. See C.R. Pennell, 'Tripoli in the Late Seventeenth Century: The Economics of Corsairing in a "Sterill Country" ', *Libyan Studies*, vol. 16. (1985).
125. Rossi, 'Storia del Medio Evo', p. 341.
126. *Ibid.*
127. Rossi, *Storia di Tripoli*, pp. 218-9.
128. *Cologhli* - soldiers and senior administrators, the descendants of Turkish professional soldiers, the Janisseries and local Arab and Berber women.
129. F. Renault, 'La traite des esclaves noirs en Libye au XVIIIe siècle', *JAH*, 23, 2 (1982).
130. T. Walz, *Trade between Egypt and the Bilad as-Sudan, 1700-1820*, Cairo, 1978, p. 23.
131. *Ibid.*, pp. 17-8.
132. *Ibid.*, p. 89.
133. Renault, 'La traite des esclaves noirs'. But see also Lovejoy, *Transformations in Slavery*, pp. 59-60.
134. Renault, 'La traite des esclaves noirs'.
135. S. Dearden (ed.), *Ten Years' Residence at the Court of Tripoli*, London, 1957, p. 184.

136.   *Ibid.*, p. 40.
137.   S. Dearden, *A Nest of Corsairs*, London, 1976, p. 22.
138.   Nachtigal, *Sahara and Sudan*, I, p. 122.
139.   See *ibid.*, p. 324; Fisher and Fisher, *Slavery and Muslim Society*, pp. 83ff..
140.   J.O. Hunwick, 'Black Africans in the Islamic World', *Tarikh*, 5, 4 (1978).

# 4
# THE NINETEENTH CENTURY

*I would not have a slave to till my ground,*
*To carry me, to fan me while I sleep,*
*And tremble when I wake, for all the wealth*
*That sinews bought and sold have ever earned.*
— William Cowper

At the end of the eighteenth century, when Europeans were exploring the South Seas and establishing the first settlements in Australia, they knew less of the interior of Africa than of the earthward face of the moon. The sum of Europe's African knowledge was based on classical accounts at least 1,500 years old, the sketchy, sometimes inaccurate and by then outdated writings of medieval Muslim travellers, and on the present-day knowledge of the coasts and their immediate hinterlands. Indeed, even contemporary Egyptians and other North Africans usually had little idea of their own continent beyond the Sahara. Muslim trans-Saharan traders and other travellers could no doubt have enlarged the general knowledge of African geography, but their information was not necessarily particularly broad or accurate.[1]

When the French cartographer J.B. Bourguignon d'Anville ('possibly the greatest cartographer the world has ever known'[2]) published his map of Africa in 1749, the few details of the interior were largely based on a critical selection from the works of Ptolemy (second century) and Al-Idrisi (twelfth century). And when, in 1798, Major James Rennell ('the greatest geographer of the day'[3]) drew his map, corrected in 1802, 'showing the progress of discovery and improvement in the geography of North Africa', he incorporated all that had been added to European knowledge since the travels of James Bruce in 1768–73. But Rennell still relied on attributions to Pliny, Ptolemy, Al-Idrisi, and Leo Africanus. He confused Ghana with Kano; Kawar was misplaced by some 500 miles and shown more or less south of Augila; and his River Niger ended improbably, flowing in a loop through a pair of substantial lakes and around the land of 'Wangara'. According to the original twelfth-century description of al-Idrisi, 'Wangara'[4] was an island 300 miles long and 150 broad, rich in gold and surrounded by the 'Nile' all the year. This natural depression, 'the sink of North Africa at all seasons', was clearly the basin of Lake Chad, but not the terminus of the Niger. Rennell's difficulty with the final course of the Niger was due partly to his positioning of the 'Mountains of Kong' from east to west across half the continent, thus

55

barring any Sudanic river from reaching the Gulf of Guinea. By the 1830s, after another generation of quite extensive African exploration, the anonymous geographer could apologise, 'We are still ignorant of many of its kingdoms, the sources of several of its rivers continue uncertain, and the very existence of one of its principal cities is to this day a subject of dispute.'[5] And even some ten years later, the French geographer Joumard, commenting on the most recent French and British exploration of the inner continent, declared, 'What an immense void is found on a map bounded by these discoveries! . . . Europe scarcely knows a fiftieth part of the interior of Africa: beyond that, all is confusion and doubt.'[6]

At the end of the eighteenth century, the curiosity of the age, the vigour of British scientific inquiry, stirrings of humanitarian concern and evangelical conscience, combined with political, military and strategic self-interest and plain commercial enterprise, prompted the first concerted efforts to explore the African interior. A dozen influential and wealthy British gentlemen, 'desirous of rescuing the age from a charge of ignorance', determined on the formation of 'An Association for Promoting Discovery in the Inland Parts of Africa' in London in June 1788. As the published *Plan of the Association*[7] noted:

. . . notwithstanding the progress of discovery on the coasts and borders of that vast continent, the map of its interior is still but a wide extended blank, on which the geographer . . . has traced with a hesitating hand a few names of unexplored rivers and of uncertain nations.[8]

From the very outset Tripoli was the main point of entry for exploratory expeditions, either planned by the African Association, or carried out on its behalf. At the time, the Saharan route to the interior seemed in every way more feasible because of the even greater practical difficulties barring every other approach. After failing to establish permanent trading stations on the Atlantic coast of the Sahara, European adventurers considered advancing along the other main routes leading to the interior, the rivers Senegal and Niger. The French in due course gained control of the Senegal and the British of the lower Niger; but, besides the hostility of the Africans, there were other obstacles to penetration. The French found the Senegal, like most other African rivers, unnavigable some distance upriver because of rapids marking the river's descent from the higher lands of the interior. And the mouths and lower courses of the Niger lay in equatorial forest that proved appallingly unhealthy to any European who travelled there before the discovery of quinine as a prophylactic in the 1850s. For three centuries the European presence on the West African coasts nearest to Sudan was limited to hulks and forts on the shoreline, or to small enclaves where the climate allowed the white man to survive a stay of more than a few months. By 1800 the British government had come to understand the need to solve the Niger problem, to discover what lay upstream from the Niger delta as a means of opening trade relations with western Sudan; it had also begun to sense a threat to British interests in the French advance up the Senegal River. After the failure of Mungo Park's second expedition in 1805–6, the Colonial Office and the Admiralty each sponsored an expedition on the Niger quest. But they were so unsuccessful that by 1820 it still seemed that the Sudan was not to be as easily reached from the west and the south as from the north, by 'the long and tedious routes over the deserts of northern Africa', as it was called by Hugh Clapperton, one of the British explorers who travelled it.

Simon Lucas, oriental interpreter at the court of St James and a man of long North African experience,[9] was commissioned by the African Association to travel from Tripoli to Fezzan because of Fezzan's 'frequent and regular intercourse' with the interior. He was to 'collect and transmit by way of Tripoli, whatever intelligence, respecting the inland regions of the continent, the people of Fezzan, or the traders who visited their country, might be able to afford'.[10] He was to return by way of the River Gambia or the Guinea coast, a journey that would have been one of the most remarkable of African explorations had it been made. But Lucas never even reached Fezzan – which, as Ali Pasha Karamanli incorrectly told him, he would be the first Christian to visit. Held up in Tripoli by tribal unrest on the road to Fezzan, he later travelled to Misurata, the second port of Tripolitania, and found the road southwards still closed, a reflection of the infrequency and precariousness of all contact between the Mediterranean coast and the interior. But while in Misurata he at least took the trouble to learn much at second hand about inner Africa, gaining detailed accounts of Fezzan and Bornu, as well as the first specific report on Tibesti.[11] Not all the information was accurate, but it was 'the most substantial contribution to the geography of the interior since Leo Africanus had written his account two hundred and sixty years earlier'.[12] That such information was fairly readily available in the second port of Tripolitania was a reflection of the closeness, when conditions allowed, of the trading link with the countries described.

Following the successful first journey of Mungo Park into western Sudan (1795–9) the next approach from the north was made by a young German travelling under the auspices of the African Association, Frederick Hornemann. In 1798 he left Cairo by caravan for Fezzan, disguised as a Mamluk merchant and accompanied by an Arabic-speaking German convert to Islam, Joseph Frendenburgh. Travelling through Siwa, Augila and Temissa, after six weeks they reached Murzuk, where Hornemann stayed for seven months. He was not the first European visitor, for the Sultan's *mamluks* were mostly Greek or Genoese renegades, 'but he was the first to visit it with the intention of bringing back information'.[13] Hornemann learned much about the geography of the central and western Sudan and encountered many peoples, including Tebu, Tuareg and traders from the Hausa states and Bornu. He found the commerce of Fezzan to be considerable, with Murzuk from October to February

the greatest market and place of resort for various caravans from Cairo, Bengasi, Tripoly, Gadames, Twat, Soudan, and for other smaller troops of traders, such as Tibboes of Rschade, Tuaricks and Arabs . . . the trade with Bornu is managed by the Tibboes of Bilma. The caravans coming to Mourzouk from the south or west, bring, as articles of commerce, slaves of both sexes, ostrich feathers, zibette [civet], tiger skins [leopard skins], and gold, partly in dust, partly in native grains, to be manufactured into rings and other ornaments, for the people of interior Africa. From *Bornou* copper is imported in great quantity. Cairo sends silks, *melayes* [striped blue and white calicoes], woollen cloths, glass imitations of coral, beads for bracelets, and likewise an assortment of East India goods. The merchants of *Bengasi*, who, usually join the caravan from Cairo at *Augila*, import tobacco manufactured for chewing, or snuff, and sundry wares fabricated in Turkey.

The caravan from Tripoly, chiefly deals in paper, false corals, firearms, slaves, knives, and cloths called *abbes*, and in red worsted caps. Those trading from *Gadames* bring nearly the same articles. The smaller caravans of *Tuaricks* and *Arabs*, import butter, oil, fat, and corn; and those coming from the more southern districts, bring senna, ostrich feathers, and camels for the slaughter-house.[14]

Part of the revenues of the Sultan of Fezzan were derived from a tax on caravans passing through Murzuk, with the Bornu and Sudan caravans paying two 'matkals' (*mithqals*), or about one-eighth of an ounce of gold, for each slave offered for sale. Delayed in Murzuk by sickness ('seized with the country fevers': it was always an unhealthy town) he was too late to join the caravan for Bornu. With Frendenburgh dead ('led astray by wine and women') and unwilling to stay longer in Murzuk ('after the caravan had left, the most disinteresting town I ever saw'), Hornemann went to Tripoli to forward his information to London and to prepare for a fresh attempt to reach the interior. He left Tripoli in December 1799 in the company of the collector of the Fezzan tribute, the *Bey al-Nawba*, one Mohammad al-Mukni.[15] He intended to go from Fezzan to Bornu, then westwards to the Niger and Timbuctu. By January 1800 he was in Murzuk and in April left with the Bornu caravan. No more was heard of him till years after when it was learned that he had travelled through Bornu and almost right across Africa, only to die suddenly of dysentery towards his journey's end.[16] His most valuable contribution to African knowledge was the information gained during his first stay in Murzuk, as Hallett confirms:

That which he acquired during this time was exceedingly valuable, throwing a clear shaft of light on to the people and states of the central Sahara and central Sudan, confirming much that Leo Africanus and Lucas had reported before him, and supplementing their accounts with some new facts.[17]

Yusuf Pasha Karamanli had usurped the throne of Tripoli in 1794 by murdering one elder brother and banishing another; he ruled for thirty-eight years in the same ruthless manner.

A cruel and unprincipled tyrant, who never honoured his engagements unless it suited him, Yusuf was nevertheless the greatest of the Karamanli Bashaws. He had soaring ambitions for his country which he pursued ruthlessly. He used his army with such effect against the ever lawless tribes of the hinterland that his influence was felt, and his name was feared, nearly as far as Bornu.[18]

From 1795 to 1805 he consolidated his political power; from 1806 to 1817 he pacified much of what is now modern Libya and imposed his direct rule over the main trading oases of the interior; and from 1817 to 1824 he worked to project Tripoli's power across the Sahara to Sudan.[19] Early in his reign he greatly increased the power, prestige and wealth of Tripoli through an upsurge in corsairing raids on the Mediterranean shipping of the smaller European powers while the larger ones (which normally restrained such activity) were preoccupied with the Napoleonic Wars.[20] Even before British prestige had been enhanced by Nelson's victories and the expulsion of the French from Egypt and Malta, the Pasha positively welcomed British attempts to probe the African interior along the main trade routes from Tripoli. In contrast with the common attitude of North African rulers to European curiosity up to that time, he had favoured the attempts by both Lucas and Hornemann to travel into the interior; indeed Hornemann had found him 'a sensible man, and a good friend of all that is English'.[21]

The British wanted to know what lay beyond the natural barrier of the Sahara, what were the patterns of trade and the markets of the inner continent and, above all, whether the great River Niger was really a tributary of the River Nile, thus joining the western Sudan with Egypt. It is likely that the Pasha also wished to know these things, and certainly those relating to trade. Tripoli clearly would be the first to benefit if the British stimulated trans-Saharan trade with Black Africa; and even if they failed, British expeditions were a source of revenues in themselves, in the form of 'presents' and payments for any protection the Pasha might promise, or indeed provide. Moreover, the British interest in the Saharan approach to inner Africa seemed for a time to coincide with his own imperial aspirations.[22] The end of the Napoleonic wars and, following the Congress of Vienna, greater efforts by Britain and France to curb central Mediterranean piracy and the enslavement of Christians, prompted the Pasha to turn to Saharan trade, especially the trade in black slaves, as an alternative to the income once provided by corsairing. In 1814 there arrived a remarkable British consul, Colonel Hanmer Warrington, who did much in the following decades to promote this apparent coincidence of Anglo-Tripolitan interests, even if he seems never to have appreciated fully the limits to the Pasha's power and influence in and beyond the Sahara.

Caravan traffic between Bornu and Tripoli was constantly threatened by predatory Arab or arabised Berber tribes whose traditional grazing grounds, markets and spheres of political influence stretched from south-east Tripolitania and the Sirtica to the oases of Fezzan. They dominated the ancient Fezzan road through Bu Ngem and the Giofra oases, often cutting it for months on end. Foremost among them was the great Arab tribe of the Awlad Slaiman, led by the Saif al-Nasr family – elements that consistently opposed attempts by the Karamanlis to centralise power in Tripoli. In 1806–7 the Awlad Slaiman were crushed and Shaikh Ahmad Saif al-Nasr was killed. This victory prompted the Pasha to bring both Ghadames and Fezzan, as other links in Tripoli's trans-Saharan trade networks, under closer control. In 1810 he accordingly sent a military force to Ghadames which, as it had been for the past 2,000 years, was one of the main centres of Saharan trade, maintaining relations with Timbuctu, Hausaland and Bornu on one side of the desert and Tripoli, Tunis and Algiers on the other. The Ghadamsi merchants were still well able to meet the financial demands the Pasha made of them; but such demands were also limitless, and thus potentially ruinous.

In the late 1790s the Pasha had regularised Fezzan's relationship with Tripoli by appointing an old Karamanli supporter, Mohammad al-Mukni, as collector of the tribute. As such, he went down to Murzuk at the end of each year; but he soon saw that 'the sum paid as the tribute was but a very small part of the immense gains of the reigning Sultan'.[23] Al-Mukni persuaded the Pasha that efficient management by his own representative could triple the yearly Fezzan tribute from the petty 5,000 Spanish dollars' worth in gold-dust, senna and slaves that had been paid for many years, and that the province could accordingly be made to yield much of the Pasha's income that corsairing, in the post-Napoleonic era, no longer provided. There were other reasons for deposing the semi-independent sultan of Fezzan, Mohammad al-Muntasir, as an obstacle to the more effective exploitation of Tripoli's hinterland. In 1807–8, the Sultan had tried to interfere in Tripoli's efforts to promote more direct trade with Bornu.[24] Two years later, he was openly supporting some of the Awlad Slaiman in their rebellion against Tripoli.[25] In 1811 Al-Mukni mounted a coup in which the Sultan was killed and other members of his family were either murdered or exiled. Al-Mukni was recognised by Yusuf Pasha Karamanli as Bey of Fezzan (with the traditional right to the title of Sultan within the province), and for nine years he ruthlessly exploited the country with little other purpose than enriching himself and raising the tribute needed to sustain his own position.

Having thus established control over Fezzan, and brought some other parts of what is now modern Libya under his direct rule, the Pasha in 1817 embarked on his most ambitious project, of extending Tripoli's power right across the Sahara to the central Sudan. This was the only feasible outlet for an expansionist regime in Tripoli whose other neighbours were either too powerful or too friendly to be annexed. To the east lay the rising military power of Mohammad Ali's Egypt, and to the west Tunis under the friendly allied regime of the Hassainid Beys.[26] But directly to the south, the empire of Bornu had long been encroached upon by the rising power of its eastern neighbour, Wadai, and in 1808 also suffered serious defeat by the forces of the Fulani *jihad*, a militant Islamic revival. Out of this disaster, however, arose a remarkable leader, Shaikh Mohammad al-Amin al-Kanemi, who rallied Bornu's political and religious resistance and over the next twenty-five years revived the empire. He was, in the words of Bovill, 'an astute and far-seeing dictator . . . who refused to usurp the throne of the sultan whose kingdom he governed so ably'.[27] Al-Kanemi was born in Fezzan of Kanemi and Arab descent, and after his education in Egypt he settled in Kanem. Seeking allies against threats from Bagirmi to the south-east and from Fulani pressure to the west, he turned to Tripoli, and proposed to Yusuf Pasha Karamanli a uniting of forces to conquer Bagirmi. (Bornu already looked to Tripoli to supply the guns and ammunition that gave it a certain local military superiority.)

But this initiative had the unforeseen consequence of encouraging Yusuf Pasha's own designs on Bornu.[28] The Pasha and his advisers estimated the campaign would require 6,000 troops and cost £25,000, and in mid-1820 he asked the British government (through Consul Warrington) to make this sum available. He baited his appeal with the prospect of ending the Saharan slave trade, arguing that Bornu 'and Sudan' would provide enough legitimate trade (especially in gold-dust) once they were under his rule, although the part of 'Sudan' he intended to annex, in addition to Bornu itself, is not clear.[29] But what is clear is that the Pasha was looking to Bornu to provide him with revenues beyond even the greatly increased sums Fezzan and Ghadames were yielding, although he must have known that legitimate commerce with Bornu was unlikely to match the estimated $10,000 a year that the slave trade brought in. In the event, Britain decided not to support his imperial ambitions.

In 1816 Commander W.H. Smyth, who visited Tripoli to collect Roman antiquities the Pasha wished to present to the Prince Regent,[30] had been impressed by the extraordinarily close and confidential relationship Consul Warrington had apparently established with the Pasha during his two years in Tripoli. Indeed, the French Consul was to declare that his British colleague was 'more master of the country than the Pasha himself, so much so that a gesture on his part is enough to make the Pasha tremble'.[31] Smyth reported to his superiors in London the Pasha's standing offer – an offer based on his professed friendship with Shaikh al-Kanemi of Bornu and with Mohammad Bello, Sultan of the Sokoto empire further west – to help any British exploration in his territories, adding:

I am becoming still more convinced that here – through this place and by means of these people – is an open gate into the interior of Africa. By striking due south of Tripoli, a traveller will reach Bornu before he is out of Yusuf's influence; and wherever his power reaches, the protecting virtues of the British flag are well known.[32]

Smyth set a high value on the Pasha's offer because he, and Warrington, believed the Pasha's influence extended much further into the interior than it in fact did.[33] Warrington seems to have been convinced the Pasha's authority stretched as far as Bornu to the south and Timbuctu to the south-west. But Major Alexander Gordon Laing, who travelled from Tripoli to Timbuctu in 1825-6, established by personal experience that the Pasha's power reached south-westwards no further than Ghadames, a fact that Warrington never apparently accepted. But even Laing was convinced that the Bornu road was 'a regular trading road, under the power of the Bashaw [Pasha] along which a child might travel'.[34] Warrington tended to under-estimate the difficulties of exploring regions of which he had no personal experience. He once informed his masters in Whitehall that 'the road from Tripoli to Bornu was as open as that from London to Edinburgh'.[35] Even as late as 1845, when Warrington was nearing the end of his long consulship, the British traveller James Richardson reported that

Colonel Warrington boasted of being able to do anything and everything in Tripoli . . . he had the Bashaw under his thumb, or hooked by the nose . . . Colonel Warrington under-rated the difficulties and dangers of travelling in Tripoli and Central Africa, making the road from Tripoli to Bornu as safe as the road from London to Paris.[36]

The extraordinary dangers of desert travel, even over the quite short distance from Tripoli to Fezzan, had been made plain by the

Ritchie-Lyon mission of 1818–20. It was led by a young surgeon and 'gentleman of great science and ability', Joseph Ritchie. Accompanied by Captain George Lyon, his main duty was to establish himself as British vice-consul in Fezzan 'with a view to the successful prosecution of the discoveries now attempting in the interior of Africa'; his objective was to reach the River Niger and determine its course. The party's third member was accordingly an English shipwright from the Malta dockyard, John Belford.

In the twenty years since Mohammad al-Mukni had escorted Frederick Hornemann to Murzuk, his star had risen higher. Although his position as viceroy of Fezzan was highly profitable, Al-Mukni needed to take between 4,000 and 5,000 slaves yearly from 'all his defenceless neighbours' in order to keep up a much increased burden of tribute.[37] Unable to obtain these by the usual means, and having also his own 'insatiable ambition and excessive avarice' to satisfy, he had started great slave raids into the remoter parts of Sudan. 'From one of these slave hunts into Kanem he had just returned to Tripoli, with a numerous body of captives and many camels, and was, in consequence, in the highest favour with the Bashaw.'[38] He was indeed preparing for another such expedition when the Ritchie-Lyon mission arrived in Tripoli, and he agreed to escort the British travellers to Fezzan. Arrived in Murzuk (despite its importance, a mere village of only 2,500 people, mostly blacks), both Ritchie and Belford soon fell ill with fever; Ritchie eventually died there, and Belford became stone-deaf. During the months he spent in Murzuk, Lyon gathered much new information about the countries of inner Africa: Bornu and, further off, Kanem, Mandara and Bagirmi to the south and east of Lake Chad which at that time were the main source of slaves, not least because of the conflict between the larger power of Bornu to the west and the rising power of Wadai to the east.[39] The regular slave caravans from the south to Murzuk were in the hands of Tripoline Arabs and Tebu, some from Fezzan and others from along the road through Kawar to Lake Chad.[40]

The only first-hand exploration was a five-week journey by Lyon and Belford through Zawila and Gatrun to Tegerri, about 100 miles south of Murzuk, where they made the first contacts with the Tebu. This short expedition, and the mission's return journey to Tripoli, taught Lyon much about the Saharan slave trade, 'his report on this traffic was perhaps the most valuable part of his published narrative'.[41] The main revenues of the Sultan of Fezzan were derived from slaves, general merchandise and dates. Lyon tells how:

For every slave, great or small, he receives, on their entering his kingdom, two Spanish dollars. In some years the number of slaves amounts to 4,000 . . . on the sale of every slave, he has, in addition to the head money, a dollar and a half, which, at the rate of 4,000, gives another 6,000 dollars . . . add to this his annual excursions for slaves, sometimes bringing 1,000 and 1,500, of which one-fourth are his.[42]

In his account of his Fezzanese travels, Lyon refers to the apparently new Fezzanese practice of raiding for slaves into suitable Tebu country, or even into the Sudan proper, rather than relying only on Arab and Tebu dealers to obtain slaves from countries further south. While in Murzuk, Lyon reported,

Great preparations were now making all over the kingdom, to forward an expedition which the Sultan intended to send against the tribe of the Tiboo Borgo, a country about a month S.E. Bodies of Arabs arrived from Sockna, and the towns in that direction; a party of horse also came from Benioleed,[43] and Morzouk was all confusion.[44]

When it finally left Murzuk on 12 July 1819, the raiding army comprised 300 horsemen, 800 foot and nearly 2,000 camels; six months later, Lyon witnessed its return from slave raiding into Borku and Bahr al-Ghazal:

They had brought with them 800 lean cripples, clad in skins and rags, between 2,000 and 3,000 Meherries [riding camels], and about 500 asses . . . nearly 1,000 camels and many captives, had died on the road, besides children; the death of the latter was not included, as they are not considered of any importance.[45]

The climax of Yusuf Pasha Karamanli's imperial aspirations in Sudan coincided with the most ambitious and successful African expedition so far sent out by the British government, the Bornu mission of 1822–5. In 1821, Shaikh al-Kanemi of Bornu had proposed a joint campaign with Tripoli to crush the rebellious kingdom of Bagirmi. The Pasha reacted to this prospect of a slave raid on a massive scale by sending a force of 450 cavalry and 1,300 infantry, led by the newly-appointed Bey of Fezzan, Mustafa al-Ahmar. If the assault on Bagirmi was less decisive than Al-Kanemi had perhaps hoped, Yusuf Pasha was doubtless pleased that his troops had penetrated further into the Sudan than ever before, had gathered a large booty in slaves, and had gained the military experience needed for the invasion of Bornu.[46] After the Bagirmi campaign, relations between Tripoli and Bornu deteriorated, partly because Al-Kanemi's family, originally sent to Fezzan for safety, were being held there as virtual hostages. It was at this juncture that the British Bornu Mission arrived in Tripoli at the start of its African journey, with Yusuf Pasha apparently intending to use it as a means of furthering his imperial designs on Bornu.[47]

There were three members of the mission. Dr Walter Oudney, an

Edinburgh surgeon, was to become British vice-consul in Bornu, 'with a view', according to his Colonial Office instructions based on those given earlier to Ritchie,[48] 'to the successful discoveries now attempting in the interior of Africa and the extension of our commerce in the Interior of that Continent'. African exploration was by then also being justified on commercial grounds, and Oudney carried with him specimens of British trade-goods; he was also asked to familiarise the natives with the British 'name and character'.[49] Lieutenant Hugh Clapperton, R.N., and Lieutenant Dixon Denham were to explore the African interior and were in particular to trace the course of the River Niger: Denham and others in London accordingly confidently expected the mission eventually to reappear on the River Nile in Egypt.[50]

For better communications between Tripoli and Britain's proposed permanent resident in Bornu, the Colonial Office approved Consul Warrington's suggestion of establishing a permanent vice-consulate at Murzuk. This would offer greater possibilities 'than any other course of promoting knowledge of the interior of Africa, and the advancement of British interests in that Quarter'. Although the Treasury initially turned down the proposal, it is significant that the Colonial Office was even then concerned with 'British interests' in the central Sahara and beyond.[51]

The mission was to reach Bornu 'under the full sanction and protection' of the Pasha of Tripoli. For the very handsome fee of £5,000, the Pasha proposed to send an escort of 1,000 men with the mission to Bornu and back to Tripoli, a proposal that did not necessarily reflect the true state of the security of the Tripoli-Bornu road. For the Pasha no doubt hoped that his troops, sent across the Sahara at British government expense, would indulge in widespread slave-raiding (despite contrary assurances to the British), or would even prepare the way for an invasion of Bornu. In the event, when the mission finally left Murzuk for Bornu in November 1822, it was escorted by 200 of the Pasha's troops. Although the Pasha had failed in his attempt to have the travellers accompanied by what would have amounted to an army, the 200 men sent with the mission were seen in Bornu as a reconnaissance party likely to be followed by an army of invasion as soon as the British had departed.[52] The mission and its escort were accordingly met outside Kuka (Kukawa, the new capital of Bornu, west of Lake Chad) by 'a considerable body of troops; both as a compliment to the bashaw, and to show his representative how well prepared he [Al-Kanemi] was against any of those who chose to be his enemies.'[53]

The British travellers had been told that Al-Kanemi's soldiers were 'a few ragged negroes armed with spears who lived upon the plunder of the Black Kaffir countries'. Instead, they were met by a splendid force of cavalry which 'surrounded the little body of Arab warriors so completely, as to give the compliment of welcoming them very much the appearance of a declaration of their contempt for their weakness'.[54] Although the Pasha of Tripoli clearly did not have the means to overcome such military power on the far side of the Sahara, he did have a superiority in firearms that Al-Kanemi was eager to remedy with help from Britain.

Dr Oudney died in Bornu in January 1824, but Lieutenants Denham and Clapperton explored Bornu and Hausaland before returning to Tripoli a year later. The Central Sahara, Lake Chad and the Central Sudan had been charted. The mission was 'one of the greatest achievements in African discovery', and had 'flooded with light areas which till then had been merely a subject of speculation'.[55] 'It had proved the security of the road between Tripoli and Bornu, even for Christians in European dress who made no attempt to disguise themselves; and it had demonstrated the effectiveness of Tripoli's connections with the interior. While the mission's findings stimulated merchants and confounded geographers, they also agitated the Colonial Office and the humanitarians about the slave trade and its abolition'.[56] It was accordingly suggested that the abolition of the slave trade in the northern part of Africa should be encouraged with 'a pecuniary compensation to a limited extent'. The difficulty, as outlined by Denham, was that North African traders in Sudan wanted only slaves, and as long as they refused any other exchange, the slave trade would continue.[57] Not for another twenty-five years was the British government able merely to end the dealing by officials in slaves at Tripoli; the trade itself was to continue through various parts of Libya for another century.

After the abolition of the Atlantic slave trade, the anti-slavery campaign of Sir Thomas Fowell Buxton in the 1830s drew the attention of the British public for the first time to the horrors of the long-established Saharan slave routes. Basing his figures on the accounts of British travellers, Buxton estimated that 20,000 slaves were being driven across the desert every year to 'Barbary' (Tripoli and the Maghrib) and Egypt, with approximately 42 per cent dying en route.[58] The fact that in 1835 Ottoman Turkey had deposed the last Karamanli Pasha and re-established its own direct rule over Tripoli made no apparent difference to the conduct of the slave trade. In 1840 and again in 1843, the British and Foreign Anti-Slavery Society called on all the Barbary rulers and the Sultan of Turkey to abolish the trade. Under diplomatic pressure from Britain, Tunis soon did so; Morocco, as a much greater and less vulnerable power, did not. The reactions of the Turkish authorities, both in Tripoli and Constantinople, were more ambiguous.

To discourage the slave trade and encourage its substitution by legitimate commerce, the British government eventually acted on Consul Warrington's long-standing suggestion by establishing vice-consulates at the two main slave entrepôts of Murzuk (in 1843) and Ghadames (in 1850). These appointments reflected the emergence of a clear British policy of developing large-scale trading contacts across the Sahara from Tripoli to central and western Sudan, while at the same time denying any similar opportunities to the French, then expanding their military occupation in Algeria towards the Sahara.[59] It was 'to ascertain how and to what extent the Saharan Slave Trade was carried on' that James Richardson visited Ghadames, Ghat and Murzuk in 1845–6 as agent of the Anti-Slavery Society.[60] He found in Ghadames that most of the slaves were from Bornu, others from 'Soudan' and Timbuctu; their greatest delight was in 'exchanging their various lingos'.[61] Ghadames at that time was well beyond the reach of the anti-slave-trade laws,[62] and slavery was still of vital financial importance to the oasis, especially with the Tunis outlet by then closed by the Bey and those of Algeria coming under French control. Richardson found that slaves lately brought from Bornu

. . . were as much like merchandize as they could be, or human beings could be made to resemble it . . . all were nearly alike, as so many goods packed up of the same quality. They were very thin, and almost skeletons, about the age of from ten to fifteen years, with the round Bornouese features strongly marked upon their countenances. These slaves are the property of a Tibboo . . . the Tibboo bought the slaves on speculation in Bornou; now he could sell then at from forty to fifty dollars each . . . there was nothing in him to denote that he was a common trafficker in human flesh and blood.[63]

During his two months in Ghadames, Richardson realised that fully to understand the slave trade and its workings he would have to penetrate much further into the interior: 'Unless I go to the first-hand traffickers in human flesh – to the heart of Africa itself – I can never get the information which I require . . . cannot see any danger if I stick close to the Ghadamsee merchants.'[64] In Murzuk, he found the traffic in slaves under the watch of the British vice-consul, G.B. Gagliuffi.[65] 'Unquestionably,' Richardson wrote, 'the establishment of English consuls throughout the desert and all the great cities of the Interior of Africa, would be an immense benefit to humanity, whilst it would equally promote British trade and interests, and the commerce of the entire world.'[66] Gagliuffi believed 'one of the greatest obstacles to the suppression of the slave trade was the facility which it afforded Moorish and Arab merchants to indulge in 'sensual armours'. Although a merchant would get no profit by his long and dreary journeys over Desert, he would still carry it on for the sake of indulging in the lower passions of his nature.'[67] Gagliuffi also considered the

Tebu even worse slave-drivers than the Tuareg of Air, or even many Tripolines.[68] Richardson himself reported that the slave trade was on the increase in the Great Desert and that 'slaves are the grand staple commerce of the Sudan and Bornou caravans, and without slaves this commerce could hardly exist.'[69]

Richardson, who considered the traffic in slaves 'the most gigantic system of wickedness the world has ever seen', published his findings in a report to the committee of the Anti-Slavery Society[70] and in his two-volume *Travels*. His evidence was supported from Murzuk by Gagliuffi, who in 1849 reported the death from thirst of a whole caravan of 1,600 slaves travelling up from Bornu; six months later, he reported that another 800 slaves had died on the same route, also from thirst. The widely-known purpose of Gagliuffi's presence in Murzuk did not necessarily decrease the flow of slaves across the Sahara, but resulted partly in their being driven by less-known and thus, if anything, even more difficult routes to the Mediterranean. The German traveller Heinrich Barth, in Bornu in 1851, witnessed the departure for Fezzan of a caravan of about 750 slaves, and noted that they were still the country's main export.[71] In 1858, the British consul in Tripoli estimated that slave-trading still represented more than two-thirds of the caravan trade across the Sahara;[72] indeed, the Tripoli port returns for 1850 showed that the number of slaves being shipped from there to Albania, Rhodes, Cyprus, Constantinople and the Levant was actually increasing. At the same time, Benghazi, as the northern terminus of the newly-developed trans-Saharan route from Wadai, became a more important outlet for black slaves, with the British vice-consul there reporting in 1849 the deaths of 400 out of one group of 1,600 slaves on the march from Wadai.

Through British pressure, the Turkish Sultan in 1855 prohibited the transport of slaves from Tripoli, Benghazi and Derna to Crete for onward shipment to other parts of the Ottoman empire; this was followed by a decree prohibiting the sending of slaves by land or sea between Tripoli and Turkey, and in 1857 by the abolition of slave-dealing, but not slavery, within the empire. Wilhelm Heine, a German artist who visited Tripoli in 1859, found:

Since the prohibition of the import of slaves into the Regency, caravans coming from the interior have diverted their traffic eastwards, to Egypt, or westwards, to the Moroccan coast, and as a result transport has lessened and imports have fallen off considerably.[73]

The principal outcome of the reports of James Richardson was the despatch of the Central African Mission of 1850. Richardson led it, and was accompanied by two Germans in the service of the British government, Dr Adolph Overweg and Dr Heinrich Barth. Leaving

Tripoli in March 1850, the mission travelled through Murzuk and Ghat to Air. While Barth went on to the great trading city of Kano, Richardson marched towards Kukawa, capital of Bornu, but died on the way. Barth and Overweg then explored the country round Lake Chad and, after the latter's death in November 1852, Barth travelled through Sokoto to Timbuctu, which he reached in September 1853, and where he stayed for six months. On his return journey he met a five-man party under the leadership of Dr Edward Vogel, another German in British government service. This was a supplementary mission to the Central African Mission, and while Barth returned to Tripoli and then to England in the autumn of 1855, Vogel continued the work of the mission in Sudan (he was killed in 1856 and all the members of his party were dead by the following year).

Within two years of his return to England, Barth published the first volume of his monumental five-volume account of his work, *Travels and Discoveries in North and Central Africa*, which confirms him ('nothing but a foreign gentleman', as he described himself) as the greatest European traveller in the Sahara and the western Sudan. Due largely to Barth, the Central African Mission stands as the successful climax of seventy years of British efforts to penetrate those parts of Africa from Tripoli. As A. Adu Boahen commented:

The mission cleared once and for all the mystery about Timbuctu and the areas further south. It dispelled any doubts entertained about the populous and fertile nature of the regions south of the Sahara, the standard of civilisation and, above all, the attitude of the African rulers. It renewed and strengthened British influence and prestige in the Western Sudan. Finally, not only did it prepare the way for future enterprise . . . but it also pointed out once more the possibility of opening up a shorter and more practical route from the south to the rich markets of Hausaland and Bornu.[74]

This route was the eastern tributary of the River Niger, the Benue, which, as Barth noted, led several hundred miles into the interior.

So Britain soon abandoned the political gains achieved in the Sahara over many years, turning again to the penetration of inner Africa by way of the Niger-Benue river system. In 1854, while Barth was still making his way home, a specially constructed iron steamship of 260 tons, the *Pleiad*, sailed for four months up the Niger-Benue. As a voyage of trade and exploration, it was not a success, but the *Pleiad* showed that the Niger-Benue system could be opened up by steamer, and because quinine was used as a prophylactic against fevers rather than as a cure for them, not one of the sixty-six members of the expedition died. At the time, such a record would have been remarkable almost anywhere in Africa, and was all the more so for having been achieved on the notoriously unhealthy Nigerian rivers, then justly known as the 'white man's grave'. Steam-power, quinine and in due course the breech-loading rifle were to enable the British to exploit the interior of Africa via the Nigerian river system and to leave the Saharan approach to any other power that cared to make use of it.

By the late 1850s it was officially recognised in London that the Niger route was safer and swifter than the Saharan one, that it led more directly to the sources of worthwhile Sudanese trade and that, in exploiting it, Britain would be less likely to encroach on the interests of imperial France, by then starting a new phase of African expansion from her two possessions in Algeria and Senegal. When the vice-consulate at Ghadames was closed in 1860 and that at Murzuk the following year, Britain in effect formally withdrew from the central Sahara, leaving most of it open for eventual French domination. For seventy-five years Britain had been pursuing the illusion of the supposed wealth of Sudan. It was an illusion founded less on contemporary realities than on medieval Islamic accounts of the wealth and learning of Timbuctu and other trading cities. Rather than expect the conditions of the fourteenth century to persist into the nineteenth, the British in due course accepted the evidence of their own explorers. But the French, seeking compensations in Africa for the defeat of 1870, long held to their romantic illusions of the imperial potential of another India on the River Niger whose millions of peoples would respond to the benefits of European civilisation and commerce brought to them by a trans-Saharan railway from Algiers. Yet the fact remained that, without the slave trade and the institution of slavery, Sudanic Africa was to become one of the very poorest regions of the modern world.

Until the nineteenth century, relations across the central Sahara between the lands comprising modern Libya and modern Chad respectively, were largely sustained by impersonal commercial incentives. The ancient trade link between Tripoli and the Empire of Bornu through Kawar was, in modern terms, largely one between Libya and territories now forming part of the Republic of Niger, and of northern Nigeria. Lands that today are situated in the Chad Republic – notably Kanem, Bagirmi and Wadai – usually had only secondary commercial ties with Tripolitania, as fiefs of Bornu and as sources of raw materials for the Bornu entrepôt trade. But from the 1840s onwards, relations became very much closer and more personal, with tribespeople and close religio-political influences spreading from Libya into what is now central Chad, and a direct trade road opened between eastern Chad and Cyrenaica. The initiators of this closer relationship were the Awlad Slaiman tribe of north-central Libya, reacting in turn to political and economic pressures from outside the Sahara.

Descended from the Bani Sulaym Arab invaders of the eleventh century,[75] the Awlad Slaiman rose – after the tribe had ceased feuding between its main factions and had united under the leadership of the formidable Saif al-Nasr family – to a position of considerable military and political strength in the central Sahara towards the end of the eighteenth century. As with most of the larger tribes of western and central Libya, Slaiman nomadism was oriented north-south, between the pre-desert steppes of the Sirtica – where camels, horses, sheep and barley were raised in the relatively fertile *wadis* – and the date-producing oases of northern Fezzan. During the seventeenth century the tribe had established a patron-client relationship with the peoples of Semnu, Temenhint and the Sebha oases, from whom they obtained the fine, dried dates that were so widely traded, or kept as the staple diet for long desert journeys.[76] Trading interests were linked with the Giofra oases of Hon, Waddan and Sokna on the western marches of the Awlad Slaiman *dira* (tribal land), and with the oasis of Zella to the east, on the road to Augila and Egypt. Only the larger and more powerful tribes (usually a cluster of small tribes acknowledging a central tribal authority) could maintain such extended politico-economic links on a regular annual cycle of trade and transhumance. Lesser groups had access only to the resources of Tripolitania or northern Fezzan[77] unless they in turn established a wider presence by linking up with other groups.[78] From the early nineteenth century four main tribes – the Awlad Slaiman, the Gadadfa and the Magarba of the Sirtica, together with the Orfella of south-east Tripolitania – often joined forces, while preserving their separate identity, in the face of other tribes or perceived external threats. This alignment, the *Saff al-Fauqi*, brought together tribes whose grazing-lands lay in inner Sirtica and who were usually hostile to the *Saff al-Bahr*, the alignment of tribes nearer to the Mediterranean coast.[79]

Although a large tribe by Saharan standards, the Awlad Slaiman was never able to field more than a few hundred men in battle at any one time; a raiding party of 300 was considered large. In times of peace, tribal survival depended on free movement between the two ecological zones of the north Sirtica steppes and the oases of Fezzan,[80] involving the regular annual migration of much of the tribe over distances of at least 500 km. The main trade route between Tripolitania and the central Sudan more or less marked the eastern limits of Awlad Slaiman power, and thus enabled the tribe to widen its margin of survival by demanding 'protection' from caravans, or by raiding those failing to pay it. In war, when success depended on the mastery of people rather than territory, survival was a matter of mobility: the ability to attack and raid with speed and surprise using a combination of horses and camels. Defence relied equally on mobility and the ability to evade pursuit in the desert.

Another source of tribal resilience was the remarkable capacity for swift recovery from disaster. From the late eighteenth century, the Awlad Slaiman suffered a series of devastating defeats, and seemed finally to have been annihilated;[81] yet less than twenty years later, a people with few material encumbrances had recovered their numerical strength, raising the same formidable challenge to outsiders seeking to control the central desert between the Mediterranean and the Fezzan. Given a few seasons of good pasture, lost herds were quickly re-established, while within fifteen to eighteen years both the free tribeswomen and the slaves, who commonly survived massacres of the warriors, had raised a new generation of young fighters, as ferocious and mobile as the old, augmented by the adoption of prisoners of war.[82]

Moreover, the tribal leadership, the family of Saif-al-Nasr, was well and widely connected, with a tradition of marrying younger sisters to the Sultans of Morocco and of establishing marriage alliances with notables throughout the Saharan borderlands. The Awlad Slaiman and their tribal allies had always opposed Karamanli attempts to centralise power in Tripoli, and particularly resented paying annual tribute. Although the tribe's relationship with Tripoli between the 1780s and the 1840s often seemed inconsistent, its main objectives were simply to be left free, with the right to political and economic influence in central Libya recognised.[83] The first of a series of tribal revolts led by the Saif-al-Nasr against the Karamanlis started in 1781 and ended with the formal recognition of Awlad Slaiman rights, thus enabling the tribe to take advantage of the social and political disasters of Ali Pasha Karamanli's regency to control, and occasionally cut, the trade route to Fezzan through Misurata. In establishing Tripoli's control over the Libyan interior, Ali's successor Yusuf Pasha Karamanli had to mount a series of campaigns against the Awlad Slaiman and their allies between 1805 and 1816. After its eventual resounding defeat, the tribe was dispersed and seemed to have been destroyed. But one of the grandsons of Shaikh Saif-al-Nasr, Abd-al-Jalil, was taken to the Karamanli court as a hostage; his outstanding military abilities brought him command of the Pasha's slave raids into Kanem in the 1820s.

In 1831, in one of those remarkable revivals of tribal strength, Abd-al-Jalil turned against the Karamanlis, by then fast losing their political and economic power in the closing years of Yusuf Pasha Karamanli's long reign. By the end of 1831, Abd-al-Jalil had seized Fezzan and had set himself up as an independent Sultan at Murzuk. Although soon forced back into the desert, the Awlad Slaiman remained at large in Fezzan, and with the experience gained on earlier forays under the Karamanlis, began raiding on their own account into Kanem and Bornu, while Karamanli control over Fezzan and the vital trade routes southward towards Lake Chad and south-westwards towards the Niger lands was lost. Abd-al-Jalil was a remarkable military commander:

Highly principled and a strict disciplinarian, he could conjure order out of anarchy. Despite all the odds of desert life and the fissiparous tendencies characteristic of nomad people, Abd-al-Jalil did not only organise and hold his troops together, he also gave them excellent training and maintained a very high standard of discipline among them.[84]

He had long impressed the British consul, Warrington, with his leadership, and by 1831 Warrington was offering to mediate between Yusuf Pasha Karamanli and the rebels, an offer at first rejected because of the consul's close personal relations with Abd-al-Jalil. As mentioned above, the consul had over many years built up such relations with various tribal leaders of the interior who were in the habit of visiting his country house south-east of Tripoli. Abd-al-Jalil seemed at the time ready to offer Britain a protectorate over Tripoli in return for help in gaining control over the rest of the country.[85]

Faced with continuing revolts and economic collapse as a result of the international curbs on piracy and increasing insecurity of the desert trade routes, Yusuf Pasha Karamanli abdicated in favour of his son, Ali, in July 1832. But the country was still in chaos and Tripoli itself in revolt when in March 1835 the Ottoman government sent a fleet to reimpose direct rule from Constantinople, thereby ending 120 years of the independent Karamanli state.

After the fall of Algiers to the French in 1830 and Mohammad Ali's attainment of near-independence for Egypt, Turkey's first motive in reoccupying Tripoli was to prevent further loss of nominally Ottoman North African territory.[86] But the Ottoman governors, like the Karamanli Pashas before them, soon found that the tribes, while quite willing to pay homage to the Sultan at Constantinople, were quite unwilling to pay his taxes or submit to his authority. The revolt of the Awlad Slaiman and other peoples continued and in the 1830s, when the Awlad Slaiman had attained their greatest power, Abd-al-Jalil was effectively ruler of all Fezzan. He maintained direct trade relations with Bornu and diplomatic contact with Mohammad Ali's Egypt and with the French in Algiers, thereby leading the Ottomans to fear the complete diversion of trans-Fezzanese caravan traffic away from Tripoli to other North African outlets. Abd-al-Jalil consolidated his control of the central Sahara by marriage alliances with his neighbours: he himself married the sister of the Sultan of Bornu in 1835;[87] two of his own sisters married influential Bornuese; while another was married to a Tebu notable in Tibesti.[88] Moreover, Abd-al-Jalil was by then seen by Consul Warrington and the British government as a most promising agent for the total abolition of the trans-Saharan slave trade and slavery within the central Sahara; the promotion of legitimate commerce, and the persuasion of other rulers to do the same. At a meeting with Warrington in the Sirtica in April 1842, Abd-al-Jalil undertook these commissions, on the understanding that he would be given free access to the coast (and especially the port of Benghazi) and recognition by the Sublime Porte as Bey of Fezzan.[89] But all these projects, which would have given Britain direct political and commercial access to the central Sudanese states through Tripoli or Benghazi and Fezzan, came to nothing.

Like the French in contemporary Algeria, the Turks in Tripoli adopted at first a dynamic and interventionist Saharan policy, rather than a passive and defensive one. After occupying Misurata in 1836, they were faced with rebellion in three main centres: at Tarhuna in Msellata south-east of Tripoli; among the mainly Berber communities of the Western Gebel; and in the Sirtica and Fezzan. The Turks were 'a new and more formidable master'[90] than ever the Karamanlis had been, although the harsh methods they used against rebels did not facilitate their task. But in May 1842, shortly after his meeting with Warrington, Abd-al-Jalil was surprised by a Turkish force in Orfella country between Sirte and Bu Ngem. In the ensuing battle, Abd-al-Jalil, his brother Saif al-Nasr, two of their sons, and other rebel leaders were killed,[91] an episode long recalled in the tribal poetry and song of central Libya.[92]

According to Richardson,[93] it was on Warrington's advice that Abd-al-Jalil's son Mohammad led some of the surviving Awlad Slaiman and their tribal allies quite beyond the reach of the Turks into Borku and Kanem, country they knew from their raids of the 1820s. In removing themselves some 1,500 km. into Central Africa, certain sections of the Awlad Slaiman and other tribes from the Sirtica (notably Orfella and Gadadfa) found a pre-desert country quite like their own, where they could 'replicate their northern lifestyle in a most remarkable fashion'.[94] Politically, their new homeland was far removed from the conditions they had left behind. Instead of the Ottoman Turks, and beyond them the diplomatic and economic pressures of the European Powers, they had only to contend with the decaying authority of the Empire of Bornu and with the rising, expansionist threat of Wadai to the east. The local Tebu and Kanembou people were no match for the formidable aggressive strength of the Libyan Arab and Arab-Berber migrants. The newcomers were relatively few, for many of their number had chosen to remain in the Sirtica and come to terms with the Turks. The various factions of the

Awlad Slaiman in Kanem are said to have had only about 170 tents (households), with about another thirty tents of Gadadfa and Orfella allies and vassals.[95] The Libyans probably owed much of their local military superiority to their firearms;[96] certainly no other nearby nomadic groups could compete with them. Their most formidable neighbours were the Kel Owi Tuareg confederation, centred on the Air massif to the west. In 1849 the Awlad Slaiman, supported by other tribesmen from central Libya attracted by the prospect of booty, raided the great annual caravan, the *Azelai*, organised by the Kel Owi to supply Kawar salt to the Hausa states. They made off with several thousand camels, but should have known better than to provoke the Tuareg. At the beginning of 1850, the Libyan raiders were surprised by a force of 7,000 Kel Owi and their allies at Wadi Alala and massacred: 'only the least brave and youngest were left'.[97] Shaikh Mohammad was among those killed, and he was succeeded by Ghayth, the twenty-year-old son of Saif al-Nasr.

Heinrich Barth visited the Awlad Slaiman soon after this disaster, and devoted a whole chapter of his book of travels to this 'band of robbers'.[98] After settling in Kanem, they were 'joined by a great many adventurers from all the Arab tribes from the Rif as far as Fezzan'.[99] According to Barth's estimates, the tribe was able to put between 900 and 1,000 horsemen into the field. To ensure its survival, it sought further allies among local fractions of the Tebu. It offered its services to the Shaikh of Bornu against the encroachments of Wadai from the east, and was in effect given responsibility for the defence of the province of Kanem that Bornu itself could no longer provide.[100] In actual practice, the tribe became quite skilled in playing off one settled or nomadic group against another, so much so that by 1871, when visited by Nachtigal, the Awlad Slaiman once again dominated Kanem and Borku, where they terrorised the local nomadic and sedentary communities. But they were also able to raid at will over a much wider area, enjoying an authority that brought them much more freedom of action than they had ever known in the Sirtica.[101] Nachtigal described how the tribe attracted recruits from its kinsfolk in Libya:

With admirable tenacity and enterprise, they fought one after another all the tribes living between the Chad and the southern boundary of Tibesti on the one hand, and between the Bornu road and that leading from Benghazi to Wadai on the other, and they did all this with a force which did not exceed 500 horsemen and as many footsoldiers. Indefatigable, they were found now at the date harvest in Borku, now fighting with the numerous tribes of the Bahr al-Ghazal, now on a journey to the markets of Bornu or the Hausa states. The lowlands of Egei and Bodele, rich in vegetation and with abundant though brackish water, favoured rendezvous for the camel-rearing tribes of the southeast desert, were more and more deserted, for what the ruthless Arabs had stolen since their arrival there defies calculation. Desert and steppe had to supply them with their favourite possession, the camel, and the nearby Sudan with its sedentary population offered to their rapacity many a treasure trove, rich for that region, of silver, amber, coral and cotton goods. Reports of their successful forays, exaggerated through distance to fabulous proportions, penetrated to their old home, and drew to them fellow-countrymen, adventurers eager for plunder, from the borders of Egypt to Tripoli and Fezzan, who joined for a time in their enterprises. Urfilla, Qedadifa, Ferjan, Jawazi, Meqariha, did not shrink from the toil and privations of migration or from long separation from home and family, and appeared in the far south as temporary allies to return home after a few years laden with booty.[102]

An important source of Slaiman power thus lay in maintaining close ties with their own people in Libya. While members of the tribe and their allies occasionally returned to the Sirtica, greater numbers of reinforcements were attracted, either temporarily or permanently, from Libya by the reported successes of their kinsfolk in the south. In 1861 a large number of Magarba tribespeople moved from their camel-raising country north-east of Agedabia to northern Kanem;[103] thus they lived and raided in Chad in rather uneasy alliance with the Slaiman.[104] And in Bornu in 1872, Nachtigal heard of a 300-man raiding party arriving from the Sirtica to join their tribal allies in Kanem.[105] This practice of treating Kanem, Borku and neighbouring territories as a *chasse gardée* for Libyan tribal marauders seems to have continued until nearly the end of the century. Theirs was a freebooting variant of the more regulated but no less inhumane exploitation of the human and natural resources of the Nilotic and eastern Sudan by the nineteenth-century Egyptian state.

As in the Sirtica, the Awlad Slaiman and their associates survived in Chad by pillage, extorting tribute, by regional trading and transhumance between the ecological zones of the southern Sahara and northern Sudan, and by intermittent control of the nearest stages of the main Tripoli-Bornu trade route. Their greatest strength lay in their ability to raid nomadic and settled communities almost with impunity: such raids brought in booty, while the terror they inspired ensured regular payments of tribute. If other nomads, including the Tuareg and Tebu, could put the same mobility to use in their own raiding, the Awlad Slaiman combined the use of horses, camels and firearms to give themselves an almost undisputed superiority in the central Chadian lands. A common tactic was to ride to an objective by camel with a riderless horse in tow, the fresh horse being used only in the final assault and subsequent escape. The raiders thus gained the advantage of the endurance of the camel and the swifter, short-range performance of the horse, combined with the use of firearms against peoples usually equipped with only the so-called 'white weapons' – lance, spear, sword and dagger.[106] By employing these tactics the Awlad Slaiman, although probably never able to field more than 1,000 warriors at a time, came to dominate Kanem and the routes northwards for nearly fifty years. In doing so, they established a tradition of Libyan aggression and freebooting among the peoples and territories on the far side of the Sahara exposed to their raids.

Arabs had been living in the Sahelian lands of Chad for centuries before the coming of the Awlad Slaiman. They began arriving from the Nilotic Sudan and Egypt in the fourteenth and fifteenth centuries, although only in large numbers from the seventeenth century, and there followed successive waves of Arabs up to the early twentieth century. They have long been divided into two main occupational groups: the *abbala* (camel-herders) of the northern Sahel, and the *baggara* (cattle-herders) of the rather better-watered south, grouped in about twenty main tribes of nomadic, semi-nomadic and sedentary peoples. Although they have long roamed largely within the bounds of the great Sahelian sultanates (Kanem-Bornu, Bagirmi and Wadai) and have become very mixed with other peoples, they have always maintained a remarkable degree of cultural cohesion and political exclusivity. They have played little part in the processes of state-building, but were traditionally attached to local kingdoms to the extent of paying tribute and providing men in time of war. In their economic life, they infiltrated all sections of Chadian society and maintained close trading ties with neighbouring Muslim countries. In the late nineteenth century, Magarba and Zuwaya tribesmen from eastern Cyrenaica (misnamed 'Fezzani' in Chad)[107] infiltrated Sahelian lands as traders, and have remained there ever since. According to Chapelle:

The Arab people cross Chad from east to west like a carelessly-thrown scarf or like the Milky Way in the midst of the constellations. They come into contact with all other peoples, nomad or settled, with whom the Arabs often overlap, with whom they occasionally share lifestyles and resources, and with whom material and cultural exchanges are constant.[108]

Although the Arabs have probably never represented more than one-third of the population of the lands now comprising the Republic of Chad,

they play an important cultural role, due to their language and the traditional teaching of the Koran. Up to the colonial period, Arabic was the only written language in Chad. It was spread as a language of religion by

Muslims of other races without destroying the mother-tongue of those Muslims, except in a few cases. Arab herdsmen and their women are frequent visitors to the Sahelian-zone markets, where they exchange their produce, cattle, milk and butter, for foodstuffs, textiles and various manufactured goods. Their language thus spread as a trading tongue under a popular and misshapen form called *Tourkou*.[109]

Thus all Arabic-speakers in Chad were not necessarily 'Arab', although regard for Arabic as his 'natural' language may be taken as one definition of an 'Arab'. A further definition may be the claim to an Arab identity, an awareness of being 'Arab'.[110]

## NOTES

1. For Egyptian ignorance of the Sudan in the early nineteenth century, see Walz, *Trade between Egypt*, pp. 228–30; for contemporary European ignorance, see R. Hallett, *The Penetration of Africa*, I, London, 1965, pp. 37–125.
2. Hallett, *ibid.*, p. 94.
3. E.W. Bovill, *The Niger Explored*, London, 1968. p. 5. For Rennell's map, see M. Park, *Travels in the Interior Districts of Africa*, London, 1799, app.
4. Dozy and De Goeje, *Déscription de l'Afrique*, pp. 9–10.
5. *The History of Africa*, London, 1830, p. 3.
6. Quoted in J. Bell, *A System of Geography*, Edinburgh, 1844, p. 288.
7. See R. Hallett, *Records of the African Association, 1788–1831*, London, 1964, pp. 42–7.
8. *Ibid.*, p. 44.
9. *Ibid.*, p. 26.
10. *Ibid.*, p. 56.
11. Hallett, *The Penetration*, p. 208.
12. *Ibid.*, p. 208.
13. *Ibid.*, p. 259.
14. E.W. Bovill, *Missions to the Niger*, vol. 1, Cambridge, 1962, pp. 99–100.
15. *Ibid.*, p. 109.
16. For his probable route, see *ibid.*, map I.
17. Hallett, *The Penetration*, p. 259.
18. Bovill, *Missions*, vol. I, p. 150.
19. K. Folayan, *Tripoli During the Reign of Yusuf Pasha Karamanli*, Ile-Ife, 1979, p. 78.
20. *Ibid.*, ch.2.
21. Quoted in Bovill, *Missions*, vol. I, p. 29.
22. See Folayan, *Tripoli*, ch.4.
23. G. Lyon, *A Narrative of Travels in Northern Africa in the Years 1818–1819 and 1820*, London, 1821, p. 3.
24. Folayan, *Tripoli*, p. 83.
25. *Ibid.*, p. 52.
26. *Ibid.*, p. 78.
27. Bovill, *The Niger*, p. 63.
28. Folayan, *Tripoli*, p. 85.
29. See *ibid.*, pp. 85–6.
30. See A. Thwaite, *The Deserts of Hesperides*, London, 1969, p. 2.
31. Quoted in Bovill, *The Niger*, p. 44.
32. Quoted in *ibid.*, p. 40.

33. *Ibid.*, p. 39.
34. Laing to Warrington, 13 Sep. 1825, quoted in Bovill, *Missions*, vol. I, p. 242.
35. *Ibid.*, p. 158.
36. J. Richardson, *Travels in the Great Desert of Sahara, 1845 and 1846*, London, 1848, vol. I, p. 326.
37. Lyon, *Travels*, p. 4.
38. *Ibid.*
39. Trimingham, *A History of Islam*, p. 214.
40. *Ibid.*, pp. 120–1.
41. Bovill, *The Niger*, p. 66.
42. Lyon, *Travels*, pp. 188–9.
43. Beni Ulid, south-east of Tripoli, and 'centre' of the Orfella tribe.
44. Lyon, *Travels*, p. 103.
45. *Ibid.*, pp. 249–50.
46. Folayan, *Tripoli*, p. 89. For the horrors of the campaign, see F. Rodd, 'A Fezzani Military Expedition to Kanem and Bagirmi in 1821', *Journal of the Royal African Society*, XXXV, CXXXIX (April 1936).
47. Folayan, *Tripoli*, pp. 90–1.
48. For the full text, see Bovill, *Missions*, vol. II, pp. 19–20.
49. A.A. Boahen, *Britain, the Sahara and the Western Sudan, 1788–1861*, Oxford, 1964, pp. 54–5.
50. See Bovill, *The Niger*, p. 73.
51. See Boahen, *Britain, The Sahara*, p. 56.
52. Folayan, *Tripoli*, p. 92.
53. Bovill, *Missions*, vol. II, p. 243.
54. *Ibid.*, pp. 243–4.
55. Bovill, *The Niger*, pp. 145–6.
56. Boahen, *Britain, The Sahara*, p. 68.
57. See Bovill, *Missions*, vol. III, p. 533.
58. T.F. Buxton, *The African Slave Trade and its Remedy*, London, 1840, pp. 37ff. His figures are much disputed.
59. Boahen, *Britain, The Sahara*, p. 163.
60. Richardson, *Travels*, vol. I, p. xii.
61. *Ibid.*, p. 148.
62. Fisher and Fisher, *Slavery and Muslim Society*, p. 166.
63. Richardson, *Travels*, vol. I, pp. 258–9.
64. *Ibid.*, p. 153.
65. *Ibid.*, vol. II, p. 360.
66. *Ibid.*, p. 361.
67. *Ibid.*, p. 348.
68. *Ibid.*, p. 312.
69. *Ibid.*, p. 478.
70. Published in *The Anti-Slavery Reporter*, Sept.-Nov., 1846.
71. H. Barth, *Travels and Discoveries in North and Central Africa* (5 vols.), London, 1857, vol. II, p. 339.
72. Boahen, *Britain, The Sahara*, p. 127.
73. E. Leva, 'Tripoli in Una Descrizione di Cent'Anni Fa', *Africa*, XXII, 1 (March 1967).
74. Boahen, *Britain, The Sahara*, pp. 211–12.
75. Le Rouvreur, *Sahéliens et sahariens*, p. 297, has a different account.
76. D.D. Cordell, 'The Awlad Sulayman of Libya and Chad: Power and Adaptation in the Sahara and Sahel', *Canadian Journal of African Studies*, 19, 2 (1985).
77. A. Cauneille, 'La semi-nomadisme dans l'Ouest Libyen (Fezzan-Tripolitaine)', *Nomades et nomadisme du Sahara*, Paris, 1963, p. 102.

78. *Ibid.*
79. E.L. Peters, 'Cultural and Social Diversity in Libya' in J.A. Allan (ed.), *Libya since Independence*, Beckenham, 1982, p. 108.
80. Cordell, 'The Awlad Sulayman', p. 325.
81. Lyon, *Travels*, p. 54, said that in 1812 the tribe had been almost completely destroyed; see also Bovill, *Missions*, vol. II, p. 163.
82. Cordell, 'The Awlad Sulayman', pp. 335-6.
83. *Ibid.*, p. 325.
84. Folayan, *Tripoli*, p. 119.
85. *Ibid.*, p. 120.
86. J. Wright, *Libya*, London, 1969, p. 103.
87. Boahen, *Britain, The Sahara*, p. 137.
88. Cordell, 'The Awlad Sulayman', p. 328.
89. Boahen, *Britain, The Sahara*, p. 136.
90. Richardson, *Travels*, vol. II, p. 352.
91. Rossi, *Storia*, p. 304; Richardson, *Travels*, vol. II, pp. 352-3; and Nachtigal, *Sahara and Sudan*, vol. I, p. 160, give differing accounts of Abd-al-Jalil's death.
92. Rossi, *Storia*, pp. 304-5.
93. Richardson, *Travels*, vol. II. p. 355.
94. Cordell, 'The Awlad Sulayman', p. 329.
95. Le Rouvreur, *Sahéliens et Sahariens*, p. 297.
96. H. Carbou, *La région du Tchad et du Ouadai*, (2 vols.), Paris, 1912, I, p. 85.
97. Barth, *Travels and Discoveries*, vol. II, p. 275.
98. *Ibid.*, ch.XL, 'The Horde of the Welad Sliman'.
99. *Ibid.*, p. 273.
100. Cordell, 'The Awlad Sulayman'; Zeltner, *Pages d'histoire*, p. 241.
101. Cordell, 'The Awlad Sulayman', p. 332.
102. Nachtigal, *Sahara and Sudan*, vol. II, p. 313.
103. Cordell, 'The Awlad Sulayman', p. 334.
104. Zeltner, *Pages d'histoire*, p. 246.
105. Nachtigal, *Sahara and Sudan*, vol. III, pp. 13-14.
106. Cordell, 'The Awlad Sulayman', p. 333.
107. Le Rouvreur, *Sahéliens et Sahariens*, p. 368.
108. Chapelle, *Le peuple*, p. 175.
109. *Ibid.*, p. 171.
110. See M. Rodinson, *The Arabs*, London, 1981, p. 45.

# 5

## SANUSI, FIREARMS AND SLAVES

*'We wish to ask you to obey what God and his Prophet have ordered'*
— the Grand Sanusi

If the Awlad Slaiman and their associates represented the cruder aspects of Libyan exploitation of what is now central Chad, a rather different form of domination – indeed, almost a civilising mission – came from Libya through the missionary activity of the Sanusi confraternity. For some decades, much of what is now northern and central Chad shared with large areas of Libya the common experience of Sanusi theocracy, a phenomenon brought to an end only in the early years of this century by French expansion into the central Sahara from the south, and by Italian expansion from the north. The Sanusi confraternity was established in Cyrenaica about 1843 by Sayyid Mohammad bin Ali al-Sanusi, an Algerian divine known to his followers as the Grand Sanusi. His was a strictly orthodox order of Sufis, a revivalist rather than a reformist movement dedicated to spreading religious enlightenment into places where Islam was at best only lightly observed. Their mission was to 'remind the negligent, teach the ignorant and guide him who has gone astray'.[1] Nachtigal described them as 'essentially only a Muslim missionary society, home and foreign, in so far as it preaches no dogmatic or ritualistic deviations from the orthodox sects, but has as its sole purpose the revival and extension of the faith'.[2]

In concentrating their influence away from the main political centres of the Mediterranean and Nilotic Africa, and among more inaccessible peoples of the Sahara and Sudan, the Sanusi seemed eager to separate as much as possible their own activities from those of the neighbouring powers. As early as 1864, the French explorer Henri Duveyrier asserted that the Sanusi objective was to 'preserve the peoples of the Sahara and central Africa from all contact with Europeans'.[3] This tendency of the order to withdraw into the remoter refuges of the Sahara seems to have echoed a certain theme in Islamic history: flight from malign influences, and emigration (physical, spiritual, or both) to places of safety in the face of perceived and otherwise irresistible dangers and challenges.

It is not rebellion that the Sanusi shaikhs preach, but emigration. For, in their eyes, emigration is the sole means of rejoining the *Dar al-Islam* that is open to believers living under the Christian yoke or that, no less damnable, of Muslim

81

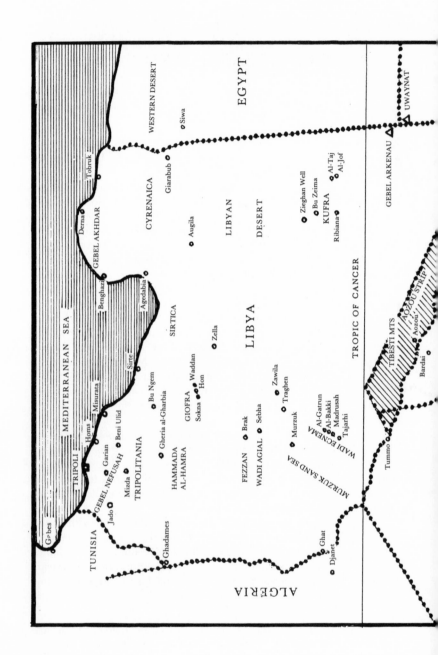

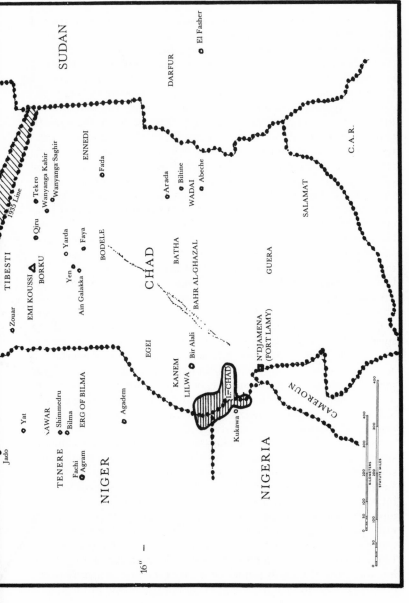

The Central Sahara and Sudan

sovereigns . . . who are at the mercy of European powers and subject to their pernicious influences.[4]

Behind such revivalism and retreat seemed to lie a deep mistrust of the modern world and all its works, and an inability to come to terms with them. From the onset of their African mission the Sanusi followed the easiest approaches into the interior. They infiltrated the tribal structures of the nomadic, semi-nomadic and oasis peoples of Cyrenaica, the Western Desert of Egypt, the Fezzan and, to a less extent, Tripolitania,[5] while the trans-Saharan trade routes took them to the central and eastern Sudan. In preaching and practising a return to primitive Islam, the order came inevitably to exercise a secular function, as well as a primarily religious one. It found the most ready following in the ungoverned tribal areas where obedience to it in due course came to imply the tacit acceptance of a greater political authority, with practical obligations on both sides, than had ever been known there before. Moreover, because the semi-barbarous places it penetrated usually lacked all but the most basic administration, the order had to create its own, and at the same time enforce a measure of peace, security, justice and economic stability.[6] In exercising such authority, the order avoided close contact, and the risks of conflict, with neighbouring powers: Turks in northern Tripolitania and Cyrenaica, the French in Algeria, British diplomatic missions in the central Sahara, and Egyptians in the Nile Valley. The order achieved its religious and political predominance without any conquests, but merely through spiritual persuasion.[7] Its instruments were the brothers of the order, the *ikhwan*, whose missionary teaching carried the message of Sanusism through large parts of Islamic and pagan Africa, and the *zawias*. These were lodges built at tribal centres, or at watering places and junctions on the trade and pilgrim routes, and served as monasteries, schools, hostels, sources of advice and mediation and, in due course, as administrative centres.

Most Europeans who came into contact with the order during the second half of the nineteenth century were hostile and critical, seeing sinister motives behind every Sanusi action. Writing in the 1880s, Louis Rinn considered the order to have the most dangerous political influence;[8] Nachtigal, during his stay in Murzuk in 1869, had forebodings about the 'pertinacity with which these fanatics embrace a great part of Africa in their jesuitical web and the threatening selflessness with which they serve their cause'.[9] By far the most hostile European observer was Henri Duveyrier, the French Saharan traveller, who from the 1860s prompted a strong French antipathy to the order that may in turn have encouraged at least some of the vigour with which the French military destroyed it and all its works in Central Africa some forty years later.[10]

In 1856 the Grand Sanusi moved his headquarters from the original site in the Gebel Akhdar of Cyrenaica to the oasis of Giarabub, about 250 km. south of Tobruk. Although Giarabub had few resources, and little water, it stood on important trade and pilgrim routes. The site impressed a modern visitor as 'an impregnable fortress surrounded entirely by deserts known in detail to members of the Sanusi, and completely alien to their enemies'.[11] Giarabub was the intellectual centre of the order, and continued to be so even after the transfer of the headquarters to Kufra in 1896; the university founded by the Grand Sanusi became second in Africa only to Al-Azhar in Cairo. At Giarabub, the *ikhwan* were trained in missionary work on behalf of this revivalist rather than revolutionary order, which sought to gain a following among receptive peoples before the rising forces perceived to be hostile to pure Islam could do so. Such forces included the material-ism of nineteenth-century civilisation, rapidly expanding European Christian imperialism, and even the decaying Ottoman imperialism that was failing in its duty of protecting the *Dar al-Islam* from outside interference. In preparing their defence against such perceived threats, the Sanusi were not averse to stocking Giarabub, and prob-ably other *zawias* as well, with European firearms. This was a practice that gave European travellers the basis for their reports of the order's militancy, reports which were reinforced by the hostility that many European travellers in the Sahara experienced from tribesmen acting on Sanusi orders to exclude all foreigners. The traveller Rosita Forbes visited Giarabub in 1920 while on her extraordinary journey to Kufra. She found it was 'a university pure and simple'.[12] But writing some forty years earlier, Duveyrier was convinced that the great *zawia* was a veritable fortress, from which a fighting force of nearly 3,000 men, including slaves, could be raised, and which had within it an arsenal containing 'quantities of hand-guns, stores of gunpowder and 15 can-non bought at Alexandria'.[13]

The transfer from the Gebel Akhdar to Giarabub reflected the increasing importance of the order's Saharan and Sudanic interests. Having established a wide following in Libya and Egypt north of the Sahara, the Grand Sanusi moved his headquarters to this remote oasis mainly to direct his missionary activity southwards. The natural channels for such expansion were the populous pagan and semi-pagan countries of the Sudan and Central Africa.[14]

The way was opened for Sanusi missionary work by two Cyre-naican tribes long engaged in trans-Saharan trade, the Magarba and the Zuwaya, whose northern commercial outlets were in Augila and Agedabia. Long known as 'the brigands of the Sahara', the Zuwaya had in the early eighteenth century seized the Kufra oases from their original pagan Tebu inhabitants and made them 'the chief centre of brigandage in the Libyan Desert'.[15] Zuwaya power stemmed from their position as 'keepers of the keys of the Sahara' and controllers of its trade routes.[16] The Magarba, known as 'the merchant princes of the Libyan Desert', had 'a wonderful business instinct'.[17] As an Italian observer noted, 'their activity is phenomenal. There is not a neighbouring country they have not visited; there is not a caravan trail, no matter how long or difficult, that they do not know perfectly.'[18] Their range of Saharan and Sudanese trading contacts eventually reached from Agedabia in the north to the Sultanate of Wadai in the south-east, and the great trading city of Kano in the south-west.

By winning the confidence of these two tribes, the Sanusi gained access to the communications network of the central Sahara. For, as Ross E. Dunn has pointed out, no desert oasis, however lonely and unimportant, was isolated from the lines of trade: 'To describe the commercial system . . . in terms of particular routes and specializing groups is certainly to oversimplify it, for caravans, large and small, went everywhere that people lived. Traders carried not only merchandise, but also news, ideas and opinions.'[19]

The Zuwaya, who had large date groves at Kufra, promised the Grand Sanusi donations of palms and water rights if he would found a *zawia* there, and the *Zawiat al-Ustaz* (Zawia of the Master) was accordingly built at the village of Al-Jof. At Kufra, as at every place they gained a following, the Sanusi brought law and order, curbed raiding, encouraged peaceful trade, sank wells and promoted agriculture; theirs was a remarkable civilising mission amid unpromising surroundings.

Sanusi expansion coincided approximately with the ascendancy of the Sultanate of Wadai, due south of the Sanusi spheres of influence in the eastern Sahara. With the help of Cyrenaican traders and cooperation from the Tebu, the dangerous road from Wadai to Kufra and the Mediterranean was made safe under Sanusi protection, and wells were dug on the longest of the waterless stretches under their supervision. The Wadai-Kufra-Benghazi road was never an easy one,[20] but it provided land-locked Wadai with a more direct outlet to the Mediterranean than the route through Darfur and Egypt, or the roundabout route through Fezzan. It took on greater importance as the ancient Tripoli-Lake Chad road to the west became less secure in the mid-nineteenth century, when the Mahdist movement in the Nilotic Sudan eventually cut all the easterly outlets to the Nile Valley, Egypt and the Red Sea, and when after 1882 the British in Egypt began to curb the slave-trade from the Upper Nile.

A leading agent of Sanusi expansion in the eastern Sudan was the Sultan of Wadai, Mohammad Sharif (1835–58). Wedged into marginal land between Kanem and Bagirmi to the west and Darfur to the east, Wadai was in the seventeenth century penetrated by Islamic influence from the kingdom of Sennar on the Upper Nile.[21] As in other Sudanic states, in Wadai many diverse peoples were only held together by firm, centralised rule.[22] At the end of the eighteenth century, Wadai expanded westwards towards Kanem and southwards into the pagan lands of Dar Sila, Dar Kouti, Dar Runga and Salamat; in the early nineteenth century it annexed Bagirmi. Wadai's prosperity and importance lay mainly in its ability to capture large numbers of slaves on raids into the remoter and more primitive lands to the south (as far off as the modern Central African Republic) and re-export them to Egypt and Cyrenaica. In doing so, Wadai pushed forward the frontiers of Islam against weaker pagan peoples, using religious proselytisation as a rationale for this type of raiding warfare.[23] Slaves exported to Cyrenaica went by the route through Kufra that the Sanusi protected, and close Sanusi involvement with the trans-Saharan slave traffic, as well as use by the order of slave labour and skills, were well established.

There are two not necessarily incompatible accounts of the origins of Sanusi influence in Wadai. One tells how, while at Mecca in the 1830s, the Grand Sanusi met and befriended the future Sultan of Wadai, Mohammad Sharif.[24] The friendship was renewed after the Sanusiya became established at Giarabub, and thereafter successive Sultans of Wadai maintained this special trans-Saharan relationship that seems always to have owed as much to secular interests as to pure religious commitment. The other account, by Duveyrier,[25] tells how the Grand Sanusi bought a caravan of slaves on the march from Wadai to the Mediterranean, and had them freed, instructed and eventually returned to Wadai as missionary *ikhwan*. 'After this', says Duveyrier's contemporary reporter on the Sanusi, Louis Rinn, 'the negroes of Wadai came spontaneously, like servants, to the Sanusi *zawias*, and the Sultan of Wadai became one of the most faithful disciples of Shaikh Sanusi.'[26] Yet the strength of the Sanusi following in Wadai should not be over-estimated. Despite the early, mutually advantageous and prestigious relationship between the Sanusiya and one of the leading nineteenth-century political entities of the eastern Sudan, the degree of spiritual and political influence the order actually wielded there has never been made clear. While successive Sultans may indeed have been true supporters of the order's teachings and ideals, annually sending large presents to the head of the order as tokens of esteem and friendship, there is little evidence of an extensive Sanusi following in the Sultanate and its tributary territories as a whole. And it is likely that most of the 2.5 million people estimated by Nachtigal to have been subjects of Wadai at the time of his visit had no direct experience of the Sanusi at all: certainly the claim that the order had as many as 3 million adherents seems greatly exaggerated.

Nachtigal was in Wadai for several months in 1873, and again in 1874, more than forty years after the first reported meeting at Mecca between the Grand Sanusi and Sultan Mohammad Sharif. In his fairly detailed account of the sultanate[27] he makes no mention of the order and its work, apart from remarking that Sultan Ali Ibn al-Sharif (1858–74) was 'the most faithful adherent of the Sanusiya'. Although the order eventually established a total of 146 zawias in north-east Africa and the Hijaz,[28] only one of these centres for the propagation of the order's teachings and influence has been known for certain to exist in Wadai, at the post-1850 capital Abeche. According to Rosita Forbes, the Sultan of Wadai, while prepared always to be the friend and ally of the order, opposed the building of zawias in his realm, seeing them as a possible preliminary to conquest.[29] Carbou, referring to a late phase of Sanusi-Wadai relations, suggests that 'the most perfect accord does not always reign between the Sultan of Wadai and the representative of Sanusism at Abeche.[30] As Nachtigal described it, society in Wadai in the 1870s was still at least half pagan and barbarous, with only a veneer of Islam; there was no suggestion of Sanusi influence on the ordinary people, even in Abeche. He wrote of the 'great freedom enjoyed by women and girls', despite Sultan Ali's strictures, and added: 'Just as the natives, despite their religious fanaticism, have with the greatest tenacity clung to the use of alcoholic drinks, so, despite the Quran, they have not been able to cast off the easy-going principles which characterised their social life in old times.'[31] Such passages hardly suggest that a religious society noted for the strictness with which it imposed its religious and social disciplines on its adherents elsewhere, had much of a popular following in the Sultanate. Under Sultan Ibrahim (1898–1901) the Sanusi tried to impose their strict social rules on the ordinary people, forbidding in particular smoking and drinking of merissa, the Sudanese beer; but on being told that rather than give up their drink, the people would prefer to be without Sanusi guidance, Sidi al-Mahdi wisely decided not to persist.[32] Moreover, Nachtigal makes no suggestion that religious education, which he reports to have been 'much more general and more advanced in Wadai than in Bornu and practically all the other central African countries' was in any way under Sanusi control.[33] Significantly, perhaps, writings for higher studies were not imported from any Sanusi centre, but from Egypt.

The Grand Sanusi died at Giarabub in 1859. His eldest son, Mohammad al-Mahdi, who was then only about fifteen, succeeded him after a period of regency. Under Al-Mahdi's forty-three years' leadership, the order reached the zenith of its power. His brother, Mohammad al-Sharif, continued to preside over the university at Giarabub. A *zawia* had in the meantime been opened in 1845 at Mizda, in the pre-desert south of Tripoli (Barth saw it in 1850);[34] it provided access to southern Tripolitania and Fezzan and seems to have been a subsidiary centre for further Sanusi expansion in the west.[35] Similar lodges were later opened at more important commercial centres on the central Saharan trade routes from which Sanusi teachings could easily spread: Sokna, Zawila and Murzuk, Ghadames and Ghat;[36] but the relative commercial importance of all these places was being eroded in the mid-nineteenth century by the decline of the central Saharan trade. They were, moreover, too close to expanding French interests in the Algerian Sahara and, after 1882, in Tunisia, as well as to the growing Turkish presence in southern Tripolitania and Fezzan.

Nachtigal describes how, after seeking to 'effect an entry among the inhabitants of the western desert', the Sanusi 'strove gradually to establish their spiritual supremacy over the tribes of the eastern desert':

First of all they set up one of their stations on the road from Jalo to Wadai, and occupied the deserted oasis of Kufara, whose date plantations moreover offered them a means of livelihood; they colonised the Wäu oasis north of Tibesti, and established a centre in the great Tubu oasis of Kawar on the road to Bornu. From Kufara they moved forward to Wanyanga, and even to Wadai, whose King Ali ranked as one of their most ardent adherents. Along this road it remained for them to reform, or rather to islamise, Borku and the Daza region to the west, and the Ennedi region with its population of Bedayet to the east.[37]

The oases of Kufra became the forward base for Sanusi expansion in the eastern Sahara well before the headquarters of the order moved there in 1895, for, despite extreme remotness, they had some unique advantages. They were nearly at the centre of the growing Sanusi sphere of influence, yet apparently beyond the reach of any other power: the nearest wells in any direction were at least five days' travel away.[38] With their ground sources of fossil water the oases supplied fresh produce and water to travellers crossing the Libyan Desert – the largest true desert in the world. Kufra was about half-way (in travelling time, if not actual distance) from Benghazi in the north to Abeche in the south,[39] and thus was an essential halt for caravans on the direct road northwards from Wadai to the Mediterranean. Under Sanusi control, ten trade routes eventually radiated from Kufra:three leading into Chad territory, three to the oases of the Western Desert and so to the Nile valley, and four to various parts of Libya.[40] Rosita Forbes, while on her journey to the oases in 1920–1, came to realise how they represented 'the spider at the heart of the web, whose threads were the long caravan routes spreading out in every direction from Tripoli to the Sudan, from Lake Chad to Egypt . . . Kufra controls the desert trade of half the Sahara'.[41] Eventually, the number of *zawias* in these oases increased from the original foundation at Al-Jof to a total of six, including the last centre of the order, the 'massive block' of the fortress-sanctuary at Al-Taj ('the crown').

The aims of the order's missionary drive into the south were set out in the letter the Grand Sanusi wrote about 1850 to the people of the oasis of Ounianga in Borku, on the Kufra-Wadai road.[42] Significantly, the letter was addressed to *all* the people of the oasis, old and young, male and female; for the Sanusi appreciated the importance, at least in certain mid-Saharan societies, of directing their appeal to the women and girls, who often led more open and public lives than in the Arab or Arabised north, and more sedentary lives than their own men and boys, and who were accordingly better able to absorb and pass on the Sanusi message. The Grand Sanusi had nothing out of the ordinary to ask of these nominal Muslims of Wanyanga. He merely wished, he wrote, to ask the people of the oasis 'in the name of Islam' to obey God and his Prophet:

We wish to ask you to obey what God and his Prophet have ordered, making the five prayers, keeping the month of Ramadan, giving tithe, making the *Hadj* to the sacred home of God [Mecca] and avoiding what God has forbidden . . . In following these, you will gain everlasting good and endless profits which will never be taken from you.

Some. men of your country had asked us to send with them some of our *ikhwan* in order to remind them of God and teach them what God and his Prophet have ordained and guide them rightly. We decided to do this because it is our profession [mission] for which God has put us, i.e. to remind the negligent, teach the ignorant and guide him who has gone astray.

The Grand Sanusi also made known his intention 'to make peace between you and the Arabs [presumably the Awlad Slaiman] who invade you and take your sons and your money'. And if the people followed Sanusi teaching, they were told, 'you will then not fear anyone'. This promise to protect and mediate was vitally important in persuading the would-be followers of the Grand Sanusi and his successors of the worldly as well as the purely spiritual advantages to be gained from their teaching, especially by tribes and communities living on the very margins of survival and under the constant threat of violence. Quite apart from its religious preeminence, the order's temporal power, prestige and authority thus lay in providing the poor, the weak, and the vulnerable with a form of protection all the more effective in its reliance on spiritual and moral, rather than physical, superiority. The order was similarly a respected source of mediation in the numerous tribal, communal and familial disputes that caused much strife among desert and pre-desert peoples living beyond all but the most rudimentary rule of law.

Hassanein Bey, the Egyptian traveller who made two remarkable journeys through the Libyan Desert in the early 1920s, found that the power of the Grand Sanusi and his successor, Al-Mahdi, 'lay in themselves and in the spiritual influence that radiated from them . . . Until this day the Beduins fear the Senussi family not so much because of any temporal power, but on account of the spiritual powers with which they credit them.'[43] Furthermore, he found that:

There can be no question that the influence of the Senussi Brotherhood upon the lives of the people of that region is good. The *ikhwan* of the Senussis are not only the teachers of the people, both in the field of religion and of general knowledge, but judges and intermediaries between man and man and between tribe and tribe . . . The importance of these aspects of the Senussi rule in maintaining the tranquillity and well-being of the people of the Libyan Desert can scarcely be over-estimated.[44]

The Sanusi could apparently pacify and control even the most unruly and predatory Saharan peoples, including the Zuwaya of Kufra – who were said to 'own the desert'[45] – the Awlad Slaiman and eventually even the Tebu of Tibesti. Under Sanusi government, Rosita Forbes wrote, the Zuwaya

were obliged to give up their organised brigandage, but with such a long history of murder and plunder behind them – half the tragedies of the Sahara may be laid at their door – it is not to be wondered at that they are still lawless and wild. Every man fears them and only a power as great as the Senussi could hold them in check.[46]

The head of the order was deeply respected for his dual leadership, and Forbes asserts that the tribesmen 'must feel convinced that there is one being on earth who blends spiritual and temporal power so that he can himself dwell in a sort of mystic security'.[47] A rather more cynical view of the Sanusi exercise of power was expressed by the American anthropologist, Lloyd Cabot Briggs:

The Senoussi, whose iron hand clothed in the velvet glove of religion and old-fashioned diplomacy has . . . ruled most of the eastern half of the Sahara so effectively for a hundred years, are merely another manifestation of the profound affinity of Moslems for government by dictatorship, preferably though not always based on magico-religious prestige, which is rooted in a power concept, the cult of The Strong Man.[48]

While the Sanusi thus came to exercise a close spiritual and political authority over the tribes of Cyrenaica, and eventually welded them into an incipient nation-state, the degree with which they exercised such control elsewhere in the Sahara and Sudan was much more problematic. The French colonial official, Henri Carbou, accused the Grand Sanusi's successor, Sidi al-Mahdi, of 'trying to establish in the Muslim states of central Africa an influence more political than religious'; but he also judged it to be 'almost impossible for Sidi al-Mahdi to exercise an effective authority on groups so dispersed'.[49] It has been suggested that Sidi al-Mahdi persuaded the people of Wadai and other sub-Saharan regions not to support the Sudanese Mahdi, Mohammad Ahmad,[50] and that he warned his followers near the borders of the Mahdist state to resist all its encroachments. In a letter to the Sultan of Borku, he pointed out the dangers of civil war weakening the Muslim community.[51]

In 1870 Nachtigal was in the oasis of Kawar, where he found the 'spiritual lord' to be the *shaikh* of the Sanusi *zawia* at Shimmedru, a village near Bilma. There, he wrote,

it was all the easier for the chief of the *zawia* to acquire and preserve great influence, since he could easily maintain an oversight over the oasis, the inhabitants had gained from the caravan trade some degree of sociability and a higher level of understanding, and since they could look to him for at least some protection against their hereditary Arab enemies [presumably the Awlad Slaiman]. In fact, already during the most recent Arab raids Shimmedru and the inhabitants of the neighbouring villages who had sought refuge there had suffered very much less than the rest of the region.[52]

Sanusi protection was obviously welcome, despite the fact that, as Nachtigal reported, 'the pride and arrogance' of the Sanusi *shaikhs* 'who appear to have taken a lease of genuine piety, are beyond belief', and that the *zawia* (which 'excelled in its banqueting arrangements') had to be wholly supported by the people of Kawar.[53]

Under Sidi al-Mahdi, the Sanusi became predominant throughout eastern and southern Libya and much of what is now eastern and northern Chad: theirs was effectively a theocratic empire of vast extent but few subjects. The number of *zawias* is estimated to have increased fourfold during the four decades of Sidi al-Mahdi's leadership. While these lodges continued to offer a model of spiritual and social conduct, the close but impartial involvement of their *shaikhs* in the life of the local community gave them power and responsibility well beyond their main purpose. The accumulation of tithes and gifts, the encouragement of settled and more efficient agriculture, and participation in regional and trans-Saharan trade made the order wealthy, especially in annual offerings from *zawias* in the richer oases and in the coastal zone of Cyrenaica, where the order soon became by far the biggest landowner.

As the most powerful religious and political entity in the pre-desert and Saharan hinterland of north-east Africa, the Sanusi had to adopt policies towards neighbouring governments and movements that allowed the order to safeguard its integrity within its own sphere of influence. This was achieved by cooperating with those it could not afford to offend and by rejecting those whom it could. In northern Cyrenaica, where there was no question of keeping the Turks at arm's length, or denying them their sovereignty, the Sanusi accordingly collaborated in providing a rudimentary administration wherever the Turks were unable to do so, with the tribal areas in effect becoming a Turkish-Sanusi condominium.[54] Such collaboration implied no approval of Turkish policies in Cyrenaica or elsewhere. Thus the order resisted Turkish demands for assistance in fighting the Russians in the war of 1876–8; it ignored appeals by Arabi Pasha for help against the British occupation of Egypt in 1882; and it rejected German and later Italian diplomacy urging joint action against French African interests. Moreover, when the Mahdist revolt overwhelmed the Nilotic Sudan after 1881, Sidi al-Mahdi found no kindred spirit in the self-proclaimed Mahdi Mohammad Ahmad.[55]

The rise of Sudanese Mahdism from the Red Sea to as far west as Darfur threatened the Sanusi by creating a hostile state to the east of their main sub-Saharan spheres of influence. At the same time, all normal contact along the east-bound trade routes across the Sudan to the Red Sea and the Hijaz was cut off. The personal antagonism between Sidi al-Mahdi and Mohammad Ahmad arose when the Sudanese leader tried to recruit the Sanusi order to his cause. In a letter sent to Giarabub by special messenger (probably in 1881), Mohammad Ahmad appointed Sidi al-Mahdi his fourth *caliph* (successor) and invited him to report forthwith to claim the honour – appointments that the Sanusi leader rejected outright.[56] A second approach in 1883 was ignored. Lord Cromer, the British agent and consul-general in Egypt, remarked that it was natural that the Sanusi leader 'should view with disfavour the pretensions of any rival'.[57] And Sidi al-Mahdi declined to intervene in the affairs of the Sudanese Mahdist state even when rebels there tried to enlist his support.[58] The Sanusi seem in fact to have been alienated from the Sudanese Mahdist movement not so much by religious or political differences as by the destructive violence of the dervishes.[59]

There were, according to Evans-Pritchard, ten Sanusi *zawias* in what is now Chadian territory, with half-a-dozen elsewhere in the southern Sahara and Sudan.[60] Writing in 1889, Ernesto Farina counted a total of twelve *zawias* in Tebu-land, Ennedi, Wanyanga,

Shimmedru (Kawar) and 'on the road from Murzuk to Cucava' (Kuka, capital of Bornu).[61] These are few compared with the forty-five lodges Evans-Pritchard found in Cyrenaica, or even the fifteen in Fezzan; but the number of *zawias* in any region did not necessarily reflect the intensity of the order's local following, particularly among nomads. In 1899 the British traveller Silva White described Tibesti, Wanyanga and Borku as among 'the chief Sanusi centres'.[62] After the very early Sanusi contact with the sultanate of Wadai, the chronology of the order's penetration of the south is not clear; nor is the extent of its influence on the pagan lands of Central Africa. But in those parts there was great prestige simply in becoming a Muslim: 'The fact of having embraced Islam confers a certain nobility'.[63] Penetration of Fezzan from about 1850 onwards inevitably led the Sanusi south-wards down the central Saharan trade route to the oases of Kawar. The order began its work there by opening a girls' school, as the most effective means of infiltrating a Saharan society very different from the Arabised north. Fortunately, the local Tebu were well-disposed towards the order, since it represented at least moral protection against the assaults of the Muslim Awlad Slaiman.[64] As early as 1866 there was a functioning *zawia* at the village of Shimmedru in Kawar.[65]

Continuing down the trade road from Kawar, Sanusi missionaries were welcomed 'with good grace' by the non-Arab Muslims of Kanem and even, according to Duveyrier, by the Awlad Slaiman. These Libyan Arabs could not appear less fervent Muslims than the local black peoples, although such a display of fervour 'certainly cost more to the persecutors than to the persecuted'.[66] Nachtigal tells how, when he was in Kanem in 1871, 'two emissaries of the fanatical religious society, the Sanusiya' came 'to appeal to the conscience of the godless Arabs in favour of the Teda, the Daza and the Bidayet'. The Sanusi missionaries intended to open *zawias* in Borku and Ennedi,

and for this needed some guarantee from the Awlad Slaiman for the security of their protégés. They had been unsparing in their appeal to the consciences of the Awlad Slaiman, holding out to them the prospect of the eternal torments of hell as punishment for their shameful actions against true believers.[67]

Penetrating even further south, the order's missionaries encoun-tered lands and peoples in an even greater state of anarchy than Kanem was. In 1896–8 the order tried without success to proselytise Sultan Abd-al-Rahman Gaurang of Bagirmi, whose country was by then reported to be 'fanatically Mohammedan',[68] and Sultan Rabah Ibn Fadlallah. The latter, a slave-dealer from the Nilotic Sudan, had conquered Bornu in 1893 and set up a loose 'Mahdist' state in the Chad region founded on slave-raiding and the slave trade.[69] The Sanusiya had a rather ambiguous influence among even more undesirable 'followers' further south. There the name 'Sanusi' could be used to invoke spurious Muslim respectability and authority in largely pagan lands, where indeed Islam itself could be used as a rationale for war against peoples vulnerable to enslavement. Such was the case in the state of Dar Kouti, centred on the settlement of Ndele to the south of Wadai, and now largely within the Central African Republic. Ndele in the late nineteenth and early twentieth centuries was an entrepôt for the collection and re-export of slaves and ivory, attracting traders from as far away as Libya, and an important halt on the pilgrim route to the Hijaz.[70] Sultan Mohammad al-Sanusi had come to power there as a trusted lieutenenant of Sultan Rabah. With an arsenal of 5,000 modern rifles imported from the north, his was another state founded on slave-raiding into the surrounding 'cannibal country'. Dr Karl Kumm, who visited Sultan Mohammad at Ndele in 1909, explains his title:

Sultan Sinussi of Ndele, who everywhere in the Sudan is spoken of as *the* Sinussi, was formerly a trader in Darfur, but he is no relation of the religious leader Sinussi. He simply bears the title 'Sinussi' in the same way that every other follower of Sinussi, whether he is called Abdulla, Mohammad, Ali or Suleiman, adds, after his professed adherence to the Sinussi movement, the word 'Sinussi' to his name and calls himself Abdulla Sinussi, Mohammad Sinussi, Ali Sinussi, or Suleiman Sinussi, as the case may be.[71]

The Sanusi had been trying to build up a following in Kanem from the late 1860s; but they had no permanent presence there till the hostility of roughly half of the Awlad Slaiman was ended with the assassination of their anti-Sanusi leader,Shaikh Abd-al-Jalil, in 1895, and the subsequent split of the tribe and its Tripolitanian allies into two rival and warring groups. Sidi al-Mahdi used this opportunity to establish a following among the more receptive members of the Awlad Slaiman by sending one of his most influential lieutenants, Sidi Mohammad al-Baruni, into southern Kanem. He founded an important *zawia* in the great palm-groves at Bir Alali in the district of Lilwa, an area north and east of Lake Chad under Awlad Slaiman control. In the same year the headquarters of the order moved southwards from Giarabub to Kufra. The prime purpose in moving into Kanem was to gain the support of the Awlad Slaiman (still a formidable fighting force, despite internal quarrels) in the by then almost inevitable armed struggle against the French advance into Central Africa. The same urgent need to meet the French challenge prompted the further move of the order's headquarters from Kufra to the obscure oasis of Qiru in Borku in 1899.

In the mean time, beginning in the 1870s, the order had made considerable missionary progress further north in the central Saharan lands of Borku, Ennedi and Tibesti, whose Tebu and similar peoples had up till then been largely immune from such outside influences, religious or otherwise. According to Duveyrier, the first *zawia* in Ennedi was planned in 1871, and ten years later there were many lodges in existence; possibly they did not survive long, for the claim is not supported by later research. The first of two *zawias* eventually established at Wanyanga (Wanyanga Kabir and Wanyanga Saghir) was founded in 1871 or 1872;[72] the lodge at Ain Galakka dates from 1871, while 'Ngurma' became the site of a 'nomadic' *zawia* for the benefit of the Awlad Slaiman.[73] Visiting Borku in 1871, Nachtigal tells of a Sanusi missionary he saw there, 'in the midst of the Arabs, who, like naughty children, accepted his teachings and reproaches'.[74] Borku was considered by Carbou to have been particularly important to the Sanusi, as it was their only source of grain in the south.[75]

The Sanusi moved finally into Tibesti after almost encircling the massif with *zawias*. The *Derde* Chai Bogar-Mi, paramount chief and chief of the Tomaghera Teda clan, who from 1895 to 1939 exercised a varying degree of political-religious authority over the peoples of Tibesti,[76] was one agent of Sanusi penetration. From journeys to the Sanusi centres at Giarabub and Kufra in the 1890s, he brought back 'lists of indemnities and penalties and long and precise lists of misdoings, among them drunkenness, brawling, abetting murderers, etc.'[77] He also encouraged Sanusi merchants to visit Tibesti, where they had enormous influence, revitalising Islam among a semi-pagan people, even if they failed to eradicate the Tebu habits of drinking alcohol and stealing cattle.[78] Chapelle, drawing on the reminiscences of elderly Tebu, tells how Sanusi missionaries gained a following among these people, perhaps the most difficult of all their converts, who only knew outsiders as enemies:

The Sanusi, by contrast, who enjoyed the protection of the *Derde*, arrived with all sorts of money and bundles of those precious stuffs which, before they arrived, the Tebu had been obliged to seek a long way off. The Sanusi paid for all services rendered, made gifts to those who attended the Friday prayer, and fed the pupils who followed their teaching. But things became awkward when one of them wanted to take part in administering justice, and the *Derde* had him recalled. He was not replaced.[79]

As for Sanusi influence among the Tebu, Chapelle quotes one opinion of the benefits the *ikhwan* brought:

They taught the true way, commanded the performance of the *salaam*, showed how to do it (before that, one didn't know how), recommended fasting in Ramadan, hard work in the vegetable gardens, good behaviour in the home, no lying and no use of force against poor folk. Those who ignored these rules became poor and died young; those who followed them grew old and rich.[80]

In 1912 Henri Carbou considered the Tebu to be 'very fanatical Muslims', a judgement that seemed to reflect the efficacy of Sanusi religious tutelage, since it hardly corresponded either to their previous or to their subsequent reputations for irreligiosity.[81]

Apart from their religious mission and coincidental political influence, the Sanusi penetrated the Sahara and the lands to the south of it through trade. Because the Sanusi was the sole organisation spanning the full length of the Cyrenaica–Wadai road, it provided merchants with a common legal, social and commercial system, and even a postal service. It was uniquely placed to use its moral influence and prestige to protect commercial traffic, even sometimes persuading caravan-robbers to restore stolen goods. The order itself gained by levying tolls, leasing storage-space, and by receiving gifts from merchants, while peaceful trading gave a certain unity to the lands under Sanusi influence.[82] As Hassanein Bey reported:

The difficult and waterless track between Buttafal Well near Jalo and Zieghen Well just north of Kufra became in Al-Mahdi's time a beaten route continually frequented by trade caravans and by travellers going to visit the centre of the Sanusi Brotherhood . . . Al-Mahdi strove to make desert travel safe, and in his day . . . a woman might travel from Barka [Cyrenaica] to Wadai unmolested.[83]

By the late nineteenth century, the Benghazi-Kufra-Wadai route had become commercially and culturally the most important of all the trans-Saharan trade links.[84] Having used Cyrenaican traders such as the Zuwaya and the Magarba to open the way to Sudan, and having extended their moral influence to protect it, the Sanusi themselves became closely involved in trade: the northbound slave trade and the southbound trade in manufactured goods, and particularly in arms. As Henri Carbou wrote, 'It was evident that the occupation of Wadai by our troops threatened to ruin the Sanusiya by suppressing their two great resources: the trade in slaves and the smuggling of arms.'[85] While the Sanusi themselves needed domestic slaves in the *zawias*, and others to work the prosperous oasis-gardens and accompany caravans, further slaves were always needed to supply the export markets. It is estimated that during most of the nineteenth century a varying traffic, but averaging about 10,000 slaves a year, was needed to meet the demand of the Ottoman market for household slaves (Ottoman military slavery having by then come to an end). According to Toledano, 'The great majority of slaves imported into the Ottoman empire during those years were African women, although African men in small numbers were still being acquired until the 1890s.'[86]

It has been estimated that about 2 million black slaves were exported to the Islamic lands of North Africa and the Middle East in the nineteenth century. Of these, perhaps one million came from the Upper Nile and Ethiopia, one-third of a million from East Africa, and the remaining 650,000 were brought across the Sahara from the Sudan.[87] It is not easy to estimate the number of slaves exported via the Wadai-Cyrenaica route, largely because the traffic passed through such remote country, far from the interference of European (and especially British) consuls, with the exception of the incumbent at Benghazi. But even consular reports do not necessarily clarify all the facts. From the mid-nineteenth century, Benghazi became an increasingly important outlet for the Saharan slave trade as others were shut down as a result of European diplomatic pressure. In 1847 the British consul in Tripoli reported that 1,200 slaves had been shipped through Benghazi in the previous year, the same number as was estimated to have left Tripoli itself in 1847;[88] but in September of that year the British vice-consul in Benghazi reported:

Caravans arrive here every second year from Waday. From 800 to 1000 slaves are brought by each caravan . . . small caravans come at irregular periods two or three times in the year from Fezzan, each of which brings . . . about 150 slaves . . . on an average, about 700 are exported from Benghazi in the year, chiefly to Constantinople and Canea [Crete].[89]

One implication of such reports is that slave exports could vary considerably from one year to the next, for even the highest estimates of the Wadai-Cyrenaica traffic hardly begin to add up to an average yearly export of 6,500 slaves from all nineteenth-century Saharan outlets, many of which were closed by mid-century. It is true that European officialdom failed to witness and record the shipment of slaves through smaller Cyrenaican anchorages, and notably the little port of Derna. The combined yearly total of exports through such outlets was unlikely to have been greater than Benghazi's, for as the British vice-consul, Dupuis, reported to London in 1879, 'within the recollection of the oldest inhabitants, Benghazi has always been a hot-bed of slavery'.[90] Early in the twentieth century, the Italian geographer Arcangelo Ghisleri reported that the negroid or Sudanese element was largely represented in the population of Benghazi as a result of the caravan trade with the interior.[91]

The oasis of Jalo, about six days' march south-east of Benghazi, was in the second half of the nineteenth century an essential entrepôt for trans-Saharan slave traffic. Turkish measures in the 1850s were effective in halting the trade through Tripoli, where European diplomatic pressure was strongest; but such measures were almost without effect in the remote territory of Cyrenaica. Jalo thus became a slaving centre not only for the established traffic between Wadai and Benghazi, but also for traders from Bornu and Fezzan, and from the

Niger via Ghat, who were no longer able to ship their slaves through Tripoli. Caravans went forward from Jalo either to northern Cyrenaica, or to Egypt via Giarabub and Siwa. In a despatch in 1883, the British consul in Benghazi called Jalo 'the great and only slave centre in northern Barbary'.[92] It was 'where the slaves were dressed after their horrible march of a few months through the desert and taught a few words of Arabic'.[93] When he went to Jalo in 1852, the British traveller James Hamilton found the gains from the slave trade to be very large, 'and many of the Jalese [sic!] have amassed in it large sums; which sums, however, they have no means of spending'.[94] Siwa was another important slave entrepôt, as this report by Silva White, who was at the oasis in 1898, testifies:

Slaves work in the fields, slaves live in the town . . . and slaves pass through Siwa on their way to Alexandria and Constantinople. All these slaves come from the Sudan, via Jalo or Jarabub. None can be bought or sold, legally, in Siwa. But that they are brought to the oasis, by the Mojabra, and fed up for the market, after the exhausting desert march, there can be little doubt.[95]

Egypt, White wrote, could not enforce the strict letter of the law in an oasis so remote and as lightly held as Siwa was without raising serious political issues, 'although, at the same time, the more serious abuses of this traffic are checked and controlled'.[96]

The Wadai road survived as an artery of the slave trade longer than any other, largely because it was well beyond the control of any outside power committed to its abolition, including even the Turks. Indeed, despite official Turkish prohibitions, Benghazi remained a centre of unconcealed slavery and slave-trading till the late nineteenth century, if not later. As Nachtigal put it, 'The profit represented by the slaves, amounting to three or four times the purchase price, is so substantial that enterprising merchants do not allow themselves to be deterred even by the risk of confiscation.'[97] And as the British consul Dupuis reported in March 1879, 'this consulate is constantly besieged by runaway slaves, seeking my protection and intervention with the Turkish authorities to obtain their freedom.'[98] Two weeks later, Dupuis reported:

Almost every Arab notable, without exception, residing in this town is a slave owner, and . . . the sale and purchase of negroes is freely though quietly carried on among the natives . . . even the local government actually permits all its functionaries, to the utter disregard of all Firmans and vizirial orders, to possess as many slaves as their circumstances will enable them to maintain.[99]

Slaves freed in Benghazi through the intervention of Dupuis came from Bornu, 'Sudan', Darfur, Wadai and Bagirmi, or were classified as 'Tibboo'.[100]

Most of the slaves driven across the Sahara in the nineteenth century were women and young girls destined for domestic and/or sexual services. In 1847 the vice-consul in Benghazi, T.H.Gilbert, estimated that three-quarters of the slaves in any caravan were 'young females' who were slaves either born in Wadai or kidnapped from Bornu. 'Those from Bornu are most esteemed as being in general more docile and better tempered than those born at Wadai', he wrote.[101] Well into the twentieth century, the negro quarter of Benghazi was in the extreme northern suburb of Sabri, and was characterised by domed straw huts more reminiscent of Central rather than Northern Africa. However, the Italians destroyed this quarter during the early years of their occupation (there was a similar 'Sudanese' village at Tripoli).[102]

As mentioned above, slaves exported from Cyrenaica represented only a fraction of the total taken from Central Africa. Accounts of nineteenth-century European travellers suggest that loss of life on slave raids and in the processes of delivery to the various Sudanic slave-marshalling centres was enormous: 'It is the frightful atrocities committed in the process of capture . . . the inhuman barbarity with which the slaves are treated on the march . . . it is the gradual depopulation of large districts of Central Africa . . . the scenes of desolation which mark this accursed traffic.'[103] Some northbound slaves were bought for domestic service or heavy labour in the oases on the way: 'There is not a cultivator or trader who does not possess a certain number of slaves in proportion to his wealth, to whom is entrusted the heaviest and most tiring work'.[104] But those who had to make the full Sahara crossing faced 'an ordeal no less hideous than the so-called middle passage of the ocean' with an average mortality rate estimated at anything between one-fifth and more than half.[105]

It has been argued that many slave deaths on the road were the result less of ill-treatment than of natural causes, such as sharp variations in desert temperatures, shortage of water, and sandstorms in which whole caravans could be buried alive.[106] In 1847 the vice-consul in Benghazi gave a further explanation:

I have been told that the chief reason for so many [slaves] being abandoned on the journey is not so much scarcity of food and water, but that from the swelling of their feet in traversing the hot sands, they are unable to keep up with the others, and there being no spare camels to carry them, they are left to die in the Desert.[107]

The slave trade on the Wadai-Cyrenaica route was remarkably enduring, and persisted to some extent even after Wadai fell to the French in 1909, and after the Italian invasion of Cyrenaica in 1911. Enver Pasha, commander of the Turco-Libyan force that encircled the Italian bridgehead around Derna in the war of 1911–12, tells in his diary how the head of the Sanusi order sent him 'greetings and gifts

. . . two negresses, ivory, etc.' And this otherwise resourceful soldier asks: 'What shall I do with two negro ladies?'[108]

In practice, it took France and Italy many years to control their respective ends of the trade route, while its middle sections were not brought under an effective European authority till even later: the French were only fully in control of Borku, Ennedi and Tibesti well after the First World War, while the Italians did not occupy Kufra until 1931. Ten years earlier, Rosita Forbes described how in Jalo she had seen 'smuggled slave boys and girls of eight to ten years . . . solemn little beings with chubby black faces peering out of the pointed hood of minute camel's-hair burnuses'.[109] Hassanein Bey learned at Kufra in 1923 that the price of a slave-girl varied between the then very considerable sums of £30–£40 sterling. The price had greatly increased since his travels in 1916, when he had been offered a girl for six gold louis (120 francs, or £5 sterling), 'because there were no more slaves coming up from Wadai on account of the French authorities in that province'.[110] Knud Holmboe, the Danish Muslim traveller who was in Libya in 1930, learned that slavery was still endemic in Kufra. A large slave market was held there every Thursday, but a good slave cost up to only 1,000 lire (about £15 sterling).[111] The Wadai-Cyrenaica slave trade was another means by which peoples on both sides of the Sahara remained in contact; this was especially so in the late nineteenth century. It was characterised by the usual exploitation of the Black African by his (or, more usually, her) 'white' Arab or Arab-Berber neighbour from across the desert, but was perhaps also of some lasting benefit in exposing the enslaved pagan Africans to the Islamic civilising mission.

Of all the manufactured goods carried across the Sahara in the later nineteenth century, arms, and particularly modern breech-loading rifles, were the most coveted. These were imported into the Sahara in large numbers. Every warrior wanted to carry one as a symbol of his manhood; every Sudanic ruler wanted an arsenal of them as a means of enforcing his political authority, as adjuncts to festivities and ceremonial, and as a means of increasing his economic resources by using them in slaving and in procuring ivory in Central Africa (although elephants tended, in practice, to be killed with traditional weapons). Guns first reached Bornu across the Sahara from Tripoli, and from Bornu spread to Hausaland; Darfur and the Nilotic Sudan imported their guns from Egypt. But there appears to have been no regular arms traffic with Wadai until the reign of Abd-al-Karim Sabun in the early nineteenth century, when the direct trade route to Kufra and the Mediterranean was opened up. Early in his career, Sabun was persuaded by North African traders of the advantages of firearms over the traditional 'white arms', an advantage that was not always apparent before the introduction of the rapid-firing breech-loading rifle in the late nineteenth century. Sultan Sabun bought guns in quite small numbers from North African traders, at the same time arranging for his slaves to be trained in their use.[112] But in the first half of the century, at least, Wadai seems largely to have relied on North African musketeers.

The trans-Saharan arms trade proceeded at quite a modest level until about 1875. The Egyptian government, and the Turkish authorities in Tripoli, aware that the import of arms into the Sahara and Sudan threatened their own security and ambitions in the south, had long tried to stop the trade; indeed the Turks seem to have stemmed the flow of arms into the central Sudan after their return to Tripoli in 1835.[113] From about 1870, European armies began to replace their traditional muzzle-loading muskets and rifles with breech-loading metal-cartridge rifles. These were at first single-shot, but from the 1880s had magazines holding five or more rounds, allowing rapid rates of fire. Large stocks of muzzle-loaders thus became available for supply to Africa, the Middle East and elsewhere. The Sanusi connection undoubtedly helped successive Sultans of Wadai to acquire guns, despite Turkish and Egyptian attempts to suppress the traffic. While Sultan Mohammad al-Sharif, who died in 1858, apparently owned only 300 guns, his successor Sultan Ali (1858–74) had 4,000 good-quality flintlock muskets imported mainly from Tripoli, while Sultan Doudmourra (1902–9) had an arsenal of 10,000 rifles, including Martinis, Colts, Remingtons, Winchesters and Gras.[114] According to Nachtigal, however, Sultan Ali had scarcely 1,000 men capable of using his 4,000 muskets. The Sultan's twelve bronze cannon, cast locally by Egyptian and Turkish soldiers and mechanics, lacked gun-carriages and gunners, and were thus quite useless.[115] Nachtigal nevertheless found the Sultan's favourite topics of conversation to have been 'gunpowder, the manufacture of cannons and guns, steamships and the like'.[116] A few of these firearms had been acquired as gifts: Nachtigal tells how he decided to present 'a pair of cavalry pistols with gold inlay, a telescope and a revolver carbine' to Sultan Ali.[117] But most guns were traded from Tripoli, 'for the percussion weapons imported by the Nile merchants were of very poor quality'.[118] If guns were used to acquire slaves (largely by inspiring terror in people wholly unused to them),[119] slaves were used to acquire guns, by providing the most acceptable exchange for imported weapons. In 1907 one slave from Wadai was the exchange for an 1874-model French rifle in good condition, with forty cartridges included.[120] In 1881 the Italian traveller Giuseppe Haimann learned in Cyrenaica that Italian high-precision rifles were greatly prized in Wadai, their value increasing by up to ten times after crossing the Sahara, although he doubted whether such an advantage would be sustained if the trade were to grow.[121] Despite the rapid fire, greater accurancy and other advantages of late nineteenth-century breech-loaders, the regular supply of the various different calibres of ammunition to the far side of the Sahara was usually difficult and expensive. Even in Cyrenaica, Haimann found the local *beduin* armed with 'the long flintlock, which they prefer to modern arms, even when they can obtain them, because of the difficulty in procuring percussion caps and cartridges, while they can easily obtain smuggled gunpowder'.[122]

The Sanusi had first become involved with the illicit arms-trade as a means of acquiring weapons for themselves, and especially for stocking the great arsenal at Giarabub. They maintained their trade in arms for commercial reasons, and finally encouraged it as a means of providing their followers in the central and eastern Sudan with weapons to resist the French military advance from the late 1890s onwards: European arms to fight European colonialism. In particular, the Sanusi introduced large stocks of arms into Wadai at the turn of the century. The traveller Karl Kumm reported seeing in Tripoli in 1905 'large quantities of cartridges and Winchester rifles which had been smuggled into the country by Italians and sold to Sanussi. Everybody in Tripoli seemed to know about these smuggling operations.'[123] Hanns Vischer, a Swiss subject who travelled across the Sahara from Tripoli to Bornu in British service in 1909, learned that 'European guns and rifles of every pattern and origin . . . can be found in most towns along the North African coast and will be supplied by unscrupulous agents of respectable firms as long as there is a profit.'[124] Arms were also smuggled into Cyrenaica along the coast from Alexandria and other Egyptian cities. In 1899, 250 cases of Winchester rifle ammunition worth £1,750 sterling and 200 cases of Martini ammunition worth £800 were sent into Cyrenaica in this way.[125] The French, even after they had occupied most of Wadai, still complained in 1910 of the difficulty of suppressing the exchange of guns for slaves by the Sanusi. Yet the fact remains that guns and ammunition have always been expensive and therefore rare in the Sudan because of the distances over which they had to be carried; North African technicians were usually needed to look after guns in the royal arsenals, while privately-owned firearms were often misused and therefore ineffective. Only in the late nineteenth century did guns become so cheap and generally available as to affect the balance of power in the central and eastern Sudan permanently.[126]

The fact that black slaves were the mainstay of trans-Saharan trade became apparent when the traffic was suppressed and merchants tried to rely solely on 'legitimate' commerce: within fifty years or less, the international trade of the Sahara had nearly come to an end. Other factors contributed to this collapse but, as the French diplomat Pierre-Paul Cambon asserted, 'Without the slave trade, the commerce of the Sudan is not enough to supply the caravans. They disappear everywhere a power opposed to slavery installs itself.'[127] The value of the largely unrecorded trade across the Sahara in the nineteenth century is not easily assessed. The African Association reported in 1793:

A lucrative commerce, the extent of which is unknown, but which, from the best information appears to be much under rated at a million sterling per annum, is carried on from the different States of Barbary to the Nations on the Banks of the Niger, and . . . the large compensation which the profit affords has constantly yielded an ample encouragement, and has uniformly upheld the trade.[128]

Boahen believes the nineteenth-century caravan trade to have had only a fraction of its former value, the total annual two-way exchange across the Sahara being worth no more than £125,000 sterling,[129] not least because the gold trade was by then 'almost negligible'. But Rossi quotes the Swedish consul in Tripoli in the 1820s as reporting the arrival of 1,500 ounces of gold in Tripoli from the south every year, not counting the gold tribute of Fezzan and Ghadames.[130] At the end of the nineteenth century, Henri Schirmer estimated the absolute maximum of two-way trade across the Sahara at 9 million French francs a year (then equivalent to about £360,000 sterling), or the equivalent of a port of the twentieth order.[131] Yet, ironically, the supposed wealth of the trans-Saharan trade, and of the countries beyond the Sahara contributing to it, was one factor that prompted the European intervention which eventually led to the ruin of the whole operation. The French in Algeria (with their impractical, if grandiose schemes for a trans-Saharan railway linking the Mediterranean to the Niger), and later the Italians in Libya, believed they could revive the trade once they had conquered and 'pacified' the desert.[132] In actual practice, no outside power involved in the Sahara could ever sustain the political, economic and social conditions for prosperous trading once the new European railways and shipping-lines serving both the east and west coasts of Africa had disrupted the ancient communications of the inner continent.

Like that of previous centuries, trans-Saharan trade of the nineteenth century continued to be an exchange of North African and European manufactured goods for the unprocessed raw materials of the interior. As the century progressed, industrial Europe came increasingly to dominate the southbound trade with a widening range of cheap trade goods. At the same time, Africa's few exportable commodities still had only limited appeal, especially when the supply of both slaves and ivory became more difficult, and when other raw products, perhaps cheaper and of better quality, could be more readily obtained from other, newly exploited tropical regions elsewhere. In

1817 Dr Paolo della Cella, an Italian surgeon attached to a military expedition sent overland from Tripoli into Cyrenaica by Yusuf Pasha Karamanli, noted that caravans from Misurata were trading with Fezzan, Wadai and the Niger states. Their southbound loads included cottons, *baraccans* (the traditional, toga-like woollen garment of Libya), carpets and Venetian coloured glass jewellery for the 'belles of Timbuctu'.[133] Apart from the glass, the goods seem to have been local: the carpets and *baraccans* from Misurata itself and the cottons from Egypt. Della Cella found the trade of Benghazi limited to local produce, because use of the direct route to Wadai through Kufra had at that time hardly begun. The range of goods traded across the Sahara was far wider than Della Cella had found. Edward Rae, a Briton travelling in Tripolitania in the 1870s, reported that Tripoli was then the centre of all the caravan trade of northern Africa, Tunis and Algiers having 'for various causes lost their footing in this lucrative business'. The commercial caravans, Rae reported,

. . . carry coarse European cloths, silks, baraccans or Arab wraps, powder, muskets, glass, hardware, beads, toys, looking-glasses, paper, real and false corals, imitation pearls, turbans, amber, porcelain, coffee cups, copper vessels, kaftans, embroidered muslins, handkerchiefs and cotton goods, essence of roses, and spices.[134]

Textiles also included calicoes and printed cottons from England, and French muslin, linen and silk thread. Other trade-goods were Venetian writing-paper, German and English sword-blades (to be fitted with local handles), mirrors, needles, and small European metal tools and implements.[135] In the Sudan, Venetian paper was used not only for writing but also as money: literally a paper currency. But according to Giuseppe Haimann, the medium of exchange used by the Arab (Libyan) merchants in Wadai were sheets of English calico and coloured handkerchiefs. He complained that a few years earlier, Venetian glass beads had circulated as currency in Central Africa, 'but are now much less valued because the hairstyles of negresses are also subject to the changing caprices of fashion'.[136]

According to British consular reports, eight caravans left Benghazi for Wadai in 1893, carrying merchandise worth £10,885; in 1894 nine southbound caravans carried goods with a total value of £34,300. In the 1890s, among the principal goods sent across the Sahara by this route, in addition to arms and ammunition, were lump sugar imported from France and English green tea (the Libyan habit of tea-drinking having by then presumably penetrated into and beyond the Sahara), drugs, spices, perfumes from Austria, textiles, glass beads, hand mirrors and paper.[137]

Tripoli's own central Saharan trade was in serious decline by the late nineteenth century, and so merchants tended increasingly to export to Wadai through Benghazi (many of the Benghazi merchants were in fact agents of Tripoli trading-houses), which was linked with Tripoli by a regular Società Rubattino steamship service in 1881. There was a difficult but little-used direct route between Tripoli and Wadai, via Tummo and Arada by which the round trip took up to ten months. Unlike other Sudanese routes, there were no fresh camels to be hired on the Benghazi-Wadai trail south of Jalo, so the caravan for the whole journey had to be fitted out in Cyrenaica; Kufra provided only dates and water.[138]

Apart from slaves, goods carried northwards included ostrich feathers and ivory, kola nuts, gums, wax, raw perfumes (including civet), cloth, skins, hides, and leather goods; by the late nineteenth century however, only ivory and feathers were still important. The trade in ostrich feathers was, according to Haimann, a 'source of considerable earnings' and was controlled by Jewish merchants in Benghazi.[139] The value of the feathers increased fourfold between Wadai and Tripoli,[140] where they were cleaned and sorted for shipment to London and Paris. But the trade was vulnerable to shifts in demand and to competition from sources that were more easily exploited, notably the South African ostrich farms. The Jewish visitor Nahum Slouschz reported that in Tripoli at the beginning of the twentieth century, 'about 100 families made a living by cleaning and dyeing ostrich-feathers, but by 1907 I found nearly four hundred girls, who were in this trade, out of work'.[141] He also found that 'in 1906 there were only eight houses in Tripoli doing a trade with the Sudan, and by 1909 there were even fewer.'[142] At about this time, Hanns Visher learned that 'Murzuk has now lost its last source of income and the Turkish administration of today is faced with the difficult problem of the confidence of the people in the value of their own country independent of the Arab trans-Saharan trade.'[143]

By the time the Italians finally conquered Fezzan in 1930, they found that the Saharan trade was all but dead. There was little caravan traffic, apart from some business by local merchants, and the only remaining market of any size was at Murzuk. 'Today [1934] almost all commercial movement takes place along the motor-tracks; the southern caravan trails are used only for the greatly-reduced trade between Fezzan and Tibesti and Fezzan and Tidikelt [southern Algeria].'[144] The degree of prosperity of the trans-Saharan trade routes reflected political, military, social and economic conditions at both ends, and along their intermediate stretches. The incentives to trade were often finely balanced, and troubles on one route could prompt traffic to use another. But the central Saharan routes, after enjoying varying fortunes in the first half of the nineteenth century (the Bornu-Tripoli route was almost closed between 1830 and 1842) enjoyed a noticeable boom in the 1860s and '70s before going into a terminal decline in the 1880s, accelerated by the awful depredations of Sultan Rabah Ibn Fadlallah and others in the central Sudan in the 1890s.[145] After the abolition of the slave trade, traffic across the Sahara was finally halted by external forces, and particularly by the British and French penetration of the west and central African river-systems. By the late nineteenth century, the trade of inner Africa was being diversified westwards and southwards along the new, secure railways and river steamer routes to ports on the Atlantic coast and thence to the worldwide trading system. A similar process took place in the Nilotic Sudan in the wake of the British conquest, with trade being drawn from the central Saharan trade-routes to the Red Sea. The modern, independent states of Africa have been unable to correct this disruption of some of the oldest and most important of trans-continental trading relations. Small wonder that in 1897 the British traveller in Tripolitania, Swainson Cowper, described the country as 'waterless, treeless . . . nearly tradeless'.[146]

In the nineteenth and early twentieth centuries, the peoples of the lands now forming Chad and Libya were more closely linked than they had ever been before. The relationship was based partly on one-sided exploitation – of the more primitive, pagan or semi-pagan Saharan and Sudanese peoples and their natural resources by their Arab or Arab-Berber Muslim neighbours, who in turn were responding to external demands for the goods of inner Africa. This last phase of the exploitation of Africans by Africans before the European colonial intervention was generally less systematic and efficient, and even more wasteful of human life and natural resources, than the worst European colonial practices.

If Karamanli ambitions of trans-Saharan imperial conquests in the early nineteenth century were thwarted, the Awlad Slaiman and their tribal allies from central Libya managed to establish their own preserve on the southern fringes of the desert by the middle of the century. They came to terrorise and exploit the central Chadian lands at least as effectively as they might have done as the shock troops of Yusuf Pasha Karamanli's Saharan imperialism, while continuing contact with their homeland helped to sustain the Libyan character of their transposed, predatory culture.

At about the same time, the Sanusi confraternity, in its own selfless way, was taking the message and enlightenment of Islam into parts of Africa that were only nominally Muslim, and, simultaneously, was opening a channel for the penetration of inner Africa by undesirable influences. The central Sudanic slave trade and the traffic in arms needed to procure slaves from black Africa flourished as they did, because the Sanusi profited from ensuring secure commercial access to the Mediterranean. At great risk to themselves, enterprising North African traders carried across the Sahara the desirable products of European industry, but their business methods were such that they needed royal protection in Wadai, where the inhabitants looked on foreign merchants as 'intruders and parasites who lived sumptuously at their expense'.[147] Libyan merchants, who are still familiar figures in the market-places of Chad, have rarely earned the goodwill or esteem of their clients.[148]

## NOTES

1. See R. Forbes, *The Secret of the Sahara: Kufara*, London, 1921, app. D, pp. 334-5 (trans. of original MS letter of Sidi Ben Ali es Senussi to the people of Wajanga).
2. Nachtigal, *Sahara and Sudan*, vol. I. p. 175.
3. H. Duveyrier, *Les Touareg du Nord*, p. 300.
4. L. Rinn, *Marabouts et Khouan. Étude sur l'Islam en Algérie*, Algiers, 1884, p. 497.
5. See E.E. Evans-Pritchard, *The Sanusi of Cyrenaica*, Oxford, 1949, ch. III.
6. *Ibid.*, p. 9.
7. Khazanov, *Nomads and the Outside World*, p. 233.
8. Rinn, *Marabouts et Khouan*, p. 495.
9. Nachtigal, *Sahara and Sudan*, vol. I, p. 176.
10. See H. Duveyrier, *Les Touareg du Nord* and *La confrérie de Sidi Mohammed Ben Ali Es Senousi*, Rome, 1918.
11. P. Ward, *Touring Libya: The Eastern Provinces*, London, 1969, p. 71.
12. Forbes, *The Secret*, p. 293.
13. Duveyrier, *La Confrérie*, p. 19.
14. Evans-Pritchard, *The Sanusi*, pp. 14-15.
15. Hassanein Bey, *The Lost Oases*, London, 1925, p. 64.
16. Peters, 'Cultural and Social Diversity' in J. A. Allan (ed.), *Libya since Independance: Economic and Political Development*, London, 1982, p. 111. For an account of Zuwaya trading patterns, see J. Davis, *Libyan Politics: Tribe and Revolution*, London, 1987, pp. 188-9.
17. Hassanein Bey, *The Lost Oases*, p. 97.
18. E. Ceriani, 'Cufra', *Bollettino della Società Africana d'Italia*, XXXIX, III (1920).
19. R.E. Dunn, *Resistance in the Desert*, London and Madison, 1977, p. 130. See also Le Rouvreur, *Sahéliens et Sahariens*, pp. 368-9.
20. See Nachtigal, *Sahara and Sudan*, IV, p. 203. For details of route and length of travel stages, see F. Minutilli, *La Tripolitania*, Turin, 1912, p. 137. For an account of how the road was opened up, see R.A. Bagnold, *Libyan Sands*, London, 1935, pp. 188-9.
21. For the history of Wadai, see Nachtigal, *Sahara and Sudan*, IV, ch. X, and Trimingham, *A History of Islam*, pp. 139-40.
22. Duveyrier, *La Confrérie*, p. 41.
23. Lovejoy, *Transformations in Slavery*, p. 70.
24. N.A. Ziadeh, *Sanusiyah. A Study of a Revivalist Movement in Islam*, Leiden, 1958, pp. 49-50.

25. Duveyrier, *La Confrérie*, pp. 18–19.
26. Rinn, *Marabouts et Khouan*, p. 492.
27. See Nachtigal, *Sahara and Sudan*, IV, chs. III, IV, and VII-X.
28. Evans-Pritchard, *The Sanusi*, pp. 24–5.
29. Forbes, *The Secret*, p. 119.
30. Carbou, *La Région*, II, p. 244.
31. Nachtigal, *Sahara and Sudan*, IV, p. 139; Duveyrier, *La Confrérie*, p. 66, asserts that there was a *zawia* at Abeche.
32. F.Valori, *Storia della Cirenaica*, Florence, 1961, p. 115.
33. Nachtigal, *Sahara and Sudan*, IV, p. 189.
34. Peters, 'Cultural and Social Diversity', p. 110; Barth, *Travels*, vol.I, p. 102.
35. Ziadeh, *Sanusiyah*, p. 99.
36. Nachtigal, *Sahara and Sudan*, I, p. 176.
37. *Ibid.*
38. Minutilli, *La Tripolitania*, p. 137.
39. *Ibid.*
40. See *Handbook on Cyrenaica*, IX, K.D. Bell 'Kufra' map, app. A.
41. Forbes, *The Secret*, pp. 158–9.
42. For full translation, see *ibid.*, app. D, pp. 334–5; see also Ziadeh, *Sanusiyah*, pp. 95–6.
43. Hassanein Bey, *The Lost Oases*, pp. 66, 96.
44. *Ibid.*, p. 67.
45. Davis, *Libyan Politics*, p. 85.
46. Forbes, *The Secret*, pp. 205–6.
47. *Ibid.*, p. 256.
48. Briggs, *Tribes*, p. 101.
49. Carbou, *La Région*, I, p. 133.
50. Valori, *Storia della Cirenaica*, p. 112.
51. M. Morsy, *North Africa 1800-1900*, London, 1984, pp. 280–1.
52. Nachtigal, *Sahara and Sudan*, II, pp. 63–4.
53. *Ibid.*, pp. 64–5.
54. Evans-Pritchard, *The Sanusi*, p. 98.
55. See A.E. Afigbo *et al.*, *The Making of Modern Africa*, London, 1986, p. 207; C.C. Adams 'The Sanusiya Order' in *Handbook on Cyrenaica*, X., p. 11.
56. Ziadeh, *Sanusiya*, pp. 52–3.
57. Cromer, Earl of, *Modern Egypt*, London, 1911, p. 491.
58. *Ibid.*, p. 492.
59. Valori, *Storia*, p. 112.
60. Evans-Pritchard, *The Sanusi*, pp. 24–5.
61. E. Farina, 'I Senusi nella Storia e nella Geografia', *Bollettino della Società Africana d'Italia*, VIII, III-IV (March–April 1889).
62. S. White, *From Sphinx to Oracle*, London, 1899, map facing p. 128.
63. Carbou, *La Région* vol. II, p. 3.
64. Duveyrier, *La Confrérie*, p. 40.
65. See Nachtigal, *Sahara and Sudan*, vol. II., p. 64, n.1.
66. Duveyrier, *La Confrérie*, p. 39.
67. Nachtigal, *Sahara and Sudan*, II. pp. 337–8.
68. H.K.W. Kumm, *From Hausaland to Egypt through the Sudan*, London, 1910, p. 91.
69. Palmer, *The Bornu*, p. 269. See also W. K. R. Hallam, *The Life and Times of Rabih Fadl Allah*, Ilfracombe, 1977.
70. See S. Decalo, *A Historical Dictionary of Chad*, London, 1971, pp. 257–8; T. O'Toole, *The Central African Republic*, London, 1986, pp. 19–20; D.D. Cordell, *Dar al-Kuti and the Last Years of the Trans-Saharan Slave Trade*, Madison, 1985. For a first-hand account of Dar Kuti, see Kumm, *From Hausaland to Egypt*, pp. 170ff.

71. Kumm, *From Hausaland to Egypt*, p. 176.
72. Duveyrier, *La Confrérie*, p. 65.
73. *Ibid.*
74. Nachtigal, *Sahara and Sudan*, II, p. 386.
75. Carbou, *La Région*, I., p. 166.
76. Wilfred Thesiger, meeting him on a visit to Tibesti in 1938, found him taciturn. *The Life of my Choice*, London, 1987, pp. 287-8.
77. Chapelle, *Nomades Noirs*, p. 324.
78. *Ibid.*, pp. 93-6.
79. *Ibid.*, p. 377.
80. *Ibid.*, pp. 377-8.
81. See Nachtigal, *Sahara and Sudan*, I, pp. 402-6; Chapelle, *Nomades Noirs*, pp. 378-9; Briggs, *Tribes*, pp. 188-9.
82. See S. Baier, *A History of the Sahara in the Nineteenth Century*, Boston, 1978, pp. 27-8; D.D. Cordell, 'Eastern Libya, Wadai and the Sanusiya', *JAH*, XVIII, 1 (1977).
83. Hassanein Bey, *The Lost Oases*, pp. 64-5.
84. Boahen, *Britain, The Sahara*, p. 111.
85. Carbou, *La Région*, II, p. 169.
86. E.R. Toledano, 'The Imperial Eunuchs of Istanbul: From Africa to the Heart of Islam', *Middle Eastern Studies*, 20, 3 (July 1984).
87. Lovejoy, *Transformations in Slavery*, p. 147.
88. British Parliamentary Papers, *Correspondence Relative to the Slave Trade Class D*, 1847-8, LXIV, p. 67.
89. *Ibid.*, p. 73.
90. *Correspondence with British Representatives and Agents Abroad . . . Relative to the Slave Trade*, London, 1880, 5, p. 180.
91. A. Ghisleri, *Tripolitania e Cirenaica. Dal Mediterraneo al Sahara*, Milan-Bergamo, 1912, p. 142.
92. *Correspondence with British Representatives*, 1883-4, p. 38.
93. G. Baer, 'Slavery in Nineteenth Century Egypt', *JAH*, VIII, 3 (1967).
94. J. Hamilton, *Wanderings in North Africa*, London, 1856, p. 196.
95. White, *From Sphinx to Oracle*, p. 157.
96. *Ibid.*, p. 158.
97. Nachtigal, *Sahara and Sudan*, II, p. 233.
98. *Correspondence with British Representatives*, 1880, p. 180.
99. *Ibid.*, pp. 180-1.
100. *Ibid.*, tables, pp. 178, 179, 182, 186.
101. *Correspondence Relative to the Slave Trade*, 1847-8, LXIV, p. 73.
102. H. Bulugma, *Benghazi through the Ages*, Benghazi, 1972, p. 87.
103. R.F. Clarke, *Cardinal Lavigerie and the African Slave Trade*, London, 1889, pp. 251-2.
104. Ceriani, 'Cufra'.
105. Wickins, *An Economic History*, pp. 149-50.
106. A.A. Boahen, 'The Caravan Trade in the Nineteenth Century', *JAH*, III, 2 (1962).
107. *Correspondence Relative to the Slave Trade*, 1847-8, LXIV, p. 67.
108. Enver Pasha, *Diario della Guerra Libica*, Bologna, 1986, p. 67.
109. Forbes, *The Secret*, p. 109.
110. Hassanein Bey, *The Lost Oases*, p. 179.
111. K. Holmboe, *Desert Encounter: An Adventurous Journey through Italian Africa*, London, 1936, p. 188.
112. H.J. Fisher and V. Rowland, 'Firearms in the Central Sudan'. *JAH*, XII, 2 (1971).

113. See J.P. Smaldone, *Warfare in the Sokoto Caliphate*, Cambridge, 1977, pp. 97-8.
114. Fisher and Rowland, 'Firearms in the Central Sudan'.
115. Nachtigal, *Sahara and Sudan*, IV, p. 183.
116. *Ibid.*, p. 68.
117. *Ibid.*, p. 20.
118. *Ibid.*, p. 183.
119. See F. Rodd, 'A Fezzani Military Expedition to Kanem and Bagirmi in 1821,' *Journal of the Royal African Society*, XXXV, CXXXIX (April 1936).
120. Fisher and Rowland, 'Firearms in the Central Sudan'.
121. G. Haimann, *Cirenaica (Tripolitania)*, Milan, 1886, p. 196, n1.
122. *Ibid.*, p. 175.
123. Kumm, *From Hausaland to Egypt*, p. 115.
124. H. Vischer, *Across the Sahara from Tripoli to Bornu*, London, 1910, p. 67.
125. G. Narducci, 'Industrie e Commercio della Cirenaica e loro Avvenire nel "Dopo Guerra"', *Bollettino della Società Africana d'Italia*, XXXVII, V (1918).
126. Fisher and Rowland, 'Firearms in the Central Sudan'.
127. Quoted in F.V. Parsons, *The Origins of the Morocco Question, 1880-1900*, London, 1976, p. 362.
128. Hallett, *Records of the African Association*, pp. 144-5.
129. Boahen, *Britain, The Sahara*, p. 131.
130. Rossi, *Storia*, p. 292.
131. H. Schirmer, *Le Sahara*, Paris, 1893, p. 366.
132. J. Wright, *Libya: A Modern History*, London, 1982, p. 17.
133. P. Della Cella, *Viaggio da Tripoli di Barbaria alle frontiere occidentali dell'Egitto*, Città di Castello, 1912, p. 34.
134. E. Rae, *The Country of the Moors*, London, 1877, p. 79.
135. Boahen, *Britain, The Sahara*, pp. 122-3.
136. Haimann, *Cirenaica*, p. 196.
137. Narducci, 'Industrie e Commercio della Cirenaica'.
138. See F. Coro, 'Un Documento Inedito sull'Antico Commercio Carovaniero fra Tripoli e l'Uadai', *Gli Annali dell'Africa Italiana*, IV (1941).
139. Haimann, *Cirenaica*, p. 196.
140. Minutilli, *La Tripolitania*, p. 137.
141. N. Slouschz, *Travels in North Africa*, Philadelphia, 1927, p. 7.
142. *Ibid.*
143. Vischer, *Across the Sahara*, pp. 132-3.
144. Scarin, *Le Oasi del Fezzan*, p. 190.
145. For the reported fate of Tripoli merchants under Rabah, see H.S. Cowper, *The Hill of the Graces*, London, 1897, pp. 305-6.
146. *Ibid.*, p. 304. For an account of the decline of Tripoli-Bornu trade in the early twentieth century, see Vischer, *Across the Sahara*.
147. Nachtigal, *Sahara and Sudan*, IV, p. 57.
148. Le Rouvreur, *Sahéliens et Sahariens*, pp. 394-5.

# 6

# THE AGE OF IMPERIALISM

*'The day of small nations has long passed away. The day of Empires has come'* — Joseph Chamberlain

While the Egyptians exploited the Nilotic Sudan, the French expanded into the hinterlands of Tunis and Algiers, and the Sanusi penetrated the eastern Sahara and Sudan, the Ottoman Turks reluctantly conquered Fezzan and garrisoned the more important oases controlling the central Saharan trade routes. For as they returned to Tripoli in 1835 to reassert their sovereignty as a counter to French African expansion and to Egypt's near-independence, the Turks realised that the well-being and prosperity of their North African possessions would depend largely on their ability to attract and control central Saharan trade. But after their initial conquests in the 1830s and '40s they moved slowly, tending merely to react to the train of events that led to the division of all the Sahara and Sudan between European colonial powers. While the Turks let the Sanusi take charge of most of Cyrenaica, in Tripolitania and Fezzan they had to be alert to any moves made by the French in Algeria, and at the same time watch for signs of further British diplomatic involvement in the central desert.

In 1843 the Turks first established a claim to the oases essential for promoting a long-term Saharan and even Central African policy: Ghadames, on the main route to the Niger, and Murzuk, on the Bornu road. They could thus control most central Saharan trade and direct it towards Tripoli by favourable tariffs and other inducements. The abolition of the slave trade in both Algiers and Tunis stimulated this process; yet up to 1862 the Sultan was represented at Ghadames only by a *mudir*, while at Murzuk there was a small garrison. Meanwhile, the French in Algeria had overcome the revolt of Abd-al-Kader, and by 1848 were ready to advance into the Sahara, at that time still open to outside powers seeking political or commercial influence there. Turkey had vague claims to the hinterland of Tripoli, as did Morocco to the territories beyond the Atlas Mountains and as far east as the Tuat oases. But if the tribes of the western Sahara said Friday prayers for the well-being of the Sultan-Caliph of Morocco, as those of the central and eastern desert prayed for the Sultan-Caliph at Constantinople, spiritual supremacy was about the limit of the allegiance which these two Commanders of the Faithful could exact from the tribespeople of the great Sahara.[1] Then in 1851, under a new governor of Algeria, Marshal Jacques Randon, a phase of dynamic expansion began with the occupation of the northern oases; Laghouat (1852), Ouargla (1853) and Tougourt (1854), all outposts for a future advance into the central desert. Randon was one of the first to propose the economic development of the Algerian Sahara and the reopening of Algerian trade with the Sudan, disrupted by the French conquest; but his plans were frustrated by the hostility of the Ajjer Tuareg and Ahaggar Tuareg confederations which controlled the Algerian roads to the south.

The Turks had no such ambitions; they merely assumed a vague and undefined sovereignty over the interior, which mostly they failed to exercise in practice. In 1859 the governor of Tripoli, Ahmed Izzat Pasha, sent an expedition to assert Turkish protection over the Tibesti. But this effort was without lasting effect because Nachtigal, on his travels through the mountains a decade later, found no trace of Turkish influence; indeed he believed that the empire ended at Tejerri, south of Murzuk in the district of Gatrun.[2] However, a traveller from Tripoli to Wadai in 1873, Haj Omar al-Tarabulsi, remarked that Al-Uar (Tummo) 'is the furthest point subject to our Sultan'.[3]

In 1862 the French despatched Commander Mircher to Ghadames where, only a year or two after the withdrawal of the British vice-consul from the oasis, he signed a treaty whereby the Ajjer Tuareg confederation undertook to help protect French or native Algerian traders as far as the Sudan. The fact that the treaty was worthless was irrelevant to the Turks in Tripoli, who reacted to this latest perceived French threat to their interests by posting a regular garrison at Ghadames, which at the same time became the administrative centre of western Fezzan. In 1869 the Sultan-Caliph Abd-al-Aziz sent a manuscript Koran and a sword of honour via Tripoli to the Sultan of Bornu;[4] and in 1875 the Turks took advantage of bloody strife between the Ajjer and Ahaggar Tuareg in Ghat to establish a garrison there. By posting troops in these main trading centres, the Turks in effect broadly defined the western limits of Tripolitania and Fezzan. But Turkish pretensions to sovereignty over the Ajjer Tuareg were not accepted by the French, and certainly not by the Tuareg themselves. Nevertheless, in 1879, the Turkish governor of Fezzan, Mustafa Faiq Pasha, created two new administrative districts: of the Ajjer Tuareg at Djanet and of the Tebu Reshada at Bardai. However, neither of these had any existence in practice. Significantly, he was later recalled for what were considered to be uncontrolled schemes to bring all the Sudan under Turkish sovereignty.

The French in the meantime had conquered little of the Sahara. The massacre by the Ahaggar Tuareg of the Flatters military expedition (sent to trace a suitable route for a trans-Saharan railway) in 1881 delayed French penetration from the north till the end of the century. Indeed, the French found an easier approach to the western Sudan by way of the long-established possession, Senegal, which also provided the native *tirailleurs* necessary for further conquests. By 1883 the French were on the upper Niger, which they still half-heartedly hoped could become the artery of an African empire rivalling British India in wealth, population and prestige. Ten years later they were in Timbuctu, which by then offered little more than a romantic echo of long-vanished splendours. France could be said almost to have had active encouragement from its two main European rivals, Germany and Great Britain, to engage in such adventures as a form of harmless compensation in inner Africa for defeat by Prussia in 1870–1 and the British occupation of Egypt in 1882.

By the late nineteenth century, Turkey's place in Africa was in effect confined to a relatively narrow corridor of territory between British-occupied Egypt to the east and French Algeria and Tunisia to the west – all erstwhile Ottoman lands that the Sublime Porte had done little to protect from European occupation. But to the south, in the central Sahara and Sudan, the possibilities for asserting territorial claims still seemed almost limitless. Inspired by the pan-Islamic ideals of Sultan Abd-al-Hamid II, and adopting an assertive and forward African policy, the Turks might have denied the French access to the strategic oasis-complex of Tuat in the north-western Sahara, which was the key to further expansion to the south and was also claimed by Morocco. The Turks might equally have extended their presence, rather than mere claims, southwards from Fezzan towards Lake Chad.

In the aftermath of the Congress of Berlin (1884–5) and the European 'scramble' for African colonies, decisions on the political division of the continent were taken in Europe with little regard for African geography, and even less for local realities or interests. The first of a series of decisions leading to the formal political separation of territories now comprising respectively Libya and Chad, and drawing between them a frontier of purely European conception, came with the Anglo-French Declaration of August 1890. In allowing French Mediterranean possessions to extend as far as the lower Niger and Lake Chad,[5] the agreement removed nearly all the diplomatic objections to an eventual French occupation of the western half of the Sahara. But the Anglo-French Declaration brought a response from the Turkish Foreign Minister, Said Pasha, in the form of a Note to London and Paris. This was a strong but by no means hasty summary (it took some three months to prepare) of Turkish claims in Africa. These were perhaps more significant for their breathtaking scope than for reflecting any present reality or even future possibility. The Note asserted that the rights of the Ottoman empire must, in accordance with the 'long-standing' rules of the 'hinterland' doctrine,[6] extend to all the territories in the zone from Bir Turki on the southern Tunisian frontier, west of Ghadames and the Ajjer Tuareg; they must take in the oases of Djebabo and Agram (west of Kawar) and then pass between the frontiers of Bornu and Sokoto, emerge on the northern frontiers of Cameroun, and turn east to the watershed between Congo and Chad in such a way as to include the territories of Bornu, Bagirmi, Wadai, Kanem, Wanyanga, Borku and Tibesti, 'thereby leaving in our possession the great caravan route that goes from Murzuk to Kuka by the oases of Yat, Kawar and Agadem'.[7]

In modern terms, Ottoman Turkey was claiming the whole of Chad, a substantial piece of the neighbouring territory (the western Republic of Niger), corners of Algeria, Nigeria and Cameroun, and parts of the Central African Republic – territories which in 1890 were the objects of British, French and German colonial ambitions. Since the nearest Turkish garrisons were at that time in southern Fezzan, some 1,500 km. from Lake Chad and more than 2,000 km. from the Chad-Congo watershed, the greater part of the claim was clearly fanciful. Nor was the Turkish case strong in terms of international law. The specified hinterland was subject to no diplomatic definition; the claim was unilateral, unsupported by any treaty with another regional power, and covered regions to which the Ottoman empire had no title.[8] There was not even evidence of any recent act of sovereignty over the nearest of these claims – Borku, Ennedi and Tibesti.

Lake Chad itself became an objective of British expansion through northern Nigeria; of the Germans extending the northern borders of their colony of Kamerun; and the goal of more grandiose French ambitions, since the regions north and east of the lake represented the 'missing link' between the emerging French empires of North, West and Equatorial Africa.[9] By the late 1890s, with French expeditions slowly converging on Lake Chad from Algeria, the Congo basin and the upper Niger, the French imagination was briefly stirred by the vision of a vast African empire extending not only from the Mediterranean to the Congo, but also from the Senegal to the Red Sea. The vision was constrained only in its widest extent by the 'Fashoda Incident' of 1898 which left Britain and not France in possession of the upper Nile valley. Then, in seeking to define more precisely their respective spheres of influence between the Nile and Lake Chad, and thereby avoid the risk of a European war starting in Africa, Britain and France in March 1899 ratified a convention which, among its other provisions, established the future frontier between Chad and Libya. This was simply the mutually-recognised limit of the French sphere of interest north of the 15th parallel. It was defined as the line departing from the meeting-point of the 16th degree of longitude east of Greenwich with the Tropic of Cancer, running south-east to the meeting-point with the 24th degree of longitude east of Greenwich, and then continuing on the 24th until it met the frontier of Darfur, then still undefined but somewhere north of the 15th parallel. The greater part of Tibesti as well as the whole of Borku and Ennedi were thus in the French zone of influence, although the possibility of their military conquest and occupation was well over a decade in the future. In running north-west to south-east, the Anglo-French line cut right across the Sahara's traditional north-south communications. It was thus a potential barrier to freedom of movement from Fezzan and Cyrenaica to the lands of the central and eastern Sahara and Sudan, and it had been agreed without consultation with those likely to be most affected, whether governors or governed. While the line set an agreed limit to the zone of French influence in the direction of Kufra, the Libyan Desert and, beyond them, the Nile Valley, its existence did not necessarily imply a comparable zone of British influence to the other side. Rather, London and Paris were agreeable to recognising Turkish rights in Fezzan and Cyrenaica north of the 1899 line; so, too, was Italy. As self-appointed heir to Turkey's North African possessions, Italy accepted the Anglo-French declaration in 1902[10] in return for confirming British rights in Egypt and recognising French claims on Morocco. But Turkey, as in 1890, protested, drawing attention to its 'historic rights' over the whole zone as far south as Lake Chad, and making known its refusal to recognise a diplomatic act that violated those rights.

These European initiatives aroused the belated interest of Constantinople in the African interior and its potential. In 1886, and again in 1895, Sultan Abd-al-Hamid II sent the same envoy to Sidi al-Mahdi al–Sanusi. The missions seem to have been inconclusive[11] and even if, as the emissary later reported in a series of press articles, the Sultan was named in Friday prayers at the Sanusi centre at Kufra, and the 'Great Caliph' of Constantinople was well-regarded in the Sudan, such respect for his spiritual position in no way implied acceptance of his imperial sovereignty. The Sanusi, although fanatical defenders of Islam, were no defenders of Ottoman imperialism. They rejected the Sultan's attempts to claim leadership of the whole Muslim community through the caliphate, and his view of pan-Islamism as a means of establishing that unity.[12]

While the Sanusi could be relied upon to defend Islam, if not Ottoman interests, in the eastern Sahara and Sudan, the Turks were especially concerned to protect the central Saharan trade on which the prosperity of Tripolitania and Fezzan ultimately depended. The axial oases of Murzuk, Ghadames and Ghat had been garrisoned earlier in the century to protect the trade, and the Turkish Note of 1890 had laid stress on Turkey's control of the 'great caravan route' from Murzuk to Lake Chad.

Between 1900 and the First World War, the French conquered and occupied all the western and central Sudanic and Saharan lands due to them under diplomatic agreements with other European powers, although in many places 'pacification' and occupation were not completed till the 1920s. In doing so, they frustrated Turkish attempts at maintaining sovereignty wherever the French considered their own spheres of influence to extend, up to the line agreed with Britain in 1899. Towards the end of 1898, three great French military expeditions had set out for the interior of Africa. The Foureau-Lamy mission started from Ouargla in Algeria, and on its southward march kept just west of Turkish claims in Fezzan; the Voulet-Chanoine (Joalland) mission marched to the east from Senegal; and the Gentil mission pushed northwards from the Congo. After many bizarre adventures – battles, starvation, mutiny and massacres – all three met together at Lake Chad and in April 1900 defeated and killed Sultan Rabah Ibn Fadlallah near the present site of Fort Lamy (N'Djamena) and dispersed his army. With the annihilation of his remaining followers a year later, all the lands north and east of Lake Chad were laid open to the French advance. Also in 1900, the French finally occupied the Tuat oases: they were the key to the final conquest of the Algerian Sahara, and their occupation further isolated Turkey's African possessions, cutting Tripoli's traditional links with the Hausa states.

Kanem was now directly in the path of the French advance, and so too was the Sanusi order. The armed confrontation with European imperialism that the order had long foreseen now took its course. From its new centre at Qiru in Borku, the order inspired and directed strong local resistance to invading forces that were always small but usually had overwhelming superiority in modern arms. The Sanusi possessed no 'armies of fanatics' such as the European imagination had long attributed to them; rather, the *shaikhs* could only use their spiritual and moral influence to induce the people to take up arms and defend the Chadian outpost of the *Dar al-Islam* against the Christian threat. The French seem to have used their few artillery pieces with devastating effect, particularly against the fortified Sanusi *zawias* and other strongholds. Early in 1902 they stormed and took the southern outpost of Sanusism, the great *zawia* at Bir Alali. Its capture forced the Sanusi out of Kanem, and back to the relative safety of Borku and Ennedi. Six months later, Sidi al-Mahdi died at Qiru, possibly from grief over the turn of events in the south.[13] He was succeeded by his nephew Sidi Ahmad al-Sharif, who fought a losing battle to protect the southern marches of Sanusism against French encroachment. Sanusi military help was also given to Wadai when requested.[14]

If one of the order's objectives in moving its headquarters to Qiru in 1899 had been to make it the capital of an independent mid-Saharan state, the Sanusi achieved neither the close working relationship with the Turks nor the guarantee of a Mediterranean outlet, both of which would have been necessary for the political and economic viability of such a state.[15] Although the Turks and the Sanusi seemed to have many common interests, they remained suspicious of each other. While the Turks ignored Sanusi urgings to declare a *jihad* (holy war) against the French, the Sanusi rejected the appointment of a Turkish official to Kufra. It was only in the hope of saving Borku, Ennedi and Tibesti from the French that Sidi Ahmad al-Sharif in 1908 recognised Turkish sovereignty over what are now the three northernmost provinces of Chad, and thus opened them to their token occupation by small Turkish garrisons;[16] indeed, only after the Young Turk revolution of 1908 is there firmer evidence of a degree of coordination of Turco-Sanusi policy in the south. Sidi Ahmad al-Sharif had moved the headquarters of the order back to Kufra in 1903. At the same time, Borku became a citadel defended against the French by a line of great fortified *zawias*: one in the magnificent palm-groves at Ain Galakka, and others at Faya, Yarda and Wanyanga.[17] Meanwhile the Sanusi organised raids by the Awlad Slaiman, the Teda and Tuareg on French lines and outposts in Kanem.

Around the turn of the century, the Turks were at last becoming aware of French ambitions in the central Sahara, and began to consider defending their interests. About 1902, they considered sending a small garrison to Bilma in Kawar, commanding the main Tripoli-Bornu trade route; but the French, after occupying Agades in Air in 1903, forestalled them by annexing Bilma to the new Niger Military Territory in 1906. According to Hanns Vischer, who was in Murzuk at the time, 'the news caused a general stir . . . for Bilma nominally belonged to Fezzan and to Turkey.'[18] Only then did the Turks start to assert their claims to Tibesti, re-establishing in 1906 their nominal administration of the Reshada Tebu, paying a monthly stipend to the Derde, and providing him with a Turkish flag and an armed escort. Two years later, the French blocked a Turkish attempt to extend their influence over the Ajjer Tuareg, sending a military detachment to take the oasis of Djanet, and ordering the small Turkish garrison already in occupation of what is now part of south-east Algeria to lower its flag and withdraw. Around 1908, the Turks also posted a few troops in Bardai in the Tibesti, apparently with the approval and even patronage of the Derde, who seems to have needed the visible support of Turkish authority as much to sustain his own position locally as for protection against the French. By 1911, Turkish strength at Bardai had been increased to sixty men and six cannon, under the command of a colonel, and defensive blockhouses had been built there and for the thirty-five-man detachment at Zuar.[19]

Although the evidence is not clear and the sequence of events is confused, it seems that around 1908 the Sanusi order, regarding the Ottoman as a lesser infidel than the Christian, finally urged the Turks to help defend Borku against the French. By early 1911 the Turkish flag was flying over the 'capital' of Borku, the Sanusi *zawia* at the oasis of Ain Galakka, and a small garrison was stationed there; there was also a Turkish detachment at the nearby oasis of Yen.[20] Finally, as late as October 1912, the Ottoman civil administrator at Ain Galakka proclaimed a Turkish administration over Ennedi and set up a small military outpost at Oum Chalouba to protect caravans on the Kufra-Abeche route.[21] This was the most southerly extension of Turkish power in the central Sahara.

France in the meantime had conquered Wadai, eliminating Sanusi influence there, while Italy had invaded Turkish Tripolitania and Cyrenaica. The Italians were thus fulfilling long-cherished ambitions to establish a strategically-important settler-colony dominating the central Mediterranean narrows and the shortest overland routes to Lake Chad and Central Africa. In October 1911, Italian forces occupied Tripoli, Benghazi, Derna, Tobruk and Homs, but hopes that Turkish North Africa would become Italian simply through diplomacy and a show of force proved illusory. There was no capitulation, and far from hailing the invaders as liberators from Turkish oppression, the Libyans, led in Cyrenaica by the Sanusi, reinforced the small regular garrisons with thousands of their own untrained volunteers.

In the far south, in Borku, Ennedi and Tibesti, detachments were withdrawn to meet this new military threat from the north. All these vast territories were thus simply abandoned to the advancing French, who completed the occupation of Tibesti in the middle of 1914. As a result of the Italian invasion, a conference that was to have convened in Tripoli in the autumn of 1911 to define the southern frontiers of Tripolitania (Fezzan) was abandoned.[22] In October 1912 the Turks relinquished the largely unconquered territories of Tripolitania and Cyrenaica to the Italians, but without fully transferring sovereignty or in any way defining the southern frontiers. By 1913, when all the Turks had finally left North Africa, Rome was becoming aware that only by means of a swift advance into the interior would there be any possibility of stopping the French from trying to take the southern oases of Fezzan itself. By early 1914 the Italians had accordingly occupied the main Fezzanese centres, but with lines of supply hopelessly over-extended, and unconquered tribes still at large in the desert, they were forced right back to the coast at the end of that year. And the French, by then fully involved in the European war, and soon to face widespread revolt in their own Saharan possessions, were in no position to take advantage of Italy's failure.

In 1915 Italy entered the Great War on the Allied side under the terms of the secret Treaty of London, Article 13 of which allowed Italy to claim equitable territorial compensations on the frontiers of its African colonies (Libya, Somalia and Eritrea) adjoining British and French territories if Britain and France increased their own colonial possessions at the expense of Germany,[23] which they were then in the process of doing. Rome had long regarded Libya as the gateway to all the little-known lands between the Mediterranean and Lake Chad and even, it was suggested, as an overland link with the Italian East African empire.[24] In 1916 the Colonial Ministry in Rome prepared what it regarded as a maximum claim to some 2.5 million sq. km. of French Chadian territory, which contained 2 million inhabitants. It proposed the 'return' to Libya of the northern part of the Chad basin, including Kanem and Wadai, as well as control of the five caravan routes between the Mediterranean and Central Africa.[25] A post-war commentator considered that 'while some details of this proposal were highly indefensible, the main purpose, that Libya should have an adequate hinterland, was sound.'[26]

In the event, Italy gained even less on its Libyan frontiers than its own minimum objectives. In 1919 Paris and Rome agreed to a new frontier between Libyan and Algerian territory, ensuring that the main Ghadames-Ghat caravan route would pass entirely through Italian territory, hardly by then a gain of much practical value; and in 1926 Egypt agreed to a frontier that recognised as Italian the Sanusi centre at Giarabub. Only some years later did the Italians control all such territory. During the First World War they had been confined by hostile Libyans to Tripoli, Benghazi and a few other coastal enclaves. After the failed attempts to give Libyans a measure of self-government, the 'reconquest' of Tripolitania began in 1922 and that of Cyrenaica in 1923. In the Sirtica and Fezzan, the Italians were opposed by descendants of the same people who had fought the Turks nearly a century before: the Saif-al-Nasr family and the Awlad Slaiman, with their allies the Orfella and Gadadfa. As the Italians conquered Fezzan in 1930, history repeated itself when defeated Awlad Slaiman and other tribespeople from central Libya again sought refuge in Kanem. This time they joined up with their kin who had first settled there in the 1840s and had been living quietly under French rule for over twenty years. In Cyrenaica, the suppression of the Sanusi-led resistance and the destruction of the order itself were bloodier and more difficult. Kufra, as the last settled outpost of the order, was only occupied in January 1931, with refugees finding safety in French territory to the south or in Egypt. With the final conquest of Cyrenaica in 1932, the Sanusi order had ceased to exist as a religious, political or social organisation, in either French or Italian territory.

Two differing versions of European colonialism – an Italian fascist 'apartheid' and the French notion of *assimilation*, both in practice alien and disruptive – thus lowered administrative and psychological 'national' barriers between peoples who over many centuries had overcome the formidable natural barriers of the Sahara to sustain commercial, cultural and personal relationships between Mediterranean and Sudanic Africa. Of course the colonial frontier was permeable, and petty trade between southern Libya and Chad continued throughout and beyond the colonial period. But the traditional centres of commerce, influence and diffusion – on one side Tripoli, Benghazi, Giarabub, Kufra and the Fezzanese oases, and on the other Kawar, Borku, Ennedi and Tibesti, and the formerly independent sultanates of Kanem, Wadai and Bagirmi – were largely separated from each other by colonial powers which insisted on fixing and policing exact international frontiers across the desert where none had existed before. The Libyan people began to be drawn into an Italian culture and a totalitarian fascist world-view centred on the Mediterranean. But people south of the Sahara, and particularly the black southern Chadian peoples formerly enslaved and now more susceptible to the Christianising and Gallicising influences, were subjected to a purely French supervision of their political, economic and social evolution. Chad was a neglected and unimportant part of a colonial federation oriented firmly towards equatorial Africa. The peoples of the former independent Muslim sultanates of Chad, now living in the northern *cul-de-sac* of French Equatorial Africa, were largely outside the French 'civilising mission', resentful that the former slave peoples of the south were gaining more from French rule than they, the former exploiters and masters, were doing.

France only tried to meet its obligations under the 1915 Treaty of London some twenty years after it was signed. In January 1935 the Italian *Duce* Benito Mussolini and the French Foreign Minister Pierre Laval agreed to move the whole frontier between Italian Libya and French Equatorial Africa (Chad) southwards by about 100 km., thereby giving Italy a strip of territory some 110,000 sq. km. in extent. The strip consisted of mountainous desert in Tibesti, with a total population which could be counted in hundreds, rather than thousands.[27] But the agreement never came into force because it was not subject to final ratification,[28] following the deterioration of Franco-Italian relations over Italy's conquest of Ethiopia (1935–6) and Italy's perception of its own enhanced international status as a result of the conquest and proclamation of the empire.[29] In December 1938 the Italian Foreign Minister, Galeazzo Ciano, denounced the accords.[30]

In June 1940 Italy entered the Second World War as the ally of Nazi Germany. After the surrender of France to the Nazis two weeks later, Chad under Governor Félix Éboué became, in August 1940, the first French African territory to declare its support for the Free French cause of General Charles de Gaulle, an action that earned it a special place in Gaullist mythology. While British forces in Egypt confronted Italian and later mixed Italian and German forces in Libya, the Free French used Chad as a base from which to launch attacks against Italian garrisons in the oases of Fezzan and southern Cyrenaica, as a necessary assertion of Gaullist determination to continue to fight for France.[31] The first hit-and-run raid was made on Murzuk in December 1940–January 1941. Then in March 1941 forces under General Leclerc, which had followed the old caravan route northwards from Faya, captured Kufra from the Italians; this was a remarkable feat of logistics in that Leclerc's army was covering very difficult country never previously traversed by motorised transport.[32] Further guerrilla raids on Italian outposts in Fezzan followed early in 1942, but even if the French had been able at the time to capture the southern oases, they lacked the means to maintain such advanced positions. By mid-December 1942, with the Italian-German forces retreating westwards across Libya after the battle of El Alamein, the French started northwards from Zuar. At the end of December, with Cyrenaica in British hands and the Eighth Army pressing towards Tripoli, the French were driving the Italians out of Fezzan and by the end of January 1943 had taken Ghadames and met up with British troops who had recently occupied Tripoli.[33] The war correspondent Alexander Clifford describes how the French arrived 'in filthy, rackety trucks tied together with wire, unkempt men incredibly sunburned with great, bushy shapeless beards. Their own mothers would never have recognised them. But their trucks flew the tricolour of France and the cross of Lorraine.'[34] While the British established military administrations in conquered Tripolitania and Cyrenaica, as occupied enemy territory, the French set up their own administration in Fezzan.[35]

The area under French military control, which included Ghadames and parts of the Tripolitanian Sahara, was defined under an agreement with the British. This was a purely French and not an Allied administration,[36] based on practice in the military territory of southern Algeria, with local garrison commanders acting as political and administrative officers.[37] But Ahmad Saif al-Nasr, who had come up from Chad with General Leclerc's column, and other members of the Saif al-Nasr family were used as intermediaries.[38] By August 1943 General de Gaulle's Comité Français de Libération Nationale was claiming Fezzan's annexation to France, seeing in it the link between Tunisia and Chad.[39] And, according to Majid Khadduri, 'The Free French forces entered the area . . . in the hope that they might retain it permanently as part of the African region that included North and Equatorial Africa.'[40]

The French did much to integrate Fezzan administratively and financially into Algeria, thus isolating it from the rest of Libya.[41] Progressive French policy in economic and social affairs was accompanied by a distinctly repressive view of political activity; the fact remained that Fezzan was of considerable political and strategic importance to its new administrators. Under close French control, it formed a buffer, protecting the otherwise exposed flanks of French North, West and Equatorial Africa from hostile powers. At the same time, it provided the quickest overland route between Tunisia, Algeria, Niger and Chad. Track No. 5, linking Gabes in Tunisia to Lake Chad via Sebha, was the best route from North to Central Africa, while the airstrips at Ghadames, Ghat, Sebha and Brak offered useful staging facilities on the French African air network in an era of slow, short-haul transport aircraft.[42]

Although the French and British administrations were only supposed to be on a temporary 'care and maintenance' basis, they lasted for nearly nine years until Libya's future was finally decided by the United Nations. An independent Sanusi kingdom, bringing together Tripolitania, Cyrenaica and Fezzan, came into being in December 1951. The UN Commissioner, Dr Adrian Pelt, who supervised the constitutional preparations for Libyan independence in 1950–1, was convinced that the French were reluctant to give up their control of Fezzan because of the example its independence would set for nearby French African territories. 'As the years went by', he wrote, 'the impression spread that the French Government wanted to add the territory of the Fezzan . . . to one of the neighbouring African territories under French administration.'[43] Although any such ambitions were frustrated by Libya becoming independent, the French retained small garrisons at Sebha, Ghat and Ghadames.

In the early 1950s Paris still hoped for a base-leasing agreement in Fezzan such as Britain and the United States had negotiated elsewhere in Libya. But in the light of the growing crisis in the French Maghrib, particularly in Algeria, the government of independent Libya was extremely wary of French influence in Fezzan, and was willing to negotiate only on the basis of full evacuation. In August 1955, a treaty of 'friendship and good neighbourliness' provided for the withdrawal of French troops by December 1956. France was guaranteed certain residual air and overland transit rights, and the frontiers with French West and Equatorial Africa (Niger and Chad respectively) were confirmed. The treaty gave express recognition (but no description) to the existing frontier with Chad,[44] but made no mention of the 1935 Franco-Italian agreement and the territory that Libya would have gained from it had it ever come into force.[45]

By the end of 1960 the demands for independence reverberating through the continent had freed all the territories of French West and Equatorial Africa from formal French rule, although in practice France retained a remarkable degree of influence over them; for example, French troops continued to administer and police the unruly provinces of Borku, Ennedi and Tibesti up till 1964.

Thus Libya in 1951 and Chad in 1960 achieved independence as sovereign states. However, they practically turned their backs on each other as a result of being separated by their relatively short but very different experience of European rule. The federal Sanusi kingdom of Libya after 1951 looked to Britain and the United States for defence and indispensable financial support, and at the same time made the necessary gesture to Arab (and especially Egyptian) solidarity by joining the Arab League which was obsessed by the Palestine issue. At the same time, the outlook and alignments of the Republic of Chad were still those of the French colonial period. By 1960, two generations of newly-independent Libyans and Chadians had perhaps largely forgotten how close the trans-Saharan associations of their parents and grandparents had been before the colonial period.

## NOTES

1. Wright, *Libya: A Modern History*, pp. 17–18.
2. Nachtigal, *Sahara and Sudan*, vol. I, p. 212.
3. Coro, 'Un Documento Inedito'.
4. Rossi, *Storia*, p. 339.
5. See B.Lanne, *Tchad-Libye: La querelle des frontières*, Paris, 1982, p. 11; D.Porch, *The Conquest of the Sahara*, London, 1985, p. 127.
6. See Lanne, *Tchad-Libye*, p. 29.
7. For text, see *Bollettino della Società Africana d'Italia*, XIV, VII-VIII (July–August 1895); Rossi, *Storia*, pp. 341-2; see also *Le Sahara, Rapports et Contacts Humains*, map VII.
8. Lanne, *Tchad-Libye*, p. 29.
9. Fuglestad, *A History of Niger*, p. 51.
10. M.Muller, 'Frontiers: an Imported Concept: An Historical Review of the Creation and Consequences of Libya's Frontiers' in J.A. Allan (ed.), *Libya Since Independence*, p. 168.
11. See Rossi, *Storia*, p. 343.
12. See Morsy, *North Africa, 1800-1900*, p. 281.
13. Martin, *Muslim Brotherhoods*, p. 123.
14. Carbou, *La Région*, vol. II, p. 244.
15. Martel, 'La Politique Saharienne et Ottomane (1835–1918)' in *Le Sahara, rapports et contacts humains*, p. 136.

16. *Ibid.*, p. 137.
17. Zeltner, *Pages d'histoire*, p. 263.
18. Vischer, *Across the Sahara*, pp. 168-9.
19. Lanne, *Tchad-Libye*, pp. 37-40; Rossi, *Storia*, p. 346.
20. Rossi, *Storia*, p. 347, n.124.
21. Lanne, *Tchad-Libye*, p. 53.
22. Rossi, *Storia*, pp. 347-8.
23. See G. Ambrosini, *I Problemi del Mediterraneo*, Rome, 1937, p. 27.
24. J. Wright, 'Libya: Italy's Promised Land' in E. Joffe and K. McLachlan (eds), *Social and Economic Development of Libya*, Wisbech, 1982.
25. J. Miège, *L'Imperialismo Coloniale Italiano dal 1870 ai Giorni Nostri*, Milan, 1976, p. 107.
26. G.L. Beer, *African Questions at the Peace Conference*, New York, 1923, pp. 394-5.
27. See Lanne, *Tchad-Libye*, p. 137n.
28. *Ibid.*, pp. 159-68.
29. G. Ambrosini, 'Il Mediterraneo dal 1919 ad Oggi', *Gli Annali dell'Africa Italiana*, IV, I (1941).
30. Lanne, *Tchad-Libye*, pp. 171-2.
31. See Ingold, *L'Epopée Leclerc au Sahara*, Paris, 1948; Michelin map, *Sahara: L'Epopée Leclerc*, Paris, 1949.
32. G. Rodger, *Desert Journey*, London, 1944, p. 44.
33. See W. Kennedy-Shaw, *Long Range Desert Group*, London, 1945, pp. 229-31.
34. A. Clifford, *Three Against Rommel*, London, 1943, p. 355.
35. R. Rodd, *British Military Administration of Occupied Territories during the Years 1941-47*, London, 1948, p. 292.
36. *Ibid.*
37. *Ibid.*, p. 293.
38. M. Khadduri, *Modern Libya: A Study in Political Development*, Baltimore, 1963, p. 51.
39. J. Bessis, 'L'evolution des relations entre la Libye indépendante et la France', *The Maghreb Review*, vol.12, nos 1-2, 1987.
40. Khadduri, *Modern Libya*, p. 50.
41. N. Arsharuni, *Inostranniy Kapital v Livii, 1911-67*, Moscow, 1970, pp. 40-1.
42. Lanne, *Tchad-Libye*, p. 179; 'Libya', COI, London, 1960, p. 20.
43. A. Pelt, *Libyan Independence and the United Nations*, New Haven, 1970, p. 56.
44. I. Brownlie, *African Boundaries: A Legal and Diplomatic Encyclopaedia*, London, 1979, p. 121.
45. See Lanne, *Tchad-Libye*, p. 214.

# 7

# LIBYA IN CHAD

*'I am an opponent of the world order'* — Colonel Moammar Gadafi

Libya at independence in 1951 was a federation of three disparate and impoverished territories belonging neither to the Arab *Mashriq* from Egypt eastwards, nor to the Arab *Maghrib* from Tunisia westwards. But Cyrenaica, Tripolitania and Fezzan, in their uneasy union under the Sanusi crown, at least had the advantages of a common Arab or Arab-Berber heritage and a near-universal acceptance of Islam, the Arabic language and of Arab culture. A certain sense of nationalism had been gained during the 'anti-colonialist struggle' and national unity was in due course consolidated through the inflow of oil revenues and their more or less even distribution among the population.

Chad in 1960 was, by contrast, an artificial by-product of French political and strategic priorities elsewhere, brought into being largely because its constituent territories filled the 'left-over spaces' between the three wings of the French empire in Africa. So long as the French were in control, Chad had a certain enforced cohesion; but the divisions and tensions between inherently incompatible peoples and cultures were still apparent. The most obvious divide was between a nomadic-pastoral Muslim north and centre and a settled animist-Christian south. While not originally responsible for such divisions, France exploited rather than ameliorated them. A main source of future friction was the fact that the black southerners, protected by the French from enslavement, were more amenable to French tutelage than the disgruntled northerners, who positively resisted French modernising efforts.[1] Probably the main beneficiaries of French rule were the Sara, a group of about ten mostly non-Muslim farming and fishing clans with related languages and cultures living along the Chari and Logone river valleys of the south and representing nearly one-third of the population.[2] They took whatever opportunities the French offered for economic, social and, eventually, political advancement. With the enforced introduction of cotton cultivation into the more fertile southern lands in the 1930s, the Saras of so-called *Tchad-utile* became economically the most productive sector of an otherwise largely impoverished economy. As the country moved towards independence in the 1950s, the Sara came to dominate the army, the civil administration and the most powerful national political organisation, the Parti Progressiste Tchadien of Gabriel Lisette and François Tombalbaye.

The many tensions apparent in Chadian society at independence in

1960 had more complex origins than the dominance of the southern blacks at the expense of the northern and eastern Muslims who had previously exploited them. Nevertheless, southern bureaucratic insensitivity in the Muslim north and centre, together with widespread refusal to accept this post-colonial southern ascendancy, precipitated a national crisis. On the withdrawal of the French garrisons and military administration from Borku, Ennedi and Tibesti in 1964, they were replaced by the Chadian army and authorities. But the newcomers had not the tact, the objectivity or the experience of the French in dealing with the independent-minded northern peoples. The north resented these unschooled, inexperienced and usually corrupt representatives of a southern, Sara-dominated administration which owed its legitimacy to the original French military conquest – a legitimacy that successive post-1960 French governments were prepared to uphold – rather than to any inherent merit or superiority.

It took less than a decade after independence for a black president and black bureaucracy in the south to avenge the injury and humiliations that their ancestors had suffered at Arab hands by reducing the authority of the sultans and chiefs to their lowest level thus far.[3]

In October 1965 there was a tax revolt among the Moubi peasants of Guera in the southern Sahel. Brutal government repression prompted further rebellions in Wadai in 1966 and in Salamat in 1967. There also occurred a series of confrontations between representatives of the central government and Tebu in Tibesti, which led to a Tebu uprising in 1966 and the Tebu leader Derde Oueddei Kichidemi seeking asylum in Kufra from a conflict in which four of his five sons were to be killed. But in those early years unrest was more deep-seated in the Sahelian centre and east than in the north. The rebellion was at first largely a series of peasant revolts (in French historical terms a *jacquerie*); but it assumed a certain unity and ideology with the formation at Nyala in south-west Sudan in June 1966 of the Front de Libération Nationale du Tchad (Frolinat), a classical anti-imperialist liberation movement. Although its support was regional, Muslim and ethnic, Frolinat never advocated the seccession of the north, nor the 'Arab'-Muslim domination of the whole country. Frolinat was usually riven by internal rifts; it was never able to control all the rebel groups; and the political and military leaderships were often disunited. Its founder, Ibrahim Abatcha, was killed in the field in 1968, and in the ensuing power-struggle a former minister of education, Dr Abba Siddick, emerged as leader in 1969, with his headquarters in Tripoli. His rise to power, as the man who 'controlled the purse strings and . . . the middleman between foreign sympathetic donors to the movement and the actual fighting forces in the field',[4] marked a shift in

Frolinat's main source of support from Sudan to Libya.

For in the meantime, there had been much more dangerous revolts in Borku, Ennedi and Tibesti. In early 1969 the government had lost control to Tebu rebels in all but the main settlements of the three northern provinces. By then, all northern, eastern and central Chad was in a greater or lesser state of insurrection, and de Gaulle's successor, President Georges Pompidou, authorised French military intervention to support the Tombalbaye regime. He did so because Chad had from the beginning of the century played an essential part in French strategic thinking, originally as the junction between the three main components of the French African empire, and as a buffer inhibiting further European colonial expansion. Even in post-1960 Africa, Chad's central geographical position gave it a critical role in the French scheme of things. It provided telecommunications and air transit facilities to a former colonial power that still had unusually close ties with nearly all its former African possessions, and which was forming close relationships with other African states. Successive French administrations needed to maintain stability in Chad because of the repercussions the fall of a French-supported government might be expected to have elsewhere in Francophone Africa, and especially in neighbouring territories such as the Central African Republic, Cameroun and, above all, Niger with its rich uranium deposits. The 'domino theory' prevalent in the period of the Vietnam war influenced successive French governments, especially Gaullist ones. For them, Chad had a particular historical significance, and they needed to be seen to support the central Chadian authority, no matter how obnoxious it might be in practice. Failure to do so could have destroyed the credibility of France within all its former African possessions, which still looked to Paris, under guarantees given at the time of independence, as the ultimate guarantor of their political and military stability against internal or external threats.

Libyan reactions to, and involvement in all such events during the rule of King Idris were discreet. Idris was old and realistic enough to appreciate that after the French conquest of central and northern Chad, the Italian conquest of Libya, and the destruction of the Sanusi order and all its works on both sides of the Sahara, there was no hope of reviving Sanusi influence on the scale it had had in the late nineteenth century. But Chadian issues were still of obvious concern to the Libyan Tebu, and indeed to all Libyans who saw the Chadian conflict as a struggle between true believers and the infidels in power in Fort Lamy,[5] or who through personal, tribal, commercial or other connections were familiar with the peoples and territories of Chad. King Idris himself had cause for some concern with Chadian affairs, not least because his own royal guard was largely recruited from Tebu of the former Sanusi centre at Kufra. Indeed, after the Derde of Tibesti sought exile in Kufra and later in Tripoli in 1966, Libya became 'the centre as well as the base and the sanctuary of the Tebu rebels'.[6] Even if little moral and material help was given them in Libya, Frolinat and its leader Dr Abba Siddick were allowed to operate from royalist Tripoli in the late 1960s, although relations were never close between Siddick and the royalist regime.[7] The latter always had 'correct' relations with Fort Lamy, and in 1969 reached a series of cooperation agreements with the Tombalbaye government over communications, the upkeep of Islamic institutions in Chad and the status of Chadian workers in Libya.[8]

Such cautiously ambiguous policy was cast aside after Moammar Gadafi and his Free Officers overthrew the Sanusi monarchy and proclaimed a Libyan republic and revolution in September 1969. By then the course of the Chadian rebellion had isolated Borku, Ennedi and Tibesti economically from the rest of Chad, leaving southern Libya as their sole source of supply, welfare and livelihood.[9] It has been argued that relations between the new Libyan regime and the Tombalbaye administration should have been naturally close because the Tebu rebels in Chad had been associated with the royalist Sanusi;[10] but such simple logic rarely applies in modern Arab and African politics, and the young military and revolutionary rulers in Tripoli found more compelling reasons to continue supporting the rebels. Although the royalist regime had been discreet in its support for Muslim Chadian dissidents, revolutionary Libya was quite blatant about the help it gave – or claimed to give – to perceived 'forces of anti-imperialism' in Chad, as elsewhere. The regime was willing to commit its oil revenues to fulfilling a self-imposed, if largely ineffectual 'sacred duty towards all revolutions'. The resultant crisis in relations between Tripoli and Fort Lamy nevertheless took nearly two years to mature.

On 27 August 1971 the Tombalbaye regime foiled a Libyan attempt to mount a *coup d'état*, possibly timed to sabotage a reconciliation between the government and Muslim opposition leaders.[11] Chad broke off diplomatic relations and air links with Libya, invited all anti-Gadafi groups to establish themselves in Fort Lamy, and laid claim to Fezzan on the grounds of 'historical rights'. Libya retaliated by officially recognising Frolinat and providing it with training bases. By October 1971 the Chadian Foreign Minister, Baba Hassan, was condemning what he termed Libya's 'expansionist ideas' before the United Nations General Assembly and drawing attention to the inaccurate maps being circulated by Tripoli,[12] a fair warning of what was to come. But in April 1972, both sides were for different reasons ready to reach a 'tactical armistice' in which the French role may have been more one of persuasion than of mediation,[13] although the ostensible mediator was President Diori Hamani of Niger. Diplomatic relations were resumed, and in return for renewed Libyan friendship, withdrawal of official support for Frolinat (Abba Siddick was moved from Tripoli to Algiers), and the pledge of substantial financial aid, President Tombalbaye was persuaded to break off relations with Israel, which in fact had no important interests in Chad. But Tombalbaye seems to have been persuaded of the advantages (perhaps to himself rather than to his country) of accepting the Libyan occupation of the Aozou Strip.[14] This transfer of territory prompted remarkably little reaction at the time, despite the fact that it put into effect the terms of the unratified 1935 Franco-Italian agreement by moving the southern frontier of revolutionary Libya at least 100 km. towards Central Africa, 'and was one of the first indications of Gadafi's territorial ambitions'.[15] Libyan forces moved into the strip in mid-1973 and built an air-base near Aozou defended by ground-to-air missiles. A civil administration was set up (attached, significantly, to Kufra, although both Sebha and Murzuk were nearer)[16] which brought the benefits of Libyan citizenship and the welfare state to the Strip's few thousand poverty-stricken people. Thereafter, Tripoli issued maps showing the strip as the sovereign territory of the Libyan Arab Republic, or Socialist People's Libyan Arab Jamahariyah,[17] the name by which the country was known after the establishment of 'people's power' in 1977.

The terms by which Libya gained the Aozou Strip remain obscure, and there has since been speculation concerning a 'secret agreement' between President Tombalbaye and Colonel Gadafi. But it was only in 1988 that the Libyans revealed such an agreement to support their claim (the thirteen years that had passed since Tombalbaye's death in the military coup that overthrew him in 1975 might reasonably have been thought a long enough time to absolve them from any further obligation to keep it secret).[18] Bernard Lanne believes that there never was a formal agreement, secret or otherwise, to cede Aozou, and that Tombalbaye had his own reasons for keeping quiet about the foreign occupation of part of his own country.[19] Ian Brownlie concluded that:

In the absence of any formulated Libyan claim, it is impossible to state the issues of principle, if any, which are involved. It is possible that the Libyan government is relying, mistakenly, upon the alignment of the Franco-Italian agreement of 1935 which remained unratified.[20]

After the 1972 agreement, Libyan aid for the Chadian rebels became less overt, but they continued to find sanctuary in Fezzan and to receive arms through Kufra. Only in 1977, when the Aozou Strip had become an advance base for deeper Libyan involvements in Chad, was the issue brought before the United Nations and the

Organisation of African Unity by the regime of General Félix Malloum, which had overthrown and killed President Tombalbaye in April 1975 in a coup mounted by the Sara military and civil establishment. The Malloum regime ended some of the worst abuses of the Tombalbaye administration; it also tried to persuade the northern and central rebels that their struggle was no longer necessary, and brought about the first of several evacuations of French forces; yet such efforts were frustrated, not least by Libya and its Chadian clients. By then, effective control of the main rebel movements had passed to two northerners, Goukouni Oueddei and Hissene Habre. Oueddei was the last surviving son of the Derde of Tibesti, while Habre was a French-educated Daza-speaker of the Anakaza clan of Borku. Their origins and backgrounds were close enough for them to understand each other's motives, yet not so close that they were able to work together. Habre was a brilliant guerrilla leader who only later advocated the re-unification of Chad under his political leadership. As a hater of Libya, he was obliged to look elsewhere for essential outside support. By contrast, Goukouni Oueddei was primarily a politician, prepared to work closely with Libya, either because he could not see, or could not attract, more suitable foreign associates. For years he would not allow his own resentment at the continued occupation of the Aozou Strip to undermine his own relations with the Libyans.

Tripoli by 1978 was actively supporting Oueddei in Chad. General Malloum claimed that 'thousands' of Libyan troops had invaded his country, penetrating as far as the central provinces of Batha, Kanem and Wadai. In March 1979 the Malloum administration collapsed after fighting spread to the capital, N'Djamena. Mainly through Nigerian and Libyan efforts, government and rebel factions came together in a Transitional Government of National Unity (GUNT) under Goukouni's presidency. Although it included Hissene Habre as defence minister, GUNT also incorporated enough pro-Libyan elements to satisfy Gadafi. Ten years of intervention in Chadian affairs had at last ended Sara administrative and military domination, giving the Tebu once again the historical role of arbiters of the state, and had resulted in a broad-based regime that would recognise Libyan interests in general and the continued occupation of the Aozou Strip in particular.

In 1980, however, Hissene Habre, with Sudanese and Egyptian help, rallied his loyal forces in the east and north to challenge President Goukouni for power. The president had by then negotiated the withdrawal of the last of the French troops who might have protected him: all but medical personnel had departed by mid-May. Habre's relentless advance on N'Djamena from the east so alarmed Goukouni that he signed a defence pact with Libya allowing him to call on military help, and thereby legitimise the Libyan military presence. By the end of 1980, an estimated 7,000 Libyan regular troops and 7,000 members of the 'Islamic Legion' – raised by Libya from several Muslim countries – had confined Habre's forces to the frontier zones of Darfur and forced him into exile.

Gadafi's military intervention in Chad in 1980–1 demonstrated an impressive logistical ability and gave him his first military victory (in striking contrast with the debâcle he had suffered in Uganda in 1979) and a substantial political achievement in Africa.[21] Libya seemed to have replaced a French military presence at the geographical heart of the continent with one of its own. Having thus kept President Goukouni in power, Tripoli sought its reward in the declaration of a Libyan-Chadian union in January 1981,[22] with Gadafi proclaiming that the common borders were open, and insisting on the Arab and Muslim character of Chad and its people.[23] If Libyan military success in central Chad had dismayed many African states, the intended union (which was never allowed to take effect) was the cause of widespread alarm, especially in West and Central Africa, where 'unification' was generally interpreted as a euphemism for Libyan annexation.[24] Led by Nigeria and prompted by France and the United States, the Organisation of African Unity finally arranged for the withdrawal of Libyan troops and their replacement by an African peacekeeping force in December 1981. The Libyan withdrawal left a military vacuum, and this was swiftly filled by Habre. From their bases in Darfur, his rebuilt forces advanced across central Chad, unopposed by any OAU troops, and in June 1982 took N'Djamena. Goukouni's forces withdrew to and consolidated their control of the northern provinces with Tripoli's help, and the president himself went into exile in Libya. At a time when Gadafi was chairman-designate of the OAU, his attempts to have GUNT re-endorsed as the legitimate government of Chad at the organisation's summit meeting in Tripoli collapsed in November 1982. The necessary two-thirds quorum of African leaders failed to turn up to support the Libyan position on Chad, the majority preferring to recognise Habre's presidency. Gadafi was thereby denied the OAU chairmanship.

President Habre had in the meantime been reuniting central and southern Chad under his rule, while all the country north of the 16th parallel remained under a GUNT administration, which relied heavily on Libyan support. As Habre consolidated his authority with the help and recognition of the French administration of President François Mitterand, and the majority of African states, so the separated north took on the character of a Libyan satellite, a role estimated to have cost Tripoli some $2 million a day.[25]

The effective division of the country into two hostile entities seemed to be in danger of becoming permanent. In 1983, incursions by Goukouni's Libyan-supported forces into the central provinces controlled by Habre led to renewed intervention by French troops: they established a security belt across the country, roughly on the 16th parallel, which seemed to acknowledge the pre-existing division of the country. But while the French willingly defended Chad south of the 16th parallel against northern incursion, they refused to become actively involved in Habre's plans to invade the north: they were not prepared to fight on his behalf to oust the Libyans, who were said to have up to 11,000 men in Borku, Ennedi and Tibesti, in order to bring the whole country under his administration. At the end of 1984 both France and Libya, which had recognised the danger to their wider mutual interests in a military clash in Chad, agreed to withdraw their forces, although there is no proof that the Libyans ever did so. But further Libyan-supported incursions across the 16th parallel brought the French forces back early in 1986, together with increased United States military aid for the Habre regime. A military stalemate ensued and lasted till early 1987 when President Habre, his men re-trained by France and equipped by both France and the United States, took the initiative of invading and reconquering the north with his own forces. The Reagan administration was naturally enthusiastic, seeing any attack on the Libyan position in Chad as part of its own wider anti-Gadafi campaign. The French gave some logistical and air support to Habre's forces, but had little direct part in the military engagements. Many northern fighters defected to join Habre, and Goukouni Oueddei himself, having at last quarrelled with the Libyans, was replaced as president of GUNT. By August 1987 a series of devastating Chadian victories had restored nearly all the territory north of the 16th parallel to N'Djamena's control, with only the Aozou Strip still under Libyan occupation. In less than nine months, the whole Libyan position in Chad, built up at such expense and with so great effort over nearly twenty years, appeared to be in ruins, with a hostile regime in control of almost the whole country pledged to liberate the Aozou Strip. The evident success of France's patient policy in Chad seemed to be in inverse proportion to the scale of Libya's failure, but the events of 1987 were not necessarily as decisive as they appeared to be at the time.

Successive Libyan interventions in Chad since the early 1970s, and their very scale, have been almost unique in post-independence Africa. They have more closely resembled the obsessive behaviour of a superpower than that of a developing country, even one as rich in oil revenues as Libya was up to the early 1980s. The inexplicably large quantities of Soviet military hardware purchased by the Gadafi regime were not used to achieve the long-proclaimed objective of liberating Palestine, but rather to project Libyan power into Chad and towards Central Africa. Such ventures have been costly in financial terms, in terms of casualties (from a population of barely 3 million) and, after the military disasters of 1987, in terms of lost prestige and military credibility. Yet a consistent, purposeful policy with specific, worthwhile objectives has not always been readily discernible behind these actions. Libyans have fought and died and squandered their oil revenues on adventures for which they may have been hard-pressed to give any coherent or reasonable justification. Apart from the deliberate occupation of the Aozou Strip in 1973, Tripoli's role seems either to have been a series of hasty reactions to perceived threats from within Chad itself, or the ill-considered attempt to seize opportunities for local or regional advantage.

It is, of course, understandable that Libya, as a direct neighbour, should have been interested in and concerned about the course of events when it became clear soon after Independence in 1960 that Chad could not sustain the artificial unity imposed on its diverse peoples by the French. The close ethnic, tribal, family and personal relationships, the long historical, linguistic, religious, cultural, commercial and other connections between the peoples of Chad and Libya – for some of whom the modern state boundaries are indeed an artificial barrier – provide further substantial explanations for Libya's persistent interest in post-Independence Chad. The French commentator Jacques Latrémolière noted:

All this does not suffice to confer membership of these regions on the Libyan Jamahariya beyond reasonable doubt; but it does show that its claims to possess them are, at any rate, more soundly based than those of colonial France, and thus those of successor Chadian governments.[26]

Further explanations, if not necessarily justifications, for the scope and scale of Libyan intervention since the early 1970s perhaps need to be sought from an even broader spectrum than the record of human relationships between the two sides of the central Sahara.

Since the 1969 revolution, Libyan foreign policy has largely reflected the ideals, visions and inconsistencies of Colonel Moammar Gadafi,[27] coloured by the notions of Arab nationalism and unity of his mentor, the late President Gamal Abd-al-Nasser of Egypt. Gadafi's background led to his own unusual perceptions of his country and of its place in Africa and the wider world – perceptions not necessarily so unusual to fellow-Libyans. He was born in 1942 in the low tent of his semi-nomadic family, pitched in the open pre-desert south of Sirte. Although the Sirtica was then administratively part of both

Tripolitania and Cyrenaica, it is historically the ungovernable domain of the great warring nomadic tribes of the Libyan heartland. By virtue of being born there, Gadafi was neither a Tripolitanian, a Cyrenaican nor even a Fezzani, but a *bedu* of the open desert which is common to all Libya.[28] The closest associates of his own tribe, the Gadadfa, have long been the Awlad Slaiman, the Orfella and the Magarba, peoples who never freely submitted to the Karamanlis, the Turks or to the Italians. Around the time of independence the Saif al-Nasr family, traditional leaders of the Awlad Slaiman, had ensured its own continued dominance of Fezzanese affairs by becoming part of the Sanusi patronage system within the new federal kingdom. Lesser tribespeople of the Sirtica and Fezzan may have felt themselves denied the spreading benefits of the new-found oil wealth from the late 1950s onwards, but their horizons and contacts remained broad.

The natural boundaries of the nomadic environment in which Moammar Gadafi grew up reached further than the familiar oases of the nearby Giofra or northern Fezzan, or even the homelands of Gadadfa kinsmen and other exiled Libyans in Kanem,[29] for they were at least as wide as the Sahara itself. To Gadafi the nomad, and to those who shared his outlook, the international boundaries of the Sahara had no historical basis or practical justification, since they were merely the artificial barriers erected by European imperialism to divide the naturally united peoples of the desert from each other. The Sahara and the lands around it were an entity common to all the peoples of the Great Desert. Moreover, according to Gadafi's thinking, Saharan ethnic divisions did not exist either: Berbers, Tuareg, Tebu and others related to them could all be called 'Muslim Arabs' with a common 'Arab' ancestry and (at least in the case of Berber speech and the Tuareg dialect, *Tamacheq*) a common linguistic heritage of South Arabian (Himyaritic) origin.[30] Such lines of reasoning led Gadafi to assert in 1971 that 'the people of Chad . . . are Muslims of Arab origin'[31] and in 1981 that 'eastern and south-eastern Chad are entirely Arab, and a large section of this Chadian people [is] Arab by origin and race, while the overwhelming number is of Muslim and Arab culture in the pervading culture of Chad.'[32]

While such claims are not altogether true, they are not wholly false, even if they do tend to ignore ethnic, linguistic, cultural and historical realities, as well as the images and aspirations of those concerned. Thus when Gadafi further claimed at the time of the abortive Chad-Libya union in January 1981 that 'the borders are open between the two countries', the implication was that all Chad and its peoples (not only the 'Arabs' and 'Muslims') were again as exposed and receptive to Libyan penetration and exploitation as they had been 100 years earlier. It seemed at the time that the Libyan leader was determined to reverse all the processes of the past eighty or so years brought about by the French imperial conquest of Central Africa, including restoration of Libya's traditional links with its natural hinterland extending towards Lake Chad that had been broken by that conquest.

Colonel Gadafi's pan-Arab, pan-Islamic vision reflected a fervid anti-imperialism fired by grievances for perceived wrongs done to the Arabs, Africans and other subject peoples during the time of colonial rule. Libya has thus long been the victim of the villainy of others, and if the Italians were objects of particular opprobrium for their colonisation of the Libyan people and the destruction of the Sanusi order and all its works in the north, a rather different official resentment was directed against the French. They were held responsible for past and continuing interference with lands and peoples that had formerly been within largely unchallenged Libyan (Sanusi and/or tribal) spheres of influence and exploitation; they had, moreover, tried to annex Fezzan before Independence, and they had failed to make over the Aozou Strip to its 'rightful' owners when they could have done so in the 1950s.

As leader of the revolution that overthrew the Sanusi monarchy in September 1969, Gadafi was necessarily critical of the many perceived shortcomings of the Sanusi political system. Under the revolution, the last vestiges of Sanusi spiritual influence in Libya disappeared;[33] but, typical of the inconsistencies of logic found in Libyan revolutionary practice, the heroes of the Sanusi resistance to the Italian conquest were never denied their official acknowledgement because their struggle endowed the revolution with its own historical credentials. The spread and influence of the Sanusi in Chad and elsewhere, and in particular their defence of the Saharan-Sahelian *Dar al-Islam* against European imperialism, provided an unacknowledged yet no doubt compelling inspiration for Libyan revolutionary ambitions in and beyond the Sahara, even if Gadafi's message of popular Islamic revolution was less readily acceptable than the Sanusi practice of spiritual guidance and impartial arbitration had been a century earlier. Gadafi never appeared specifically to exploit any residual historical regard for Sanusism and its theocracy that might still have existed in north and central Chad. In fact, reliance on historical precedent in the promotion of contemporary interests may in this particular milieu have had the undesirable side-effect of reminding southern Chadians and other black Africans of their former exploitation and enslavement by their northern neighbours, including the Sanusi. It is significant that the official media of the Habre administration during the battles in northern Chad in 1987 was referring to the 'slave-driving Libyans'. There was, moreover, little evidence of the Libyan leader's specific concern for the well-being of Libyan exiles in Chad, and especially of those tribal kinsfolk who had migrated to Kanem with the Awlad Slaiman in the 1840s and again about 1930. This was despite the fact that he has claimed that one-tenth of all Chadian Arabs are of Libyan origin.[34]

Furthermore, there was not as much direct Libyan exploitation of the undoubted 'Arab' character of up to one-third of the Chadian people as there might have been. In all the years of civil strife, the Chadian Arabs have not emerged as a separate, identifiable minority with common grievances and specific objectives of their own. Only in the late 1970s did Ahmad Acyl's Conseil Démocratique de la Révolution, originally a purely Arab movement, seem to represent the political revival of the great nomadic groups of the Sahel. As such, the CDR was greatly assisted by the Libyans, who were 'more at ease in dealing with people speaking the same language and belonging to the same culture as themselves'.[35] But the CDR proved a disappointing agent and never emerged as a specifically 'Arab' group capable of promoting specifically 'Arab' interests either in combat or in negotiation.[36] The Chadian Arabs have never been sufficiently united in their socio-economic structures or in their objectives to have achieved an identifiable 'Arab' protest; for, despite their comparable numbers, they failed in every way to match the Saras' domination of the post-Independence republic. Similarly, the agents of Libyan penetration were not necessarily the Libyan exile communities of Kanem, or the Zuwaya and Magarba 'Fezzani' traders who have long been familiar (yet always alien) figures in the marketplaces of Chad.[37] When the Arabs took part in the many manifestations of civil strife that occurred from the mid-1960s onwards (ranging from traditional banditry and cattle-stealing to outright civil war), they tended to do so as part of a more generalised and 'Muslim' or 'northern' protest, displaying little separate 'Arab' identity.

Yet the Chadian Sahel is an important Arab centre. At least one million Chadians have Arabic as their first or second language, many more than can speak French. But Chadian Arabs have not really become part of the political concept of the 'Arab World', or are even generally accepted as such in the way that even the superficially Arabised non-Arab peoples of Somalia and Djibouti have been since they joined the Arab League in the 1970s. For Chad's Arabs are, for a national minority, perhaps too closely inbred with other, non-Arab neighbours, and at the same time too remote from the mainstreams of modern Arab culture, society and politics to be able to claim a recognised place in the 'Nasserist' Arab nation, despite Gadafi's expressed belief in the essential unity of the 'Arab' peoples of Chad and Libya. And a serious claim to such an association with the wider Arab world would no doubt alarm non-Arab Chadians, and especially Christian and animist southerners, as likely to expose them yet again to trans-Saharan influences that they have long had good reason to fear. Thus Libyan interests have instead been projected deep into Chad by the Tebu and their close ethnic associates. The Tebu had never been integrated into the independent Chadian state in its first twenty years of existence, but had remained dangerously detached on its fringes, just as they had largely remained outside, but with a varying degree of interest in, other political entities in the Chad region since the Middle Ages. In the late 1970s the Tebu again played the historical role of decisive interference in the re-ordering of a weak and ineffectual central authority,[38] overthrowing the Sara establishment. They did so with the support of Libya, and the Tebu Goukouni Oueddei broke with historical tradition by gaining supreme authority as president. But in the longer term it was to be Tripoli's misfortune that it supported the weaker of the two rival Tebu contenders for power; Goukouni Oueddei and Hissene Habre were incapable of sharing that power between them.

This timely exploitation of the Tebu revolt and the state of widespread dissidence and anarchy in central Chad in the early 1970s gave revolutionary Libya its initial role of arbiter of Chadian affairs. It was perhaps the failure of Gadafi's policies in the Arab World, and especially his failure to bring about the Arab unity that he believed to be the essential pre-requisite for the liberation of Palestine, that in 1972–3 prompted his interest in non-Arab Africa as a source of alliances and potential influence. A campaign to persuade the Africans to treat the Libyans, and indeed all Arabs, as natural allies and a potential source of economic and military aid, started in Uganda, where General Idi Amin Dada had come to power in a military *coup* in January 1971. The fact that Amin was a Muslim suggested to Gadafi that he was worth befriending as a possible leader of resurgent Islam in East Africa, and a useful ally of the Arab cause. Amin cooperated, breaking off previously close ties with Israel in 1972. The Israeli presence in Chad had since become one of the issues in the diplomatic crisis between Gadafi and President Tombalbaye in August 1971, and expulsion of the Israelis was part of the arrangement by which Tombalbaye was persuaded to part with the Aozou Strip in April 1972. After these initial successes, Tripoli's diplomatic offensive against the considerable Israeli presence in Black Africa became more ambitious, with most Black African states at the time of the 1973 Middle East war being persuaded of the advantages of abandoning their neutrality on the Arab-Israeli issue and ridding their continent of Zionist influence in favour of support for the Arabs.[39] By the end of 1973, nearly thirty Black African states had broken with Israel, and most of these had opened relations with Tripoli, thereby briefly offering a vision of almost the whole continent eager for the benefits of Libyan friendship.

But the vision was an illusion, with Libya's African ambitions eventually becoming more closely concentrated on Chad and other largely impoverished, ethnically disparate and partly-Islamised states of the sub-Saharan Sahel – Niger, Mali, Upper Volta (Burkina Faso) and Senegal. Despite their close ties with France, after fifteen years of independence these states seemed to Tripoli to represent a power vacuum, ready to absorb the Libyan message of revolutionary Islam.

One credential claimed by the Libyan revolution was the Islam-inspired struggle against Italian Christian colonialism, British and United States military imperialism, Zionism (particularly in Africa) and other external 'threats'. As the revolution gained strength after 1969, it took an ever wider role in the Islamic World. Using Libya's 'great store of spiritual and material wealth', it

explored all the avenues of Islamic activity from the dissemination of the teachings of Islam and the setting up of cultural and religious centres to the actual solving of concrete problems of Muslim minorities throughout the world . . . the revolution became an important factor in the world struggle, whether that struggle be between imperialism and the liberation movements . . . or between Islamic minorities and dominant powers.[40]

Yet Gadafi has always used Islam selectively as a foreign policy tool. It is only one of several weapons in his revolutionary armoury, along-side Arabism, positive neutrality and a pragmatic assessment of political, strategic and other interests.[41] He has, after all, tended to regard Islam as a singularly *Arab* religion, revealed in a purely Arab milieu (Arabia) to an Arab (the Prophet Mohammad), through an Arab medium (the Holy Koran); non-Arab nations and peoples, fired by an Islam that was not destined for them, have left their own imprints on it.[42] While insisting that Christianity was not the religion of the Arabs,[43] Gadafi also provoked controversy by suggesting that it was not the religion of Africans either.

Islam, common to all northern and most of central Chad, has obviously been an important factor in the Libyan role there. Gadafi has identified himself with what he sees as the struggle of all Chadian Muslims (whom he counts as a clear majority) against an alien and oppressive minority of Christians and animists, supported by France and, at a greater distance, by the even more malign power of the United States. According to Gadafi, 'The people of Chad . . . are Muslims of Arab origin. They are being subject to plots, divisions and minority rule.'[44] Thus the Chadian conflict became for him part of the wider defence of *Dar al-Islam* against hostile foreign forces: western imperialism in general, or in particular the continuing French presence, both of which seemed to him to be intent on subjugating and even destroying Islam, an opinion which ignored the fact that Islam made great progress in Africa in the colonial period.[45] Moreover,

Gadafi's Third International Theory, seeking a just middle way between domination by atheistic Soviet communism and American materialistic capitalism, was also supposed to offer the same militant universalism as Libyan Islam.[46]

Such an Islamic-reformist appeal may have made the desired impression on some Muslims living on or near the critical north-south divide between Africa's predominantly Islamic and predominantly Christian-animist societies. But such appeals are, conversely, a source of constant concern to the region's non-Muslims, and especially to the small, if still influential, Christian minorities. The confessional divide across Sahelian Africa has become dangerously apparent in such recent regional conflicts as the various stages of the Sudanese civil war, the Biafran war, and other inter-confessional strife in Nigeria; and Libya has undoubtedly tried to take advantage of it.[47] Instruments of the Libyan Islamic role in Africa have, in addition to economic and social aid, included an association for the propagation of Islam (the 'Call of Islam Society'), founded in 1972 to train and deploy Muslim missionaries,[48] and the so-called 'Islamic Legion'. This was largely recruited from African Muslims (mostly volunteers, but some apparently coerced) to reinforce the Palestinian *fidayin* and to support Islamic movements struggling against 'oppression'. The legion, several thousand strong, became most closely involved in Chad, where its fighting record was most noted for its ineptitude.

Colonel Gadafi's almost single-handed direction of Libyan foreign policy since 1969 has been characterised by his country's depiction of itself as the victim of malign aggression and subversion by others. This image has been cultivated to justify the excesses of Libya's own international behaviour.[49] The experience of Italian colonialism and the former British Military Administration and military bases had by the 1970s become part of the historical memory that could be manipulated to enhance the image of a small, heroic nation constantly struggling for survival. But the United States, Israel, France and their Arab and African 'allies' were still shown to be constantly threatening Libya. As Gadafi declared in 1971, 'We are threatened by the imperialist powers. The conspiracy in Chad is part of the imperialist plan to encircle the Libyan Arab Republic.'[50]

France, as the colonial power responsible for creating Chad, and still long after independence exercising a series of interlocking interests there, became Libya's main rival for the control of this strategically sensitive area near the geographical heart of Africa. Yet for all their conflicting interests in Chad, in other parts of Africa, and in the Middle East, Paris and Tripoli always avoided any military or diplomatic confrontation that could have jeopardised mutually beneficial relations elsewhere.

The Libyans have an unusually bitter and paranoid memory of their colonial experiences shared by few other formerly colonised peoples, and certainly not by other Italian colonial subjects. Libyans, and especially Colonel Gadafi, thus seemed to find difficulty in understanding how some ex-colonial peoples could still have a close and beneficial relationship with the former colonial power. As Gadafi asserted in a speech in 1981, 'France has no friends [in Africa]. It has colonial interests.'[51] Of all the former colonial powers in Africa, France alone maintained an extraordinarily close, even at times dominant, relationship with most of its former Black African territories after their independence. Up to the mid-1970s, Chad provided one of the three main French military bases in Africa, with Air Base 142 at Fort Lamy (N'Djamena) housing the special forces intended for rapid intervention elsewhere.[52] As other outside powers, and particularly revolutionary Libya, became more closely involved in the widening civil war, Chad tested to the full the commitments of successive administrations in Paris to those in N'Djamena.

Failure by France to be seen to give support and to defend successive Chadian central administrations from their internal and external enemies would have undermined credibility with all former African possessions. For any failure in Chad would inevitably have brought into question the value of agreements with French African colonies reinforced by the stationing of nearly 20,000 French troops in five African countries, plus naval forces in the Indian Ocean. The ascendancy of any faction in N'Djamena actually or potentially hostile to French interests not only alarmed Chad's immediate pro-French neighbours (Niger, Cameroun and the Central African Republic) and other like-minded states nearby, but also seemed to threaten French prestige, and possibly western interests as a whole, throughout Black Africa.

In broad terms, two of the six states sharing land frontiers with Libya (Egypt and Algeria) are 'strong' and populous, unlikely to be readily subverted by Libyan-inspired revolution. But three others (Chad, Niger and Tunisia) seem much more vulnerable, and France for differing reasons exercises a close interest in all three. France considers Tunisia an essential element in the stability of the Maghrib and the Central Mediterranean, and long-term concerns with Tunisia's vulnerability to revolutionary Libya were not necessarily lessened by the enforced retirement of the senile President Habib Bourguiba in 1987. The Niger Republic, besides providing uranium for the French nuclear programme, was considered to be at least as vulnerable as Tunisia to the ambitions of Libya, which has territorial claims in the far north-east (in effect the extension of the Aozou Strip) and pretensions to the leadership of the Tuareg of the Nigerien Sahara.

Apart from Chad, Libya and France have clashed elsewhere in Africa, when the French have considered their vital interests, as well as those of a particular 'client' state, to have been threatened, most notably in the Central African Republic in 1979 and in Tunisia in 1980. But, despite such tensions, Paris has managed to maintain a working relationship with Tripoli, refusing, for instance, to be associated with President Ronald Reagan's international anti-Gadafi campaign. In doing so, successive French administrations seemed to be concerned to protect fairly important – and potentially vital – economic relations with Libya, including arms supplies, and to secure other important relations in the Middle East, while acting on the assumption that a working relationship with the Libyan regime offered better chances for urging moderation than no relationship at all.[53] Nevertheless, surprising French reticence over some episodes, notably the occupation of the Aozou Strip, led some observers to suppose that Paris and Tripoli had on various occasions colluded over Chad. Tacit French recognition of a Libyan sphere of influence in the north, at least, might have been a reasonable exchange for reciprocal recognition by Libya of French interests in the south.[54]

Yet Libya's ultimate desire to take over the French position throughout Chad seemed to extend naturally to other Sahelian states, even if they were not as internally vulnerable. An amorphous Libyan objective in sub-Saharan Africa seems to have been the western states system: the European political, economic and social values and practices bequeathed by colonialism, maintained more or less intact after Independence, and thus representing the very *status quo* that Gadafi wished to overthrow.[55] Destabilisation of the inherently weak Chadian state thus promised to enhance Libyan interests in Chad itself (as the 'weak link' in the western states system in sub-Saharan Africa) and to provide a forward base for the spread of Tripoli's influence throughout the region.[56] In practice, such plans have on occasion been thwarted by the direct intervention of France (discreetly supported in the 1980s by the United States) and by the direct or proxy intervention of African states, including Arab states, also worried by the implications of the Libyan revolution gaining a grip on the heart of Africa.

As an African state, Libya should have had an inherent advantage in its rivalry with a European colonial power such as France. By the early 1970s, Libya was seen to have an 'African vocation' quite independent of the Arab-Israeli problem.[57] As Gadafi himself has asserted, 'We are Africans. We are part of Africa. Africa is our continent.'[58] He envisaged the black peoples seeking their own rehabilitation, as well as vengeance and domination for their enslavement by the white race.[59] This notion seemed to imply that Libya might abet such a historical process in Africa and elsewhere (disregarding its own slaving tradition) as part of a general anti-imperialist, anti-western impetus. But such ambitions remained unfulfilled. The seizure of power by Hissene Habre in 1982, his cultivation of his own 'image as a champion of orthodox Islam',[60] and the spread of his centralising authority over the whole country (with the exception of the Aozou Strip) in the course of the next five years, represented the biggest setbacks to Tripoli's aspirations in Chad and in Africa as a whole.

Among other discernible Libyan purposes in Chad have been worries about national security, primarily in the Aozou Strip. Security was certainly threatened once Habre's forces had taken all the north up to the disputed area in 1987. The long southern frontier, whether it lies to the north or south of Aozou, by its very length and extreme remoteness, represents a 'soft underbelly' to both Libya and Chad, open to penetration from both sides. As Gadafi himself declared in 1981, 'The security of Chad is linked to the security of Libya'.[61] The ease with which small numbers of lightly-armed Free French troops, despite their enormously long supply lines, penetrated Fezzan from Chad in 1940–3 and subsequently tried to detach it from the rest of Libya, has not been forgotten. Nor has the episode in July 1970 when leading members of the former royalist administration prepared an abortive counter-*coup* – which was to have been mounted in Fezzan by 5,000 foreign mercenaries flown in from Chad – [62] against the new revolutionary regime.

Over the years the Libyans have thus tended to support any Chadian faction that might further their interests, while undermining those – including any government – that did not; they have tried to fill local and national power vacuums as they have developed, and to acquire a base in Chad for further moves into Central Africa. Longer-term objectives have included the replacement of western practices and influences in Africa with a universal acceptance of Islam and the Jamahiri system as a means of restoring the pre-colonial sense of Sahelian-Saharan community and culture, and the development of Chadian economic resources.[63]

Certain Libyans, and particularly the Zuwaya and the Magarba, have maintained their traditional and obviously rewarding trans-Saharan trading contacts with Chad throughout this century, even if they now operate with heavy lorries rather than camel caravans.[64] By the 1970s

Fezzan tradesmen have reached out as far as Tropical Africa. With cash and letters of exchange they despise barter, sell on credit, make loans on harvests and, ultimately, hold all the desert peoples in their grasp. Whole groups, such as Tuareg and Toubou, have been ousted from commercial dealings in this way to the advantage of richer or more enterprising groups.[65]

Some Libyan traders have long-established family ties with Chad.[66] While the Sanusi missionary drive followed the path of the Zuwaya and Magarba traders across the Sahara and into the Sudan in the mid-nineteenth century, so Libyan revolutionary influence has tended to follow the same ready-made lines of approach into Chad and elsewhere, without necessarily using Libyan traders as its agents. Conversely, since the start of the Libyan oil boom in the late 1950s, many Chadians have travelled through Kufra and Fezzan to seek work and settle in a country of apparently rich opportunities, even at the risk since the 1970s of conscription into Libyan forces destined to intervene in Chad.[67]

The Aozou Strip, a remote area of extremely harsh climate and landscape, is reputed to have as its sole intrinsic attraction deposits of uranium and other minerals, apparently found by the French Bureau de Recherche Géologique et Minière in 1957,[68] but never exploited. There have long been doubts about the size and location of such deposits; but it has generally been assumed that one of Libya's main interests in the strip has been in exploiting its uranium for a nuclear programme[69] intended to supply the Jamahariyah with energy (and, presumably, bombs) after the exhaustion of its crude oil and natural gas reserves, probably early in the twenty-first century. It has also been suggested that Libya's further objective in exploiting such resources would be to consolidate its role as an energy supplier. 'Its ability to supply energy to those who control the real levers of international power or international opinion – particularly with respect to the Israel question – is as important as any issue involving Arab public opinion.'[70] The discovery of modest oilfields in south and central Chad in the 1970s – hitherto unexploited because of civil strife – was also thought to have aroused Libyan cupidity, although such oil would probably best be refined locally and not exported through any foreign outlet.

Chad may in due time develop its economic potential in southern farming, Sahelian herding and possibly in the exploitation of mineral resources. Libyan interests in the territory have primarily reflected the various goals of the Jamahariyah, including the extension to other parts of Africa of the Jamahiri experiment of popular participation in the processes of local and national government and in economic and social management.[71] Unhappily, this ideal has not been widely shared by those outside Libya for whom it is intended. A system that might well suit Libyan experience[72] is not necessarily of universal appeal elsewhere in Africa. If France and the United States are hostile to the Jamahariyah's pretensions in Chad and further afield in Africa, Arab and African states have often had their own grave misgivings about the implications of Libya establishing a series of revolutionary relationships along the ethnic, linguistic and cultural divide where Arab and Black Africa have met but only partly mingled over the past millennium.

All the Arab states of North Africa have, for various reasons, looked askance at Libya's role in Chad, although most, for their own part, have certain proprietorial interests in their own respective hinterlands: Morocco in the Western Sahara and Mauritania, Algeria in Niger and Mali, and Egypt in the Sudan Republic. The Egyptians, who have had their own quarrels with Libya, long saw a menace to Sudanese stability (and thus to their own security) in the Libyan position in Chad, and accordingly supported Hissene Habre's efforts to reunite the country under his sole authority. The former President Gafaar Numeiri of Sudan claimed for years to see Soviet influence behind the Libyan moves into Central Africa; but the Soviets, while remaining Tripoli's main source of arms and military training, have in practice consistently avoided any involvement in Colonel Gadafi's foreign ventures. After Nimeiri's overthrow in 1985, the Sudanese regional role became more ambiguous, and repeated claims that Libyan forces were using the unruly frontier zones of Darfur as a base for infiltrating central Chad had to be repeatedly denied. Algeria, too, has long been worried about Tripoli's influence in and south of the Sahara, both as a challenge to Algeria's own interests in its hinterland, and because such ventures are considered to distract Libya from the more important and realistic issue of Maghrib unity.[73] Morocco has been less directly concerned with Chad, but in 1984-6 used the issue to neutralise Tripoli's active support for the Polisario Front that contests Moroccan sovereignty in the Western Sahara.

Black African states, particularly the Sahelian states that see themselves as prime objects of troublesome Jamahiri influence and expansion, have taken a sceptical view of Libya's African mission, not least because of the unsubtle way it has been promoted. As the most powerful and populous state in Black Africa, Nigeria emerged in the late 1970s as Tripoli's main African rival for influence over the course of events in Chad. The announcement of the abortive Chad-Libya union in January 1981 caused alarm and a loss of faith in Libyan intentions in Africa, with the result that Hissene Habre's own standing as an anti-Libyan champion was enhanced. By the time he had brought nearly all Chad except the Aozou Strip under his control in 1987, the success of Libyan policy seemed to have reached its nadir, with Chad being reunited under a determined, hostile regime of a type Tripoli had long tried to keep out of N'Djamena. No wonder Gadafi in 1988 hastened to make peace with Habre.

Yet for all the ultimately fruitless attempts to subvert and dominate a vulnerable and impoverished neighbour, there were no reasons to suppose that close Libyan concern with the course of events in Chad had come to an end. For despite the distance and the difficulties of the Saharan terrain separating them, the peoples of Chad and Libya have been associated for too long and too closely for them to become wholly indifferent to each other's fate.

## NOTES

1. R. Adloff and V. Thompson, *Conflict in Chad*, London, 1981, p. 7.
2. S. Decalo, *Historical Dictionary of Chad*, London, 1977, p. 251.
3. Adloff and Thompson, *Conflict in Chad*, p. 10.
4. Decalo, *Historical Dictionary*, p. 129.
5. Lanne, *Tchad-Libye*, p. 227. Fort Lamy was only renamed N'Djamena during President Tombalbaye's 'cultural revolution' of 1972-5.
6. B. Neuberger, *Involvement, Invasion and Withdrawal: Qadhafi's Libya and Chad 1969-1981*, Tel Aviv, 1982, p. 23.
7. *Ibid.*
8. Adloff and Thompson, *Conflict in Chad*, pp. 121-2.
9. See G.N. Gatta, *Tchad: Guerre civile et desagrégation de l'état*, Dakar, 1985, p. 198.
10. See Neuberger, *Involvement, Invasion*, p. 23.
11. *Ibid.*, p. 26.
12. Lanne, *Tchad-Libye*, p. 227.
13. See Neuberger, *Involvement, Invasion*, p. 27.
14. See Adloff and Thompson, *Conflict in Chad*, p. 123.
15. Neuberger, *Involvement, Invasion*, p. 29.
16. Lanne, *Tchad-Libye*, p. 228.
17. Gadafi's neologism meaning 'state of the masses'. See 'Map of the Socialist People's Libyan Arab Jamahariyah', Beirut, n.d.
18. Lanne, *Tchad-Libye*, pp. 228-31.
19. *Ibid.*, pp. 230-1.
20. Brownlie, *African Boundaries*, p. 125.
21. J. Cooley, *Libyan Sandstorm*, London, 1983, p. 199.
22. For the text of the unification communiqué, see Neuberger, *Involvement, Invasion*, app., pp. 69-72.
23. C. Legum, 'Libya's Intervention in Chad' in C.Legum (ed.), *Crisis and Conflicts in the Middle East*, New York and London, 1981, p. 58.
24. Neuberger, *Involvement, Invasion*, p. 51.
25. *Africa Confidential*, 21 Sept. 1983.
26. J. Latrémolière, 'Tchad. Le lent cheminement des évidences', *Marchés tropicaux*, 4 Jan. 1985, p. 9, quoted in R. Lemarchand, 'A propos du Tchad: La face nord à l'histoire', *Maghreb Review*, 12, 1-2 (1987).
27. R.B. St. John, *Qaddafi's World Design: Libyan Foreign Policy 1969-1987*, London, 1987, p. 11.
28. Wright, *Libya: A Modern History*, p. 124.
29. See 'Muammar El Kadhafi', *Maghreb*, n.48, 1971.
30. See, for instance, Gadafi's speech at Yefren, one of the main Berber centres of the

Gebel Nefusah of Tripolitania, Aug. 1971. *BBC Summary of World Broadcasts*, ME/3774/A/12.

31. M. Gadhafi, *The Battle of Destiny*, London, 1976, p. 128.
32. Quoted in Legum, 'Libya's Intervention in Chad', p. 58.
33. K.S. Vikor, 'Al-Sanusi and Qadhafi – Continuity of Thought?', *Maghreb Review*, 12, 1–2 (1987).
34. *Kadhafi, 'Je suis un opposant à l'échelon mondial'*, Lausanne, 1984, p. 62. According to A Cauneille, 'Le nomadisme des Guedudfa', *Bulletin du laiason saharienne*, 32 (Dec. 1958), about 750 Gadadfa sought exile in Kanem in 1930.
35. R. Buijtenhujs, 'Le FROLINAT a l'épreuve du pouvoir: L'echec d'une révolution Africaine', 'Le Tchad', *Politique Africaine*, 16 (Dec. 1984), p. 21.
36. See *ibid.*, pp.21–22; see also R. Lemarchand, 'A propos du Tchad', pp. 22–3.
37. See Davis, *Libyan Politics*, p. 114; Adloff and Thompson, *Conflict in Chad*, pp. 120–1.
38. See p. 48.
39. Wright, *Libya: A Modern History*, pp. 168–9.
40. M.El-Shahat, *Libya begins the Era of the Jamahiriyat*, Rome, 1978, pp. 22, 38.
41. B. Scarcia Amoretti, 'Libyan Loneliness in Facing the World: The Challenge of Islam' in A. Dawisha (ed.), *Islam in Foreign Policy*, Cambridge, 1983, p. 66; St. John, *Qaddafi's World Design*, p. 95.
42. Kadhafi, *'Je Suis'*, pp. 16–17.
43. *Ibid*, p. 29.
44. Gadhafi, *The Battle of Destiny*, p. 128.
45. Clarke, *West Africa and Islam*, pp. 202, 229: 'For Islam . . . the colonial period was one of rapid expansion'; see also Trimingham, *A History of Islam*, pp. 224ff.
46. Amoretti, 'Libyan Loneliness', p. 57.
47. Neuberger, *Involvement, Invasion*, pp. 63–5; St.John, *Qadafi's World Design*, pp. 101–2.
48. For details, see M.O'Bai. Samura, *The Libyan Revolution: Its Lessons for Africa*, Washington, DC, 1985, pp. 87–93.
49. L.C. Harris, *Libya: Qadhafi's Revolution and the Modern State*, Boulder, Colo., and London, 1986, p. 83.
50. Gadhafi, *The Battle of Destiny*, p. 128.
51. Quoted in C. Legum, 'Crisis over Chad: Colonel Gaddafi's Sahelian Dream' in C. Legum (ed.), *Africa Contemporary Record, 1980–81,* London 1981.
52. Decalo, *Historical Dictionary*, pp. 126–7.
53. J. Bessis, 'L'évolution des relations entre la Libye indépendante et la France', *Maghreb Review*, 12, 1–2 (1978), p. 15.
54. See, for instance, R. Otayek, 'La Libye face à la France au Tchad: Qui perd gagne?' in *Le Tchad*, pp. 72–3.
55. M.P. Kelley, *A State in Disarray: Conditions of Chad's Survival*, London, 1986, p. 25.
56. *Ibid.*, p. 28.
57. M. Bianco, *Gadafi: Voice from the Desert*, London, 1975, p. 156; Samura, *The Libyan Revolution*, p. 44.
58. Quoted in Samura, *The Libyan Revolution*, p. 44.
59. Qadhafi, M., *The Green Book*, Tripoli, n.d., pp. 108–9.
60. Adloff and Thompson, *Conflict in Chad*, p. 149.
61. BBC *Summary of World Broadcasts*, ME/6818/A/10.
62. Wright, *Libya: A Modern History*, p. 139.
63. Kelley, *A State in Disarray*, p. 29.
64. See P.O. Lapie, *Mes tournées au Tchad*, London, 1943, p. 119; J. Davis, 'Kufrah and the Trans-Saharan Trade', Society for Libyan Studies, School of Oriental and African Studies, London, 18 May 1977.

65. R. Capot-Rey, 'The State of Nomadism in the Sahara' in I.W. Zartman (ed.), *Man, State and Society in the Contemporary Maghreb*, London, 1973, pp. 456-7.
66. See Davis, *Libyan Politics*, p. 114.
67. See *ibid.*, pp. 113-14.
68. Chapelle, *Le Peuple Tcchadien*, p. 289.
69. P.E. Haley, *Qaddafi and the United States since 1969*, New York, 1984, p. 207.
70. N. Abdi, 'Common Regional Policy for Algeria and Libya' in E. Joffe and K. McLachlan (eds), *Social and Economic Development of Libya*, Wisbech, 1982, p. 225.
71. Kelley, *A State in Disarray*, p. 36.
72. See Davis, *Libyan Politics, passim*.
73. Abdi, 'Common Regional Policy', pp. 224-7.

# BIBLIOGRAPHY

## Books

Adloff R., and Thompson, Virginia, *Conflict in Chad*, London: C. Hurst, 1981.

Afigbo, A.E., *et al.*, *The Making of Modern Africa*, vol. 1: *The Nineteenth Century*, London: Longman, 1986.

Ahmed, Akbar S., and David M. Hart (eds), *Islam in Tribal Societies from the Atlas to the Indus*, London: Routledge and Kegan Paul, 1984.

Ajayi, J.F.A. and Crowder, Michael (eds), *History of West Africa*, vol.1, London: Longman, 1971.

Alawar, Mohammad A., *A Concise Bibliography of Northern Chad and Fezzan in Southern Libya*, Wisbech: Arab Crescent Press, 1983.

Allan, J.A. (ed.), *Libya Since Independence: Economic and Political Development*, Beckenham: Croom Helm, 1982.

Ambrosini, Gaspare, *I problemi del Mediterraneo*, Rome: Istituto Nazionale di Cultura Fascista, 1937.

Bagnold, R.A., *Libyan Sands: Travel in a Dead World*, London: Michael Haag, 1987.

Baier, Stephen, *A History of the Sahara in the Nineteenth Century*, Boston: Boston University, African Studies Center, 1978.

Barth, Henry, *Travels and Discoveries in North and Central Africa: Being a Journal of an Expedition under the Auspices of H.B.M.'s Government in the Years 1849-1855*, 5 vols., London: Longman, Brown, Green, Longmans and Roberts, 1857.

Bearman, Jonathan, *Qadhafi's Libya*, London: Zed Books, 1986.

Beer, G.L., *African Questions at the Peace Conference*, New York: Macmillan, 1923.

Bell, James, *A System of Geography. Popular and Scientific, or a Physical, Political and Statistical Account of the World and its Various Divisions*, vol. III Part II, Edinburgh: A.Fullerton, 1844.

Bianco, Mirella, *Gadafi: Voice from the Desert*, London: Longman, 1975.

Boahen, A. Adu, *Britain, The Sahara and The Western Sudan 1788-1861*, Oxford: Clarendon Press, 1964.

Bono, Salvatore, *Le frontiere in Africa dalla spartizione coloniale alle vicende più recenti (1884-1971)*, Milan: Giuffrè, 1972.

Bovill, E.W., *Missions to the Niger*, 4 vols., Hakluyt Society/Cambridge University Press, 1964.

——, *The Niger Explored*, Oxford University Press, 1968.

——, *The Golden Trade of the Moors*, Oxford University Press, 1970.

Briggs, Lloyd Cabot, *Tribes of the Sahara*, Cambridge, Mass.: Harvard University Press, 1960.

Brownlie, Ian, *African Boundaries, A Legal and Diplomatic Encyclopaedia*, London: C.Hurst, Royal Institute of International Affairs, 1979.

Bulugma, Hadi M., *Benghazi through the Ages*, Benghazi, 1972.

Buxton, Thomas Fowell, *The African Slave Trade and its Remedy*, London: John Murray, 1840.

Cachia, Anthony J., *Libya under the Second Ottoman Occupation (1835-1911)*, Tripoli: Government Press, 1945.

*Cambridge History of Africa*, 8 vols. (General Editors: Roland Oliver and J.D.Fage), Cambridge University Press, 1975-86.

Canevari, Emilio, *Zauie ed Ichuan Senussiti della Tripolitania*, Tripoli: Governo della Tripolitania, Ufficio Politico Militare, 1917.

Carbou, Henri, *La région du Tchad et du Ouadai*, 2 vols., Paris: Ernest Leroux, 1912.

Chapelle, Jean, *Le Peuple Tchadien, ses Racines, sa Vie Quotidienne et ses Combats*, Paris: L'Harmattan, 1980.

——, *Nomades Noirs du Sahara: Les Toubous*, Paris: L'Harmattan, 1982.

Clark, Desmond J., *The Prehistory of Africa*, London: Thames and Hudson, 1970.

Clarke, Peter B., *West Africa and Islam: A Study of Religious Development from the 8th to the 20th Century*, London: Edward Arnold, 1982.

Clarke, Richard F., *Cardinal Lavigerie and the African Slave Trade*, London: Longmans, Green, 1889.

Cooley, John K., *Libyan Sandstorm: The Complete Account of Qaddafi's Revolution*, London: Sidgwick and Jackson, 1983.

Cordell, Dennis D., *Dar al-Kuti and the Last Years of the Trans-Saharan Slave Trade*, Madison: University of Wisconsin Press, 1985.

Cowper, H.S., *The Hill of the Graces. A Record of Investigation among the Trilithons and Megalithic Sites of Tripoli*, London: Methuen, 1897.

Cromer, Earl of, *Modern Egypt*, London: Macmillan, 1911.

Dalby, David, R.A.Harrison Church, and Fatima Bezzaz (eds), *Drought in Africa/Sécheresse en Afrique*, African Environment Special Report no. 6, London: International African Institute, 1977.

Daniels, Charles, *The Garamantes of Southern Libya*, London: Oleander Press, 1970.

Davis, John, *Libyan Politics: Tribe and Revolution. An Account of the Zuwaya and their Government*, London: I.B. Tauris, 1987.

Dawisha, Adeed (ed.), *Islam in Foreign Policy*, Cambridge University Press, 1983.

De Agostini, Enrico, *Le Popolazioni della Cirenaica*, Benghazi: Governo della Cirenaica, 1922.

Dearden, Seton (ed.), *Letters Written During a Ten Years' Residence at the Court of Tripoli, etc.*, London: Arthur Barker, 1957.

——, *A Nest of Corsairs: The Fighting Karamanlis of the Barbary Coast*, London: John Murray, 1976.

Decalo, Samuel, *Historical Dictionary of Chad*, Metuchen, NJ. and London: Scarecrow Press, 1977.

Della Cella, Paolo, *Viaggio da Tripoli di Barbaria alle Frontiere Occidentali dell'Egitto*, Città di Castello: Commando del Corpo di Stato Maggiore, 1912.

Depont, Octave and Coppolani, Xavier, *Les Confréries Religieuses Musulmanes*, Algiers: Adolphe Jourdan, 1897.

Dozy, R., and M.J.de Goeje (eds), *Description de l'Afrique et de l'Espagne par Edrisi*, Leiden: E.J. Brill, 1866.

Dunn, Ross E., *Resistance in the Desert: The Moroccan Response to French Imperialism, 1881-1912*, London: Croom Helm, 1977.

Duveyrier, Henri, *Les Touareg du Nord*, Paris: Challamel Ainé, 1864.

——, *La confrérie musulmane de Sidi Mohammed ben Ali Es-Senousi et son domaine géographique en l'année 1300 de l'Hégire - 1883 de notre Ère*, Rome: Ministero delle Colonie, Direzione Generale degli Affari Politici, 1918.

Evans-Pritchard, E.E., *The Sanusi of Cyrenaica*, Oxford University Press, 1963.

Fage, J.D., *A History of Africa*, London: Hutchinson, 1978.

Fakhry, Ahmed, *The Oases of Egypt*, vol. I: *Siwa Oasis*; vol. II: *Bahriyah and Farafra Oases*, Cairo: American University in Cairo Press, 1973, 1974.

Feraud, L., *Annales Tripolitaines*, Tunis: Librairie Tournier, Paris: Librairie Vuibert, 1927.

Févre, François, *Les Seigneurs du Désert: Histoire du Sahara*, Paris: Presse de la Renaissance, 1983.

Fisher, Allan G.B., and Fisher, Humphrey J. *Slavery and Muslim Society in Africa: The Institution in Saharan and Sudanic Africa and the Trans-Saharan Trade*, London: C.Hurst, 1970.

Folayan, Kola, *Tripoli during the Reign of Yusuf Pasha Karamanli*, Ile-Ife: University of Ife Press, 1979.

Forbes, Rosita, *The Secret of the Sahara: Kufara*, London: Cassell, 1921.

Fugelstad, Finn, *A History of Niger, 1850-1960*, Cambridge University Press, 1983.

Gadhafi, Moammar (*see also* Kadhafi, Qathafi), *The Battle of Destiny: Speeches and Interviews*, London: Kalahari Publications, 1976.

Gateau, Albert (ed.), *Ibn Abd al-Hakam: Conquête de l'Afrique du Nord et de l'Espagne*, Algiers: Editions Carbonel, 1947.

Gatta, Gali Ngothe, *Tchad. Guerre Civile et Désagrégation de L'état*, Paris: Présence Africaine, 1985.

Gautier, E.F., *Le Passé de l'Afrique du Nord. Les siècles obscurs*, Paris: Payot, 1937.

——, *Le Sahara*, Paris: Payot, 1950.

Ghisleri, Arcangelo, *Tripolitania e Cirenaica. Dal Mediterraneo al Sahara*, Milan-Bergamo: Società Editoriale Italiana, Istituto d'Arti Grafiche, 1912.

Graziani, Rodolfo, *La riconquista del Fezzan*, Milan: Mondadori, 1934.

Gutteridge, William (ed.), *Libya: Still a Threat to Western Interests?* Conflict Studies no. 160, London: Institute for the Study of Conflict, 1984.

Haimann, Giuseppe, *Cirenaica (Tripolitania)*, Milan: Ulrico Hoepli, 1886.

Haley, Edward P., *Qaddafi and the United States since 1969*, New York: Praeger, 1984.

Hallett, Robin (ed.), *Records of the African Association, 1788-1831*, London: Royal Geographical Society/Nelson, 1964

——, *The Penetration of Africa: European Enterprise and Exploration Principally in Northern and Western Africa up to 1830*, London: Routledge and Kegan Paul, 1965.

——, *Africa up to 1875: A Modern History*, Ann Arbor: University of Michigan Press, 1970.

Hamilton, James, *Wanderings in North Africa*, London: John Murray, 1856.

*Handbook on Cyrenaica*, 11 parts, Cairo: British Military Administration, 1944–5.

*Handbook on Tripolitania. Compiled from Official Sources*, Tripoli: British Military Administration, 1947.

Harding King, W.J., *Mysteries of the Libyan Desert. A Record of Three Years of Exploration in the Heart of that Vast and Waterless Region*, London: Seeley, Service, 1925.

Harris, Lillian Craig, *Libya: Qadhafi's Revolution and the Modern State*, Beckenham: Croom Helm, 1986.

Haseeb, Khair El-Din (ed.), *The Arabs and Africa*, Beirut: Centre for Arab Unity Studies, Beckenham: Croom Helm, 1985.

Hassanein Bey, A.M., *The Lost Oases*, London: Thornton Butterworth, 1925.

Haynes, D.E.L., *An Archaeological and Historical Guide to the Pre-Islamic Antiquities of Tripolitania*, Tripoli: Antiquities, Museums and Archives of Tripoli, 1965.

*History of Africa, The*, London: Henry Colburn and Richard Bentley, 1830.

Holmboe, Knud, *Desert Encounter: An Adventurous Journey through Italian Africa*, London: Harrap, 1936.

Ingold, General, *L'Epopée Leclerc au Sahara, 1940–1943*, Paris: Berger-Levrault, 1948.

Joffe, E.G.H., and K.S.McLachlan, (eds), *Social and Economic Development of Libya*, Wisbech: Menas Press, 1982.

Kadhafi, *'Je suis un opposant à l'échelon mondial'*, Lausanne: Pierre Marcel Favre, 1984.

Kelley, Michael P., *A State in Disarray: Conditions of Chad's Survival*, Boulder: Westview Press, 1986.

Khadduri, Majid, *Modern Libya. A Study in Political Development*, Baltimore: Johns Hopkins University Press, 1963.

Khazanov, A.M., *Nomads and the Outside World*, Cambridge University Press, 1983.

Ki-Zerbo, Joseph, *Histoire de l'Afrique Noire d'Hier à Demain*, Paris: Hatier, 1972.

Kumm, Karl, *From Hausaland to Egypt through the Sudan*, London: Constable, 1910.

Lanne, Bernard, *Tchad-Libye: La querelle des frontières*, Paris: Karthala, 1982.

Lapie, Pierre Olivier, *Mes tournées au Tchad*, London: John Murray, 1943.

Law, Robin, *The Horse in West African History: The Role of the Horse in the Societies of Pre-Colonial West Africa*, London: International African Institute, Oxford University Press, 1980.

Legum, C. (ed.), *Crisis and Conflicts in the Middle East*, Beckenham: Croom Helm, 1981.

Le Rouvreur, Albert, *Sahéliens et Sahariens du Tchad*, Paris: Berger-Levrault, 1962.

Lethielleux, J., *Le Fezzan. Ses jardins, ses palmiers*, Tunis: Publications de l'Institut des Belles Lettres Arabes, 1948.

*Le Sahara. Rapports et Contacts Humaines*, Aix-en-Provence: La Pensée Universitaire, 1967.

Lewis, I.M. (ed.), *Islam in Tropical Africa*, London: Hutchinson, 1980.

Lhote, Henri, *The Search for the Tassili Frescoes*, London: Hutchinson, 1959.

——, *Les chars rupestres sahariens des syrtes au Niger par le pays des Garamantes et des Atlantes*, Toulouse: Editions des Hespérides, 1982.

*Libya*, London: Reference Division, Central Office of Information, 1960.

Lovejoy, Paul E., *Transformations in Slavery: A History of Slavery in Africa*, Cambridge University Press, 1983.

——, *Salt of the Desert Sun: A History of Salt Production and Trade in the Central Sudan*, Cambridge University Press, 1986.

Lyon, G.F., *A Narrative of Travels in Northern Africa in the Years 1818-1819 and 1820*, London: John Murray, 1821.

Macartney, Maxwell, H.H., and Cremona Paul, *Italy's Foreign and Colonial Policy, 1914-1937*, Oxford University Press, 1938.

Martin, B.G., *Muslim Brotherhoods in Nineteenth-Century Africa*, Cambridge University Press, 1976.

Mauny, Raymond, *Tableau géographique de l'Ouest Africain au Moyen Age*, Dakar: IFAN, 1961.

Merighi, Antonio, *La Tripolitania antica dalle origini alla invasione degli Arabi*, 2 vols., Verbania: A.Airoldi, 1940.

Micacchi, Rodolfo, *La Tripolitania sotto il dominio dei Caramanli*, Verbania: A.Airoldi, 1936.

Miège, J.L., *L'imperialismo coloniale italiano dal 1870 ai giorni nostri*, Milan: Rizzoli, 1976.

Minutilli, F., *La Tripolitania*, Turin: Fratelli Bocca, 1912.

Morsy, Magali, *North Africa 1800-1900: A Survey from the Nile Valley to the Atlantic*, London: Longman, 1984.

Nachtigal, Gustav (trans. and ed. A.G.B. and H.J. Fisher), *Sahara and Sudan*, vol. I: *Tripoli and Fezzan, Tibesti or Tu;* vol. II: *Kawar, Bornu, Kanem, Borku, Ennedi;* vol. III: *The Chad Basin and Bagirmi;* vol. IV: *Wadai and Darfur*, London: C. Hurst, 1971-88.

Neuberger, Benyamin, *Involvement, Invasion and Withdrawal: Qadhdhafi's Libya and Chad 1969-1981*, Occasional Papers no. 83, University of Tel Aviv, 1982.

*Nomades et Nomadisme du Sahara*, Paris: UNESCO, 1983.

Oliver, Roland, and Fage J.D., *A Short History of Africa*, Harmondsworth: Penguin, 1962.

Pace, Biagio, Sergio Sergi and Giacomo Caputo, *Scavi Sahariani. Ricerche nell'Uadi el-Agial e nell'Oasi di Gat*, Rome: Accademia Nazionale dei Lincei, 1951.

Palmer, Richmond, *The Bornu, Sahara and Sudan*, London: John Murray, 1936.

Pasha, Aftab Kamal, *Libya and the United States: Qadhafi's Response to Reagan's Challenge*, New Delhi: Detente Publications, 1984.

Pelt, Adrian, *Libyan Independence and the United Nations. A Case of Planned Decolonisation*, New Haven: Yale University Press, 1970.

Porch, Douglas, *The Conquest of the Sahara*, London: Jonathan Cape, 1985.

Pory, John, *A Geographical Historie of Africa. Written in Arabicke and Italian by John Leo, a More, etc*, London: George Bishop, 1600.

Qathafi, Muammar al-, *The Green Book. Parts One, Two and Three*. Tripoli: Public Establishment for Publishing, Advertising and Distribution, n.d.

Rae, Edward, *The Country of the Moors. A Journey from Tripoli in Barbary to the City of Kairwan*, London: John Murray, 1877.

Richardson, James, *Travels in the Great Desert of Sahara in the Years 1845 and 1846*, 2 vols., London: Richard Bentley, 1848.

Rinn, Louis, *Marabouts et Khouan. Étude sur l'Islam en Algérie*, Algiers: Adolphe Jourdan, 1884.

Rodd, Lord Rennell of, *British Military Administration of Occupied Territories in Africa*, London: HMSO, 1948.

Rodinson, Maxime, *The Arabs*, Beckenham: Croom Helm, 1981.

Rohlfs, Gerhard, *Kufra. Reise von Tripolis nach der Oase Kufra*, Leipzig: F.A. Brockhaus, 1881.

Rossi, Ettore, *La Cronaca Araba Tripolina di Ibn Galbun (sec.XVIII)*, Bologna: Licinio Capelli, 1936.

——, *Storia di Tripoli e della Tripolitania dalla conquista araba al 1911*, Rome: Istituto per l'Oriente, 1968.

Russell, Revd Michael, *History and Present Condition of the Barbary States, Comprehending a View of their Civil Institutions, Antiquities, Arts, Religions, Literature, Commerce, Agriculture and Natural Productions*, Edinburgh: Oliver and Boyd, 1835.

*Il Sahara Italiano. Prima Parte: Fezzan e Oasi di Gat*, Rome: Reale Società Geografica Italiana, 1937.

Samura, Mohammad O'Bai, *The Libyan Revolution and its Lessons for Africa*, Washington, D.C: International Institute for Policy and Development Studies, 1985.

Scarin, Emilio, *Le Oasi del Fezzan. Ricerche ed Osservazioni di Geografia Umana*, Bologna: Nicola Zanichelli, 1934.

Schirmer, Henri, *Le Sahara*, Paris: Hachette, 1893.

Scortecci, G., *Sahara*, Milan: Ulrico Hoepli, 1945.

Shahat, M. E., *Libya Begins the Era of the Jamahiriyat*, Rome: International Publication House, 1978.

Shinnie, P.L. (ed.), *The African Iron Age*, Oxford: Clarendon Press, 1971.

Sikes, Sylvia K., *Lake Chad*, London: Eyre Methuen, 1972.

*Correspondence Relative to the Slave Trade*, 1847–48, LXIV, London, 1848.

*Correspondence with British Representatives and Agents Abroad and Reports from Naval Officers and the Treasurey Relative to the Slave Trade*, Slave Trade no. 5, London, 1880.

Slouschz, Nahum, *Travels in North Africa*, Philadelphia: Jewish Publication Society of America, 1927.

Smaldone, Joseph P., *Warfare in the Sokoto Caliphate*, Cambridge University Press, 1977.

St. John, Ronald Bruce, *Qaddafi's World Design. Libyan Foreign Policy 1969–1987*, London: Saqi Books, 1987.

Stride, G.T. and Ifeka C., *Peoples and Empires of West Africa: West Africa in History, 1000–1800*, London: Nelson, 1971.

*[Le]Tchad. Politique africaine*, Paris: Karthala, 1984.

Torrey, Charles C. (ed.), *The History of the Conquest of Egypt, North Africa and Spain, Known as the Futuh Misr of Ibn 'Abd al-Hakam*, New Haven: Yale Oriental Series, 1922.

Trimingham, J. Spencer, *Islam in West Africa*, Oxford: Clarendon Press, 1959.
——, *A History of Islam in West Africa*, Oxford University Press, 1970.
UNESCO, *General History of Africa*, 8 vols:, Paris, 1981.
Urvoy, Y., *Histoire de l'Empire du Bornou*, Paris: Larose, 1949.
Valori, Francesco, *Storia della Cirenaica*, Florence: Sansoni, 1961.
Vikor, Knut S., 'The Oasis of Salt: The History of Kawar, a Saharan Centre of Salt Production', University of Bergen, unpubl. thesis, 1979.
Vischer, Hanns, *Across the Sahara from Tripoli to Bornu*, London: Edward Arnold, 1910.
Walz, Terence, *Trade between Egypt and Bilad as-Sudan, 1700–1800*, Cairo: Institut français d'archéologie orientale du Caire, 1978.
Ward, Philip, *Touring Libya: The Eastern Provinces*, London: Faber and Faber, 1969.
Warmington, B.H., *Carthage*, Harmondsworth: Penguin, 1964.
White, Silva, *From Sphinx to Oracle: Through the Libyan Desert to the Oasis of Jupiter Ammon*, London: Hurst and Blackett, 1899.
Wheeler, Sir Mortimer, *Rome Beyond the Imperial Frontiers*, Harmondsworth: Penguin, 1955.
Wickins, P.L., *An Economic History of Africa from the Earliest Times to Partition*, Cape Town: Oxford University Press, 1981.
Wright, John, *Libya*, London: Ernest Benn, 1969.
——, *Libya: A Modern History*, Beckenham: Croom Helm, 1982.
Zartman, William I. (ed.), *Man, State and Society in the Contemporary Maghrib*, London: Pall Mall Press, 1973.
Zeltner, Jean-Claude, *Pages d'Histoire du Kanem, Pays Tchadien*, Paris: L'Harmattan, 1980.
Ziadeh, Nicola A., *Sanusiyah: A Study of a Revivalist Movement in Islam*, Leiden: E.J. Brill, 1968.

## Articles and papers

Ambrosini, Gaspare, 'Il Mediterraneo dal 1919 ad Oggi', *Gli Annali dell'Africa Italiana*, IV, 1 (1941).
'Appunti sulla Tratta degli Schiavi', *Bollettino della Società Africana d'Italia*, Naples, V, II (Feb. 1886).
Baer, Gabriel, 'Slavery in Nineteenth Century Egypt', *Journal of African History* (hereafter *JAH*), VIII, 3 (1967).
Bessis, Juliette, 'L'évolution des relations entre la Libye indépendante et la France', *Maghreb Review*, 12, 1–2 (Jan.–April 1987).
Boahen, A. Adu, 'The Caravan Trade in the Nineteenth Century', *JAH*, III, 2 (1962).
Ceriani, Ettore, 'Cufra', *Bollettino della Società Africana d'Italia*, XXXIX, III (1920).
Cordell, Dennis D., 'Eastern Libya, Wadai and the Sanusiya: A Tariqa and a Trade Route', *JAH*, XVIII, 1 (1977).
——, 'The Awlad Sulayman of Libya and Chad: Power and Adaptation in the Sahara and Sahel', *Canadian Journal of African Studies*, 19, 2 (1985).

Corò, Francesco, 'Un documento inedito sull'antico commercio carovaniero fra Tripoli e l'Uadai', *Gli Annali dell'Africa Italiana*, IV, (1941).

Cuomo, Carlo, 'Hinterland tripolino: L'inerzia nostra e l'attività altrui', *Bollettino della Società Africana d'Italia*, XIX, fasc. VII–VIII (July–Aug. 1900).

Davies, Oliver, 'The Neolithic Revolution in Tropical Africa', *Transactions of the Historical Society of Ghana*, IV, II (1960).

De Agostini, Ernesto, 'Prospetto Etnografico della Popolazioni Libiche', *Bollettino Geografico del Governo della Tripolitania, Ufficio Studi*, 2 (Jan.–June 1932).

Dupree, Louis, 'The Non-Arab Ethnic Groups of Libya', *Middle East Journal*, 12, 1 (Winter 1958).

Fage, J.D., 'Slavery and the Slave Trade in the Context of West African History', *JAH*, X, 3 (1969).

Farina, Ernesto, 'I Senusi nella storia e nella geografia', *Bollettino della Società Africana d'Italia*, VIII, III–IV (March–April 1889).

Fisher, Humphrey J., 'Paganism and Islam among the Zaghawa', *JAH*, VII, 1 (1966).

——, 'The Horse in the Central Sudan', part I, *JAH*, XIII, 3 (1972); part II, *JAH*, XIV, 3 (1973).

——, and Virginia Rowland, 'Firearms in the Central Sudan', *JAH*, XIII, 2 (1971).

Folayan, Kola, 'Tripoli-Bornu Political Relations 1817–25', *Journal of the Historical Society of Nigeria*, V, 4 (June 1971).

Hess, Robert L., 'Italy and Africa: Colonial Ambitions in the First World War', *JAH*, IV, 1 (1963).

'The Itinerary of Benjamin of Tudela: A Twelfth-Century Jewish Description of North-East Africa', *JAH*, VI, 1 (1965).

Horowitz, Michael, M., 'A Reconsideration of the "Eastern Sudan" ', *Cahiers d'Études Africaines*, VII, 3 (1967).

Huard, Paul, 'Introduction et diffusion du fer au Tchad', *JAH*, VII, 3 (1966).

Hume, L.J., 'Preparations for Civil War in Tripoli in the 1820s: Ali Karamanli, Hassuna D'Ghies and Jeremy Bentham', *JAH*, 21, 3 (1980).

Hunwick, J.O., 'The Influence of Arabic in West Africa: A Preliminary Historical Survey', *Transactions of the Historical Society of Ghana*, VII (1964).

——, 'Black Africans in the Islamic World: An Understudied Dimension in the Black Diaspora', *Tarikh* (Historical Society of Nigeria), 5, 4 (1978).

Inikori, J.E., 'The Origin of the Diaspora: The Slave Trade from Africa', *Tarikh*, 4 (1978).

Lange, Dierk, 'L'Eviction des Sefuwa du Kanem et l'Origine des Bulala', *JAH*, XXIII, 3 (1982).

Law, R.C.C., 'The Garamantes and Trans-Saharan Enterprise in Classical Times', *JAH*, VIII, 2 (1967).

Lemarchand, René, 'À propos du Tchad: La face nord à l'histoire', *Maghreb Review*, 12, 1–2, (Jan.–April 1987).

'Les Hommes: Muammar el Kadhafi', *Maghreb*, 48 (Nov.–Dec. 1971).

Leva, Enrico, 'Tripoli in una descrizione di cent' anni fa', *Africa*, XXII, 1 (March 1967).

Lewicki, T., 'À propos du nom de l'oasis de Koufra chez les géographes arabes du XIe et du XIIe siècle' JAH VI, 3 (1965).

Manning, Patrick, 'The Enslavement of Africans: A Demographic Model', *Canadian Journal of African Studies*, 15, 3 (1981).

Martin, B.G., 'Kanem, Bornu and the Fezzan: Notes on the Political History of a Trade Route', *JAH*, X (1969).

Mauny, Raymond, 'Les contacts terrestres entre Méditeranée et Afrique tropicale occidentale pendant l'antiquité', *Afrique Noire et Monde Méditerrannéen dans l'Antiquité*, Dakar - Abidjan: Les Nouvelles éditions Africaines, 1978.

Munson, Patrick J., 'Archaeology and the Prehistoric Origins of the Ghana Empire', *JAH*, XXI, 3 (1980).

Narducci, Guglielmo, 'Industrie e commercio della Cirenaica e loro avvenire nel "Dopo Guerra"', *Bollettino della Società Africana d'Italia*, XXXVII, V (1918).

Newbury, C.W., 'North Africa and Western Sudan Trade in the Nineteenth Century: A Re-evaluation', *JAH*, VII, 2 (1966).

Penderel, H.W.G.J., 'The Gilf Kebir', *Geographical Journal*, XXXIII, 6 (June 1934).

Pennell, C.R., 'Tripoli in the Seventeenth Century: The Economics of Corsairing in a "Sterill Country"', *Libyan Studies*, 16 (1985).

Renault, François, 'La traite des esclaves noirs en Libye au XVIIIe siècle', *JAH*, XXIII, 2 (1982).

Rodd, Francis, 'A Fezzani Military Expedition to Kanem and Bagirmi in 1821', *Journal of the Royal African Society*, XXXV, CXXXIX (April 1936).

Shinnie, P.L. and M., 'New Light on Medieval Nubia', *JAH*, VI, 3 (1965).

Smaldone, J.P., 'Firearms in the Central Sudan: A Reevaluation, *JAH*, XII, 2 (1971).

'Sul Movimento degli Scambi fra la Tripolitania ed il Sudan Centrale', *Bollettino della Società Africana d'Italia*, XII, IX-X (Sept.-Oct. 1893).

Toledano, Ehud R., 'The Imperial Eunuchs of Istanbul', *Middle Eastern Studies*, 20, 3 (July 1984).

Vikor, Knut S., 'Al-Sanusi and Qadhafi - Continuity of Thought?', *Maghreb Review*, 12, 1-2 (Jan.-April 1987).

——, 'The Early History of Kawar Oasis: A Southern Border of the Maghrib or a Northern Border of the Sudan?', *Maghreb Review*, 12, 3-4 (May-Aug. 1987).

Wright, John, 'Chad and Libya: Some Historical Connections', *Maghreb Review*, 8, 3-4 (May-Aug. 1983).

# INDEX